Back to reality?

This volume appears at a critical moment for the future of cultural studies. The Anglo-American centres from which cultural studies first emerged have been displaced, and we are left with a series of urgent questions: Can cultural studies retain a singular identity? Can it legitimately speak in the language of the global or should it develop greater expertise in the field of the local? Should cultural studies disperse itself or can it now find a comfortable place for itself in the arena of international scholarship as it embraces the limits of thinking within a national frame? This collection re-asserts the importance of analysing concrete social practices as the basis for understanding the dynamics of broad cultural change.

In the first part of the book, Lawrence Grossberg, bell hooks, Meaghan Morris and Graham Murdock all address issues which are critical to the future of cultural studies. In the second part, a series of detailed case studies draws attention to the processes and the politics of cultural production. From rap to rave, from designer menswear to Marie Claire magazine, from rock music to sex tourism, each essay tackles issues of ideology, bodies, power and gender in contemporary popular culture. This is a powerful and lively collection which forges a new way forward for cultural studies now and in the future.

Back to reality?

Social experience and cultural studies

edited by
Angela McRobbie

Manchester University Press
Manchester and New York
distributed exclusively in the USA by St. Martin's Press

Published by Manchester University Press
Oxford Road, Manchester M13 9NR, UK
and Room 400, 175 Fifth Avenue,
New York, NY 10010, USA

Distributed exclusively in the USA
by St. Martin's Press, Inc.,
175 Fifth Avenue, New York, NY 10010, USA

British Library Cataloguing-in-Publication Data
A catalogue record for this book is available from the British Library

Library of Congress Cataloging-in-Publication Data
Back to reality?: social experience and cultural studies / edited by Angela McRobbie.
p. cm.
Includes index.
ISBN 0–7190–4454–5. – ISBN 0–7190–4455–3 (pbk.)
1. Culture–Philosophy. 2. Sex role. 3. Popular culture.
I. McRobbie, Angela.
HM101.B1853 1997
306'.01–dc20
95–39216
CIP

ISBN 0 7190 4454 5 *hardback*
ISBN 0 7190 4455 3 *paperback*

First published in 1997

01 00 99 98 97   10 9 8 7 6 5 4 3 2 1

Typeset in Great Britain
by Servis Filmsetting Ltd

Printed in Great Britain
by Bell and Bain Ltd, Glasgow

Contents

List of contributors

Meaghan Morris is Australian Research Council Senior Fellow at The University of Technology, Sydney. Her books include *The Pirate's Fiancée: Feminism, Reading, Postmodernism* (Verso, 1988), *Ecstasy and Economics: American Essays for John Forbes* (EmPress, 1992) and *Australian Cultural Studies: a Reader*, co-edited with John Frow (Allen & Unwin, 1992).

Lawrence Grossberg is Morris Davis Professor of Communication Studies at the University of North Carolina at Chapel Hill. He is the author of *We Gotta Get Out of this Place: Popular Conservatism and Postmodern Culture* (Routledge, 1994), *Dancing in Spite of Myself: Essays on Popular Culture* and *An American in Birmingham: Essays on Cultural Studies* (both forthcoming, Duke University Press). He is also co-editor of *Cultural Studies* (Routledge, 1992) and *The Audience and its Landscape* (Westview, 1996), and of the journal *Cultural Studies* (Routledge).

Graham Murdock is Reader in the Sociology of Culture at Loughborough University and Visiting Professor of Communications at the University of Bergen. He has written widely on contemporary culture and communications and is currently working on debates around modernity and the impact of new communication technologies.

bell hooks is the author of several books, including *Ain't I a Woman?* (South End Press, 1981), *Talking Back* (South End Press, 1989), *Black Looks* (South End, 1992) *Outlaw Culture* (Routledge, 1994), *Art on my Mind* (New Press, 1995), and *Killing Rage* (Henry Holt and Company,

1995). She is Distinguished Professor of English at City College in New York.

Paul Gilroy teaches at Goldsmiths College, University of London.

Dave Laing is Quintin Hogg Research Fellow in the School of Design and Media at the University of Westminster. He is an editorial board member of the journal *Popular Music* and associate editor of the Financial Times newsletter *Music & Copyright*. His books include *The Sound Of Our Time* (1969), *The Marxist Theory of Art* (Harvester, 1978), *One Chord Wonders* (Open University Press, 1985) and (with Phil Hardy) *The Faber Companion to 20th Century Popular Music* (Faber, 1995).

Vron Ware is the author of *Beyond the Pale: White Women, Racism and History* (Verso, 1992) and teaches Cultural Geography in the School of Humanities, University of Greenwich.

Maria Pini is currently doing a Ph.D. on 'Femininity and Contemporary Dance Cultures' at Goldsmiths College, London, where she is also a part-time lecturer. Other forthcoming publications include 'Dance Classes: Dancing between Classifications', in the journal, *Feminism and Psychology* and 'Cyborgs, Nomads and the Raving Feminine' in H. Thomas (ed.), *Dance in the City*.

Sean Nixon teaches Media and Cultural Studies in the Department of Sociology, University of Essex and is author of *Hard Looks: Masculinities, Spectatorship and Contemporary Consumption* (UCL Press, 1996).

Angela McRobbie teaches Sociology at Loughborough University and is author of *Postmodernism and Popular Culture* (Routledge, 1994) and *Fashion and the Image Industries* (forthcoming Routledge, 1997).

Introduction

Back to reality in this context points not to a return to a moment of purity, authenticity or absolute reality, as the title might suggest. Indeed each of the articles in the book contests reality, and argues with the various versions of reality which are continually put to us as indisputable and true. The collection does, however, insist on the political reality of doing cultural studies as it moves into a much larger and more expansive institutional space. The articles each attempt to keep a grip on this, even as politics also becomes more difficult to spell out because there are more stakes in the political field which argue for difference and diversity. Not only does political commitment in cultural studies provide a grounding for this collection, so also does the commitment to understanding the social experience of culture, the way in which culture is lived and the use of culture as a structure for the articulation of experience. Thus, just as reality might appear here in quotation marks, so also might the category of experience. We are not suggesting that such a thing exists raw, pure and simply 'expressive'. The experience of which we talk might, for example, include the work of being a cultural producer, somebody employed as a member of the production team on a popular magazine like *More!* In this context the interest is not in the whole 'experience' of those employees in the ethnographic sense; rather it would be on how they, in the context of the working day, deploy the routine knowledge of the magazine, understood as 'instinct' or 'gut feeling', to produce a cultural form which in this case produces a 'sex' which endlessly parodies itself, An interest in experience here would lead to a study of how the producers understand their role, how aware they are of the elements of irony, humour and feminist 'common sense' which are evident on these and other women's magazines pages in the 1990s.

bell hooks's contribution is also relevant here. The reality she points to is one often overlooked: that of the black studies classroom, where in this case the female body of the teacher represents a gendered experience and also an erotic one. The other contributors in the first section of the collection also offer a degree of self-reflection on the experience of cultural studies as it has (as some would argue) lost sight of reality in recent years. Indeed this volume appears at a critical moment for the future of cultural studies. The field of study finds itself necessarily moving far beyond the frames of the various nation states (Britain, the United States) from which it might have first emerged, although as Gilroy's *Aint No Black in the Union Jack* showed, that was never as uncontested as it looked. But, facing up to the responsibility of thinking beyond the local without descending into a kind of glib globalism, how does cultural studies engage with the world? Is this not in itself a ridiculously inflated ideal? Yet, as Grossberg points out, the local is in itself by no means unproblematic. What is it that might be returned to? How has the local been understood and whose local is it? And, as Grossberg also asks, what is culture anyway? On what basis did those working in cultural studies back in the late 1970s (myself included) construct something called the 'culture' of, for example, working-class girls? By virtually plucking it out of something much more amorphous and bestowing on it a shape and a reality which was as much my invention as it was a recognisable reality?

Meaghan Morris provides a detailed counterpoint here to the questions posed by Grossberg. She recognises that a good deal must be at stake in the increasing status of cultural studies inside and outside the academy judging by the ferocious critiques it has attracted in the Australian mass media and elsewhere. It is continually being asked to define itself, defend itself and at the same time argue its case against those in the academy whose response remains sceptical, distrustful, prepared to see in cultural studies an evasion of political responsibility in favour of the dubious postmodern politics of play. Yet at the same time cultural studies is still reviled, as sociology was before for being too political, for providing the theoretical gloss for the tyranny of political correctness in the academy. Graham Murdock here adds a more balanced critique, one which respects the tradition upon which cultural studies was established but is fearful of the ease with which the economics of culture can slip out of the picture, assumed, as Morris has pointed out elsewhere, as already having somehow been dealt with.

The second part of the book comprises a number of articles each of which directly or indirectly answers those critics who (for some reason) imagine cultural studies as virtually incapable of touching ground, of actually engaging with social practice and concerning itself with the intensified rhythms of cultural change. Can cultural studies answer its critics by proving itself more than capable of doing the empirical groundwork without succumbing to a narrow, localised and under-theorised practice? The pieces included here make a real attempt to move cultural studies out of the typecast frame in which its many critics currently understand it to be. Paul Gilroy provides a complex and nuanced reading of the centrality of the body in contemporary black popular culture. In this way he refutes a too easy reading of black body politics as being intrinsically useful or important.

Dave Laing continues the emphasis on music but shifts his attention to the tensions and anxieties manifest in the decline in the centrality of 'rock' and its cultural studies apologists. Maria Pini also challenges the assumed centrality of males in youth subcultures, an assumption which continues into the 1990s. She does this by analysing in depth the first-person accounts of young women for whom rave culture has been a leisure space in which the female body can find an autonomy and expressivity outside the normative structures of prescribed masculinity and femininity. Far from simply re-constructing gender difference, rave, and with it the drug ecstasy, loosen it up, providing, for frequently working-class young people, possibilities for gender disruption. The love-drug, in Pini's case, in conjunction with the other features of rave, produced bodily feelings and experiences which could be understood as homoerotic or otherwise as outside the grid of normative heterosexuality. In my own piece on 'new sexualities' this theme is explored in the space of the commercial girls' magazines. What is going on, I ask, when a magazine produced for fifteen-year-old girls is publishing a feature titled 'position of the week' as though it was a soft porn magazine, and in addition when this particular magazine now far outstrips its rival in circulation figures reaching over 200,000 sales a week, and a real readership of at least twice or even three times that number? Is the need for fantasy material intensified when sexual practice is overshadowed by the fear of AIDS and the steps which have to be taken to prevent it? Or does the visual material construct this as a need, and produce these cultural forms as an answer to such a need? And finally, how can we understand the feminist voices which somehow exist alongside the more conventional and regulative tone of the magazines? I argue that we have to look at the production of the magazines, at who creates these cultural phenomena and with what kind of aim. Sean Nixon continues this interest in cultural production by considering how design in retail produces certain meanings which actively contribute to the process of shopping. However, design is not a singular or non-contradictory practice, and as Nixon has argued elsewhere we can re-conceptualise the economics of culture by considering the conflicts, antagonisms and ambivalences between creative professionals as they interact in the production of these cultural forms. Nixon also argues that in these cases economics comes to be culturally rendered and deployed in the studios and boardrooms as competing professional discourses where 'creative decisions' constitute what used to be known as the 'economic base'. Vron Ware also turns her attention to the world of glossy magazines (and also the tabloid press). In her chapter Ware discusses a complex process where liberated and sexually free white women gain this 'freedom' through having access to the bodies of poor black men as a result of the growth of sex tourism for women. Ware points to the particularly contradictory position a magazine like *Marie Claire* occupies: celebrating the courage of middle-aged white women who find 'happiness' with a young partner from the Gambia, distancing itself nonetheless from these women by representing them as old, grey-haired and unattractive, and at the same time positioning itself as a magazine for, primarily, a white female readership who will participate with some degree of voyeurism in the stories and in the images of sexual passion with beautiful young black men.

Part One

Cultural studies in an international frame

Cultural studies, modern logics, and theories of globalisation[1]

Cultural studies has entered the fast track of academic success in the United States. But the cost may be too high, for it has placed cultural studies in an untenable position. As more people jump onto the cultural studies bandwagon, it needs to protect some sense of its own specificity as a way into the field of culture and power. Yet the most obvious ways of doing this identify cultural studies with a set of theoretical and political assumptions which make it more difficult for cultural studies to adapt to the challenges facing it. Let me begin, then, by trying to free myself from this dilemma.

To begin, I would argue that cultural studies can only be defined as an intellectual practice, as a way of politicising theory and theorising politics. There are, I believe, six characteristics of this practice. First, cultural studies is disciplined in the sense that it seeks new forms of intellectual authority in the face of relativism; it does not give in to relativism. Second, it is interdisciplinary in the sense that it recognises that questions of culture and power must lead one beyond the realm of culture into fields of inquiry normally constitutive of a number of other disciplines. Third, it is self-reflective, not in terms of individual identities, but rather in terms of institutional and relational structures. Fourth, it is driven by political rather than theoretical concerns; its questions are never derived from its own intellectual practice but from its encounters with the 'real' organisations of power. Fifth, it is committed to the necessity of theory, even while it refuses to define itself in purely theoretical terms. Finally, and most importantly, cultural studies is radically contextual and this is true of its theory, its politics, its questions, its object, its method and its commitments. In fact, I would argue that context is everything and everything is context for cultural studies; cultural studies is perhaps best seen as a contextual theory of contexts as the lived milieux of power. This means, at the very least, that cultural studies cannot be identified with any particular problematic or theoretical field, whether it is communication (encoding/decoding), ideology and representation, or identity and subjectivity.[2]

By identifying cultural studies with such problematics, cultural studies is locked into the very terms which it must question if it is to face one of the most urgent challenges, namely the issue of globalisation. This is especially difficult since cultural studies has often seen itself rooted in and to particular national formations. Despite the efforts of writers such as Paul Gilroy (1993) and Jim Clifford (1988) to challenge the adequacy of the nation as a bounded unit of analysis, cultural studies has been unable for the most part to escape this spatial economy, except by theorising its transgression (e.g. in images of diaspora and border-crossing). Of course, the challenge of globalisation confronts cultural studies at many levels, not the least urgent of which is the question of how the globalisation of cultural studies should take place.[3] But the level I want to deal with involves the globalisation of contemporary culture, not merely in terms of the proliferation and mobility of texts and audiences, but rather as the movement of culture outside the spaces of any (specific) language or formation. At the very least, this reconstitution of the relation of culture and space undermines our confident assumptions about how cultural practices are working, even within their own 'native' territories. The new global economy of culture entails the de-territorialisation of culture and its subsequent re-territorialisation, but the latter seriously undermines any equation of culture with location or place.

Current thinking about globalisation is too often structured by an assumed opposition between the local and the global, where the local is offered as the intellectual and political corrective of the global. This is captured in the popular demand to 'think globally and act locally'. But I must say that I have my doubts, especially when, according to Wachtel (1986) in *The Money Mandarins*, something very similar (think globally, act short-term) defines the first two principles of the new capitalism. And I am reminded of Castell's assertion that 'when people find themselves unable to control the world, they simply shrink the world to the size of their community' (cited in Gilroy, 1993: 232). Such celebrations of the local are often under-theorised, based on either a particular definition of knowledge as facts and a model of inductive empiricism, or an assumed identification of the local with the site of agency and resistance. Of course, the latter can only be justified by either a prior identification of subjectivity and agency, an indentification which gives rise to what O'Hanlon (1988) describes as 'the virile figure of the subject-agent', or an assumed equivalence between individual will and social agency. Consequently, following Bruce Robbins (1993), we need to ask why a certain kind of work – work which identifies and celebrates the local, the specific and agency – is valorised. Robbins concludes that this defines a technology of power that legitimates the claim of intellectual work to 'public representativeness'. It creates an apparent anchor in political reality which still leaves the intellectual outside offering a description of the real. It positions them as organic intellectuals speaking for a real population.

This is not, however, to dismiss the importance of 'the local', only its articulation to a particular notion of specificity within various versions of cultural studies. Here, the local as the specific site of agency is taken to be the exemplar of the concrete, located at one extreme of a vertical relation of difference extending all the way to the abstract or the general. That is, in cultural studies, too often, the local equates an epistemological question of generalisation with a pragmatic question of agency. But there is another – geographical – articulation of the local and the specific in which the local is not opposed to the global as the concrete is to the general. Rather, there is a horizontal relation in which the local is always a comparative term, describing the different articulations at different places within a structuring of space. That is, on this model, the local and the global are mutually constitutive, although the exact nature of this 'mutual constitution' remains to be specified,[4] and has yet to be adequately theorised.

As cultural studies responds to the new political terrain opened up by the contemporary globalisation of culture, and transforms itself accordingly, it will have to face a second, equally disruptive challenge. If cultural studies was founded in large part (and certainly in Britain) as a response to the inadequacy of political economic theories of the relations between culture and economics, it has too often given up any attempt to take economic relations seriously. Consequently, it has too often reduced the field of power and politics to the terrain of culture, rather than looking to the relations between what Meaghan Morris (1988) has called the politics of culture and the politics of politics. The globalisation of culture makes the cost of displacing the economic too high. Cultural studies has to return in some way to its original problematic – to rethink the relations between the economy and culture without automatically slotting the economic into the bottom line. Of course, in such work, the economics of culture cannot be limited to questions about the cultural industries, commodity production, and surplus value. It will have to take account of the changing relations between the different forms of capital (and the different economic sectors), the changing nature of and competing forms of both the modes of production (and their subsequent contradictions) and the formations of capitalism (e.g. Fordism, post-Fordism, etc.), the changing nature of labour and consumption, and the changing nature of the global relations of both political and economic power. It will have to consider how and where people, capital and commodities move in and out of the places and spaces of the global economy.[5]

These problems have become increasingly acute as cultural studies has attempted to confront the apparently new conditions of globalisation, conditions implicating all the people, commodities and cultures of the world. At the very least, the immediate result is that the traditional binary models of political struggle – coloniser/colonised, oppresser/oppressed, domination/resistance, repression/transgression – seem inapplicable to a spatial economy of power which cannot be reduced to simply geographical dichotomies – First World/Third World, metropolitan/peripheral, local/global – nor, at least in the last instance, to questions of personal identity. All this suggests a fairly different idea of what cultural studies will have to look like in the future, for it will have to break with the current tendency to equate culture with location in the form of identity. Such theories of difference not only end up equating political and cultural struggles, they end up making politics entirely into a matter of representation and interpellation. While it is reasonable to start with questions of identity and difference in contemporary politics, it does not follow that we should end up at the same place, for even if we grant that much of contemporary politics is organised around identity, it does not follow that our task is to theorise within the category of identity. After all, it is ironic that just as we discover not only that identities are socially constructed, but that the fact or category of identity is itself socially constructed, we then devote all of our energy to organising a politics around socially constructed categories. In the face of globalisation, we need to chart a trajectory from a politics of identity and difference which leads through an analysis of the geohistorical mechanisms by which relations have been constructed as differences and politics organised by identities, to a politics organised around singularity and otherness. We have to re-theorise the relations between individuation, subjectivity and identity by thinking about the affective dimensions of belonging, affiliation and identification. We have to locate the power of identity as a political force in the broader context of the new spatial economy, in order to ask why identity has become such a privileged site of struggle. Such a politics would have to define the places people can belong to, and the places people can find their way to. It would also have to break with another deeply rooted tradition in cultural studies (and in much of the literature of the Left) which privileges the position of the outsider, the marginal, the émigré as necessarily enabling a uniquely insightful understanding not available to those defined by their position as insiders, as if anyone belonged only in one place.[6]

Cultural studies, globalisation and the modern

The emergent spatial economy of globalisation involves particular forms of internationalisation and globality, and implies as well a new organisation and orientation of both power and space. The terms within which the economy is described are by now both highly predictable and extremely variable. It is generally assumed to be comprised of two opposing vectors, generally corresponding to the local and the global. This new economy is built on the increasingly apparent autonomy and simultaneous interdependence and intersection of local, regional, national and international flows, forces and interests, and its results are the very real and painful relocations and dislocations of contemporary life. Thus, on the one hand, there is the increasing internationalisation of the circuits of mobility of capital, information, manufacturing and service commodities, cultural practices, populations and labour. It is not necessary to assume that all these mobilities are the same, nor that any single circuit is realised in the same way in different places. Moreover, there is no claim here for post-industrialisation; on the contrary, hyper-industrialisation seems a more appropriate description. On the other hand, there are the various articulations of space which interrupt such international flows – various articulations of the local as it is commonly conceived – and which are, in decisive ways, more important than ever. Here we might include not only identity politics, and the reassertion of nationalism (not quite as the nation-state as much as the nation-ethnicity), but also the promotion of new urban, regional and even national identities (and the subsequent reassertion of patriotism) in the global economy.

Obviously, such characterisations of the new spatial economy are largely commonsensical, descriptive and under-theorised. And yet, for all the talk about globalisation in cultural studies, it has rarely reflected on the theoretical grounds of its models of globalisation. It has, to varying degrees, remained within the commonsense understandings of globalisation. Consequently, it has to a large extent failed to distinguish between the historical and the theoretical questions involved in the study of globalisation. One needs a theoretical understanding of the nature and stakes of globalisation (and a theoretical vocabulary capable of describing different structures and practices of globalisation) if one is to consider whether the contemporary forms of globalisation represent anything new and different in history. Without such a theoretical framework, cultural studies is unable to recognise the multiple ways in which transnational flows and relations, in a variety of different formations of colonialism, imperialism, etc., have been and continue to be constitutive of specific formations of power. But it is not as simple as it may appear on first glance, for it may be that there are very specific reasons why, in an age of hyper-theory, so little theoretical work has been done on questions of globalisation. Thus, in order to consider the nature of contemporary globalisation, one must begin by locating the concern within a broader framework of political and philosophical questions.

The larger question behind this chapter is how one does cultural studies in such global-spatial conditions, conditions in which we intellectuals are implicated, at the very least, by the somewhat involuntary (albeit somewhat pleasurable) nomadic condition of our particular class fraction. I do not believe that the answers can be found simply through some acknowledgement of our locationality, or some renunciation of ethnocentrism, or some attempt to hide our ethnocentrism in more apocalyptic claims of postmodernity. At the very least, it is a situation in which, as Meaghan Morris (1992) describes it, Euro-American culture can 'no longer experience itself as the sole subject of capitalism or as coextensive with it'. One consquence is that globalisation can no longer be confidently described from the formations of Atlantic culture as the assumed centre of the global economy of space.

Consequently, it is necessary to reflect on the philosophical grounds of cultural studies, grounds which have, I believe, made it at least unnecessarily difficult for cultural studies to adequately theorise the concept of the global and to understand the specificity of the contemporary emergent form of globalisation. To put it succinctly, if the philosophies we have don't seem to enable us to describe our reality very well, it is perhaps necessary to imagine a different philosophy, which is not to say a new philosophy since, in many ways, such a philosophy may entail a return to philosophies articulated at other times (e.g. premodern) and other places (e.g. non-Western).[7] Such a philosophy may offer a way of describing and constructing a different reality, a reality which is still ours but perhaps with a different future. Such a project points to the paradoxical position inherent in most contemporary critical theory: wary of first philosophies, it condemns itself to remain within the assumptive grounds of the first philosophies constitutive of modern thought. Unable to escape the rationality it condemns, it must be content with asking 'whose rationality is it?', with acknowledging the multiple variations of rationality, with inquiring into the specific articulations by which the inherited discourses of rationality have been accomplished, even while remaining within the broad philosophical terrain it criticises. Nowhere is this more evident than in the immediate response that any effort to begin to move outside of the structures and categories of modern thought is likely to elicit: obviously, modern thought, articulated as it is in complex ways to the modern formations of power, tells us it is impossible, but what else would you expect?

The critique of the conceptual foundations of cultural studies, and of modern thought more generally, is an ongoing collective project, questioning concepts which, if not invented in the formations of modern thought, were radically reconceptualised and repositioned in them. In the past few years, many of the most basic concepts and assumptions of cultural studies have come under attack. Various post-colonial and critical race theorists have questioned not only notions of national cultures and 'whole ways of life', but also the possibility of constructing a singular and limited space of culture, such constructions now being seen as the product of the colonising and imperialising projects of modern Europe. Various intellectual historians and policy theorists have challenged not only nostalgic conceptions of community, but also romantic-aesthetic-ethical conceptions of culture, such conceptions now being seen as the product of specific disciplining and governmental strategies of the modern nation-state. Postmodernists and feminists have argued against the reduction of culture to the domains of meaning and representation, and in a related discussion, cultural theorists and anthropologists have questioned definitions of culture as difference, mediation and supplement. Finally, philosophers and cultural geographers have demonstrated the cost of the assumed temporality of human existence, namely the erasure of space as a crucial – if not the primary – dimension of power.[8]

It is these last two which interest me here, but first I want to say something briefly about the less sensationalised critique of cultural studies offered by intellectual historians and policy theorists, for this work portends the need for an even more radical reconsideration of the role of cultural studies in the contemporary age. Although criticisms of culture as a technology of power have had more difficulty getting a hearing (perhaps because they are not the result of marginalised voices), they may ultimately prove to be the most devastating for cultural studies, for they cut to the heart of the two dominant constitutive figures of the discourse of cultural studies itself. The first is the very figure of culture. As Raymond Williams described it, the modern notion of culture, a notion which continues to animate cultural studies, involves, on the one hand, the projection of a position constituted by a temporal displacement from some other (e.g. tradition) from which change can be comprehended and, on the other hand, the equation of that position with a standard of judgement from which one can offer a 'total qualitative assessment' of such changes. 'The idea of culture is a general reaction to a general and major change in the conditions of our common life' (Williams, 1958). That is, the very concept of culture seems to require the construction of a place which would allow one to both describe and judge the changes in everyday life; that is, it requires at the very least that we find a 'court of human appeal', some locatable 'higher' standard, to be set over the processes of practical social change, generally located within and identified with some notion of culture. But this is, of course, the very ethical foundation that critics like Tony Bennett (1993) and Ian Hunter (1988) are attacking. Perhaps the solution lies in recognising the reason why Williams did not locate himself within the 'culture and society tradition': he argued that the concept of culture was invented, as it were, as a result of the recognition of 'a practical separation of certain moral and intellectual activities from the driving force of a new kind of society', i.e. that the modern is partly constituted by the separation of culture and society. For those authors whom Williams located in the culture and society tradition, the separation is taken for granted; culture is simply appropriated and transformed into a position from which that very separation can be described and judged. But Williams refused such a separation. Cultural studies had to reinsert culture into the practical everyday life of people, into the totality of a whole way of life. Yet Williams was never able to actually escape this

separation, both in his privileging of certain forms of culture (literature) and in his desire to equate culture with some sort of ethical standard.[9]

The second figure that has been uniquely constitutive of cultural
studies, especially in its British incarnation,[10] is that which links historical transformation, the experience of mobility, and the position of
marginality. That is, unlike many other theories of the emergence of the
modern (including the 'culture and society' tradition), cultural studies
is generally characterised less by a vision of a total qualitative transformation of society (e.g. from the traditional to the modern, or from
community to mass society) – cultural studies was never about the
destruction of community – than by a concern for the consequences of
new forms and degrees of mobility. Implicitly since its emergence, but
increasingly over the past decades, for cultural studies, the most significant consequence of the mobilities of postwar capitalist societies has
been that it not only created new positions of marginality but that it
increasingly brought such marginal positions into the centre of the
social formation. It is not surprising, then, that cultural studies has
tended to equate marginality with the very position described above, a
position which culture itself can no longer define. Too often, as a result,
cultural studies has either romanticised marginality or at least ethicised
it as a new standard of political and even intellectual judgement.

Nevertheless, I want to postpone such considerations in order to consider the more manageable (which is not to say easily manageable) questions raised by the critique of the logics of mediation and temporality
as constitutive of modern thought and of cultural studies. In fact, these
two logics are closely articulated together, almost inseparable, and certainly mutually reinforcing. First, the logic of mediation. Bauman
(1990) and Rosaldo (1989), for example, have both suggested that the
invention and deployment of culture as the necessary mediation by
which culture situates itself between the person and reality as the realm
of experience and knowledge (and through which all reference to the
real is erased except as a semantic category) cannot be separated from
the emerging relations of modern power. According to Rosaldo,
modern thought conceives of culture within the 'stark Manichean
choice between order and chaos'; culture is the medium of information
– the supplement – which substitutes for the lack of genetic coding in
human beings. Without culture, reality would be simply unavailable,
nothing more than James's booming buzzing confusion. Lack, mediation and semanticisation are articulated together into a particular

philosophical logic that is one piece of the conceptual groundwork of cultural studies. This logic not only erases the real but defines every possibility as a social construction.

The logic of temporality is perhaps the most powerfully articulated and the most resonant logic constitutive of modern thought. Not only does the modern embody a specific temporalising logic and a specific temporality, the relationship goes deeper, for at the heart of modern thought and power lie two assumptions: that space and time are separable, and that time is more fundamental than space. While many would locate the beginning of modern philosophy in the Cartesian problematic of the relation between the individual and reality (or truth) which was 'solved' by postulating the existence of a self-reflecting consciousness, it is, I believe, the Kantian solution which opened up the space of modern thought. Kant identified this consciousness with the mediating position of experience (giving rise to both phenomenological and structural theories of culture and knowledge). This privileging of consciousness (beyond Descartes's) as the 'space' (only metaphorically of course) of the mediation of opposition depended upon two identifications: of opposition with mediation (later dialectics, and still later, difference), and of subjectivity with temporality. Only thus was consciousness capable of appropriating the other in order to totalise and transcend consciousness. The unity of the subject depended upon the unity of time. Moreover, this meant that reality itself, at least insofar as it was available in any sense to human beings, and hence in any sense other than purely speculative and metaphysical (which of course was excluded from the domains of knowledge and philosophy), was itself temporal. This was of course only the beginning: Hegel and Marx made reality essentially historical, while Heidegger made it into temporality itself.

Getting out of the modern?

My argument is rather simple: the articulation of these two logics has made it difficult, if not impossible, for modern thought in general and for cultural studies in particular to theorise globalisation as a *spatial* economy which has its effects in and on the *real*. Only by challenging these logics can the question of the specificity of contemporary forms of globalisation be raised and theorised. But this requires formulating alternatives to the logics of mediation and of temporality. I propose two related moves: from a logic of mediation to a logic of productivity, and from a logic of temporality to a logic of spatiality. The aim of such a proposal is to suggest that we explore the concrete ways in which different machines or apparatuses of power produce the specific spaces of power that constitute not only specific technologies, conjunctures or formations, but also specific forms of globalisation as well as specific possible articulations of the local and the global.

By a productive logic, I do not simply mean that power, rather than repressing some already existing reality, constitutes its object. Rather I mean that power produces the real, as I shall explain shortly. Thus, even at the level of specific relations of power, 'The question . . . is not whether the status of women, or those on the bottom, is better or worse, but the type of organisation from which that status results' (Deleuze and Guattari, 1987). Productive machines or apparatuses offer a different view of agency, one which is opposed to mechanical, organic as well as subjective concepts. That is, agency is disarticulated from any notion of subjectivity. Productivity here is neither active nor passive but an indication of what might be called 'the middle voice'. It is a matter of reality producing itself as the very being of both reality and power. In that sense, the logic of productivity is already deeply implicated in metaphysical questions, for it takes reality to be both real (productive) and contingent (produced). It assumes that the production of reality is the practice of power, that reality is nothing but the effects of its own articulation (as becomings or transformations). And consequently, the logic of productivity means that reality cannot be bracketed out from cultural studies, nor can it be always constructed as mediated by the categories of human intelligibility.[11]

The logic of productivity also addresses what I take to be a significant absence in contemporary cultural studies: namely an elaborated theory of articulation. Articulation is a crucial concept for cultural studies for it embodies its theory and practice of radical contextualism. For the most part, cultural studies has failed to think through the consequences and strategic possibilities of articulation as both an intellectual and a political practice. And as a result, questions about the agencies, effectivities and modalities of articulation (and power) remain largely unexamined. Articulation is not merely another version of a theory of polysemy, or a way of recognising the necessity and possibilities of decoding.[12] Articulation is too often seen merely as cultural studies' attempt to occupy a middle space between essentialist theories (which can vary from a position which asserts that all relations, insofar as they are real, are necessary, to one which simply asserts that there are some necessary relations in the world) and the anti-essentialism of post-structuralist theories (which denies the reality of any relation). I would prefer to read the notion of articulation as cultural studies' way of avoiding the debate altogether and leaving the field in which the debate is meaningful. It transforms the question of the reality of relations into a matter of practices. Articulation is the practice – and its description – of the making, unmaking and remaking of non-necessary relations and, hence, of contexts. It assumes that relations (whether in the form of identities, effects, etc.) didn't have to be the way they are (i.e. they are contingent), but the fact that they are that way makes them real (i.e. effective). Articulation is, in Foucault's terms, the relation of a non-relation. A theory of articulation transforms cultural criticism and politics from questions of texts and audiences, to explorations of events and alliances, effects and contexts, and an account of the ways certain practices and apparatuses articulate contexts – as organisations of power – as the lived milieux of everyday life.

The logic of spatiality has to be understood as more than just a move into geography, just as the logic of temporality is more than just a move into history. It involves a shift in the 'metaphysical' ground for theorising. It does not mean that we erase time and history but that we see reality as events or, in Deleuze's terms, becomings which can be mapped only as lines across space, rather than as temporal continuities and discontinuities (whether as questions of reproduction or of deferral).[13] Such lines define the attempt to describe the real as, again in Deleuzean terms, a pragmatics of the multiple. The notion of the multiple (or multiplicity) here refers to the exteriority or otherness of events, to the fact that they cannot be 'interpreted' as different (as if they belonged to some already constituted totality) but must be mapped as a 'geography'. The existence of events can only be measured – and they can be measured as it were – by their effectivity, by their ability to affect and be affected. As such, events can only be located – mapped – in space along the trajectories of the lines of their effectivities. Again, this does not render history meaningless: on the contrary, within certain geographies (including of course the geography of modern power), certain kinds of becomings or lines of effectivity which are marked as history, time and reproduction, can be invested with a great deal of intensity and even power. One can in fact reconstruct the modern as a geography of temporalities. Within a logic of spatiality, the spaces, apparatuses and effects of power have to be understood in terms of mobilities rather than change, of lines of intensities rather than identities. Reality is a matter of orientations and directions, of entries and exits, rather than processes. More concretely, it means that we have to see cultural practices as 'busy intersections' (Rosaldo, 1989), as places where many things happen, where multiple trajectories of effects and investment intersect. As Frow and Morris (1993) suggest, it means that we should take Mauss's notion of a 'total social phenomenon' more seriously, as the point of intersection and negotiation of radically different kinds of vectors of determination – including material, affective, libidinal, semiotic, semantic, etc.

The theory I am proposing examines 'machines' as technologies and organisations of becoming which produce the real as maps of power. These machines impose a particular conduct and organisation, not only on specific multiplicities, but also on particular planes of effects. They define the 'geometric mechanisms' by which different kinds of individualities and subjects (implying neither identities nor subjectivities) are produced in and articulated into specific configurations. The notion of geometric mechanisms, introduced by Kellert (1993) in his description of chaos theory, proposes a model of explanation which is neither causal nor predictive. This is similar in fact to Foucault's (1981) theory of eventalisation, where each event is a singularity, defined within a monism of practices, constituted by trajectories cutting across multiple domains of reference, determination and effects. Foucault defines an apparatus as a programming of behaviour which, at the least, involves the relations between persons, subjections and bodies. It is a heterogeneous ensemble of practices, 'the said as much as the unsaid' – the material, the discursive and the semiotic – all of which condition and modify each other's functions and effects. An apparatus is comprised of regimes or technologies of jurisdiction and of veridication. The former prescribe what can be done (procedures and strategies); the latter define discourses of truth. While particular regimes of veridication are articulated to and for regimes of jurisdiction, they are not necessarily effective. That is, there are no necessary correspondences between strategies, their legitimations, and their effects. Moreover, we cannot assume that various regimes and apparatuses are consistent, either with each other or even among themselves. I am proposing a philosophical perspective that might appropriately be called spatial materialism,[14] and which, I hope, gives both substance and form to the notion of articulation by moving it into a theoretical field defined by something other than the logics of modern thought.

Three theories of globalisation

I want now to illustrate the possibilities of theorising within these spatial and productive logics by considering three different 'models' of globalisation present to different degrees in cultural studies. I will quite intentionally leave the issue of whether these models are competing descriptions of a single organisation of globalisation, or compatible descriptions of significantly different organisations. Instead I want to do two things with each model: first, I want to consider its utility for understanding the specificity of contemporary forces and structures of globalisation; and second, I want to read each model as presenting globalisation as if it were based on a different mode of articulation, or a different machinic production of the real – coding, territorialising and stratifying.

Globalisation as a coding machine

The most common view of globalisation defines it as a relationship operating in the middle ground between an infinitely small event (the local as a totally isolated place with no lines connecting it either to an outside or to other places) and infinitely large spaces (with no distance possible between places, thus allowing for instantaneous transforma-tions across space). This middle ground is then constituted by a struggle between, on the one hand, the force of globalisation which homogen-ises, producing the same at every place, and, on the other hand, the force of localisation which heterogenises or hybridises, producing differences by rearticulating the forms of the global into the local. That is, global-isation is a relation between places, and moreover a relation predicated on an assumed distinction between two kinds of places: certain places become the apparent origins of the forces of globalisation which emanate from within them, while other places inevitably become the sites of competing forces of localisation. These different places are traced onto an already existing map of the distribution of power. Globalisation is a power that generally belongs to 'the West' (if not the United States), while localisation is a power that belongs to the so-called peripheral nations or to peripheral communities within the core nations. Too much attention to the global often leads critics to the unearned, pessimistic conclusion that the victory – of capitalism, of American imperialism, etc. – is already sewn up. Too much attention to the local often leads critics to lose sight of the fact that someone is winning the struggle and, as we all know, it is rarely the periphery.

Generally, the contemporary processes (for they are generally under-stood in temporal terms) of globalisation are assumed to continue 'the every rolling march of the old form of commodification, the old form of globalization, fully in the keeping of the west, which is simply able to absorb everybody else within its drive' (Hall, 1991). But this makes the question of globalisation into little more than a continuation of earlier debates over cultural imperialism, with its assumption that culture merely follows the circuit of commodities and capital. For the most part, when the debate assumes these terms, it operates on the assumption that the nature of globalisation itself has not changed or that all that has changed is the relative degree, speed, intensity, etc. of the relation. On the other hand, it is possible to argue that this model of globalisation is no longer appropriate as a description of the spatial economy of the contemporary world, although such an argument need not challenge the basic parameters of the model of globalisation.

For example, Stuart Hall (1991) offers one of the most sophisticated and insightful discussions, along these lines, of globalisation. Hall seems to argue that such a model of the continuing and continuous march of capitalism may be inadequate to describe even older forms of globalisation, often encapsulated in notions of mercantilism, colonial-ism, imperialism and forced diasporas, because

> The more we understand about the development of capital itself, the more we understand that . . . alongside that drive to commodify everything, which is certainly one part of its logic, is another critical part of its logic which works in and through specificity . . . So that the notion of the ever-marching, ongoing, totally rationalizing, has been a very deceptive way of persuading ourselves of the totally integrative and all-absorbent capacities of capital itself . . . As a consequence, we have lost sight of one of the most profound insights in Marx's *Capital* which is that capitalism only advances, as it were, on contradictory terrain. (p.29)

Yet, while Hall also calls for a new and distinct model of contemporary globalisation which recognises that it entails different relations, rhythms and motivations, Hall's description actually does not allow for any significant structural changes in the form of globalisation. And, ultimately, it remains within the basic logic of globalisation as a rela-tion between different places. Or more accurately, it remains within a spatial topography that assumes an absolute difference between the local and the global, and between places and spaces, and that assumes as well an equivalence between these two sets of relations which is then

collapsed into a relation between different places. It is a logic of difference in which, ultimately, all differences are equated. Actually, Hall
seems to want to move away from such a logic and he makes a promis-
ing beginning (into something more like a logic of territorialisation): he
describes contemporary globalisation as a structure which is both
global and local at the same time, involving new structures of relations
between processes of globalisation and the construction of multiple
levels of localities which both interrupt and amplify global flows. Thus,
Hall points out, the erosion of the nation-state and national identities
(the result of new forms of the migration of labour and the flow of
capital) is counterbalanced by the even stronger return of 'defensive
exclusions', new ecological relations and a new cultural practice which
constructs unity through difference. This new culture, what Hall calls
the 'global postmodern', does not speak a single language or ideology,
or rather, it is unable to construct a single dialect as proper and normal.
Instead, in order to be effective, it must both pluralise and deconstruct
itself. But as soon as Hall tries to reinsert the question of power and of
unequal relations into the model, he returns to something very similar
to the logic of difference described here. Thus, he says, we have to recognise that this global postmodern still originates from a position of
power in the West, and that it is still constructing a form of homogen-
isation (and perhaps even hegemony), although now we can say that it
is homogenising precisely by working through difference.

I want to suggest that Hall's theory is an example of a model of
globalisation which operates by setting up a particular series of differences which are then somehow made equivalent: first, a relation
between two places (or more accurately, a relation between one and
many places, usually in the form of the relationship between the United
States and the rest of the world, or between the Atlantic–capitalist
centre and the various peripheries) which takes for granted both the category of place and the existence of specific places; second, a geographical relation between two forms of spatial individuation in the form of
a relation between place and space, where the latter is often treated as
little more than the empty environment through which forces, defined
within specific places, move; and third, an articulated relation between
the local and the global, linking different places within a single determining economy of power. In fact, different versions of such a model
can be distinguished on the basis of the rhetoric of transformations
which establishes the equivalences among these three differences.

I want to describe such a model as a construction of globalization as a coding machine. Coding machines work by expanding or extending themselves into apparently independent realms which they incorporate into or bind to themselves by inscribing codes of identity and difference. They normalise every event by differentiating it from the others, and then identifying it with some. Coding machines produce disjunctive articulations: all relations are of the form 'either/or'. In fact, within such a machine, I think it is actually impossible to distinguish between older forms of globalisation and the contemporary context of globalisation. It may in fact be an accurate description of older forms of globalisation, at least for the period of modern colonialism and imperialism. Such machines of globalisation produced organisations, not only of extension but of the extension of particular forms defined in terms of relations of identity and difference. That is, here globalisation involves decoding existing forms of social and cultural relations according to the operational codes of the colonising power. In this sense, such machines also set fairly simple parameters for the relations of becoming within the space of globalisation: the colonised becoming the colonisers and the colonisers becoming the colonised.[15] Not only does such a theory fail to distinguish between old and new forms of globalisation, it also fails to offer any account of the distinctive relation between 'culture' and capitalism. Instead of seeing both globalisation and localisation as modes of articulation, as two vectors within a specific contextual economy, the former defining a force of mobility, the latter a force of enclosure or boundary production, coding machines establish a series of transformations which always return them to the relations between place and space, and ultimately between different kinds of places.

Globalisation as a territorialising machine

A second model of globalisation identifies it as a relation of space and place, or more accurately a question of movements between places, across a space, although usually this space remains largely empty and powerless. To a large extent, the question of the relation between the local and the global – the most common form in which the question of power is raised – disappears. Such theories, not coincidentally, are often closely connected to some version of postmodernism as a vision of contemporaneity and history. Thus, it is no coincidence that Arjun Appadurai's (1990) theory of globalisation begins by equating globalisation and postmodernisation. Thus, according to Appadurai, globalisation is 'close to the central problematic of cultural processes in today's world . . . the world we now live in seems rhizomatic – calling for theories of rootlessness, alienation and psychological distance between individuals and groups on the one hand, and fantasies (or nightmares) of electronic propinquity on the other'. Although the question of localisation (and hybridisation) is raised, it is given short shrift in the model of globalisation itself. Moreover, Appadurai refuses to identify the economy of globalisation with a map of power (defined by particular places) that merely reproduces the geography of the centre and the periphery, arguing instead that the power relations operating within globalisation are themselves locally specific, a matter of larger nations overpowering smaller ones.

But these issues play a minor role in Appadurai's essay. The major argument transforms the question of global forces, including 'post-industrial [cultural] productions', into a description of the dimensions of global flows. Appadurai offers five such flows in his account of contemporary globalisation: ethnoscapes involve the movement of people; technoscapes, the movement of technologies; finanscapes, the movement of money and capital; mediascapes, the movement of images; and ideoscapes, the movement of ideologies and state politics. One might ask about the selection: why is there no 'scape' for information, commodities, the military, etc.?[16] More important, however, is the fact that for Appadurai the world has increasingly come to be dominated by the transition from local to global forces which apparently necessarily operate to produce increasing de-territorialisation and displacement (e.g. in the form of 'disorganized capitalism'). Further, according to Appadurai, what is central to the politics of global culture is not only the fact that the different 'scapes' follow separate non-isomorphic paths, but that the sheer speed, scale and volume of these flows has become so great that the very unpredictabilities of the disjunctures have themselves become determining.

Thus, according to Appadurai, the nature of contemporary globalisation requires new models of cultural organisation and transformation, and he proposes fractals and chaos theory as the solutions. Fractals are scholar phenomena describing shapes which, while possessing no Euclidean boundaries, still exhibit a constant degree of irregularity across different scales. Chaos is a theory of non-linear dynamic systems with 'sensitive dependence on initial conditions'. Both describe transformations within spatial economies or what I will call relations of territoriality. Appadurai's theory offers important insights into contemporary globalisation, partly because it largely succeeds in separating questions of identity, identification and globalisation, and partly because the organisation of space has become the active site – although still not the agent – of power. But I also think it has serious limitations which are not just accidental but the result of the model on which it is predicated, and in particular of the structural similarities between the model and postmodernism. First, it can tell us nothing about the becomings of and within each of the 'scapes' or, to put it in other terms, like most postmodernisms, it actually tells us very little about the actual, specific operations of power within the particular vectors of global force. Second, it assumes the absolute autonomy of the 'scapes'; each one seems to demand and control its own logic, leaving each completely intact and unable to contact or influence those forces operating alongside it.

Appadurai seems to end up with a position (whether he intends to is a different question) that asserts, like many postmodernisms, that nothing is related to anything. In fact, I think we should consider the possibility that this may actually be a somewhat accurate description of an older form of globalisation in which, while capitalism may have been its driving force, capital was produced as only one value which could still be contradicted by other values, including geographical expansion and empire, ideological values of civilisation, etc. While these values could be and sometimes were articulated to one another, they cannot be assumed to have been – and there is no evidence they were – simply and functionally equated without contradiction. In fact, older forms of globalisation were most likely the result of multiple forces, and even multiple machines, including both coding and territorialising machines (such as Appadurai's model of 'scapes'), operating by simultaneously extending and distributing their logics. Thus, colonialism was not merely a matter of capitalism (which was largely confined within the sphere of the economic); it did not work only in the economic. And it is entirely reasonable to assume that different machines were operating in the different spheres of power on which colonialism was constructed.

I have described Appadurai's theory as built upon the model of a territorialising machine. A territorialising machine is one which is already extended across space. Rather than extending itself by tracing its codes of difference on previously external events, it performs an intensional distribution. It conjunctively links singular events into spatial relations of proximity and distance, defining what is next to what. In other words, it transforms events into places and distributes them as other (rather than different) to each other. As a result, it makes place the product of space, as it were, and space the milieu of active becoming, or more accurately, of trajectories of becoming. But in the process, it erases the effectivity of places.

Globalisation as a stratifying machine

There is another kind of postmodern machine in which the same logic or force works everywhere, thus erasing all places. Instead of a multiplicity of events in a relationship of otherness (or exteriority) to each other, such a machine denies both differences and distribution in favour of a continuous production of the same. For example, imagine a globalising machine in which everything is reduced to capital or to the image. In fact, the third model proposes that the contemporary form of globalisation is produced by a single machine operating across all of the scapes (spheres, planes or domains): 'the same machine at work in astrophysics and in microphysics, in the natural and the artificial' (Deleuze and Guattari, 1987). Here the machine operates not to erase all differences, but to produce a particular stratification or division within the real (and thus, to produce the real). It reworks the codings (identities) and distributions (identifications) that already exist, but not by recoding or re-territorialising them. What kind of a machine might this be?

I will take Deleuze and Guattari's theory of contemporary global capitalism as an example of such a theory of contemporary globalisation. Such a theory suggests at least two significant shifts from older forms of globalisation, and from the above models. First, what global capitalism produces is no longer the form of value (capital) but its substance (money),[17] for it is as money that capital is most productive today; hence, we can take note of the rapid decline in investment. What has become evident, especially since the decade of the 1980s, is the presence and power of an increasing pool of private unregulated stateless money, an ecumenical body, a 'financial Frankenstein'. According to *The Economist* (April 1993), 'traditional banking went out the window in the 1980s' (cited in Wheelwright, 1994) with the rise of the derivatives market, a market defined by various forms of futures contracts, mostly related to foreign exchange, interest rates, etc. Of course, these developments were neither totally accidental nor entirely intentional. They were the result of transformations within the logic of capital which had very specific economic, political, technological and cultural conditions of possibility. *The Economist* claims that:

the foreign exchange market [is] the world's slickest. Daily net turnover (including derivatives), was about $900 billion, only $50 billion less than the total foreign currency reserves of all IMF members, and more than the combined reserves of all the great powers. Foreign exchange trading has grown by over a third since April 1989. Less than five per cent relates to underlying trade flows; ten to fifteen percent represents capital movements; most of the remaining eighty percent is the dealing of banks between themselves.

It is not surprising then that this global market in money futures can literally determine the fate of any national economy almost overnight. Nor is it surprising that this continual circulation of money seems to be producing an infinite debt or at least 'the means for rendering that debt infinite' (Deleuze and Guattari, 1987), not as an aberration but as the necessary condition for capitalism itself.

Of course, it is possible to argue that this whole situation is merely some kind of temporary aberration of capitalism which needs to be brought under control. But it is just as reasonable to assume, with Deleuze and Guattari, that the ever-spiraling debt, which includes both the poorest and the richest nations, does not represent the failure of industrial capital but capitalism's unrestricted ability to create more money which is constantly owed to itself. This is perhaps a new development in the history of finance capital, which E. P. Thompson defines as 'an articulated combination of commercial capital, industrial capital, and banking capital, within which banking capital is dominant, but not determinant' (Wheelwright, 1994). Other economists have recognised that the power of finance capital is to unify 'the previously separate spheres of industrial, commercial and bank capital'. It is possible that the particular formation of capitalism which Gramsci referred to as 'Fordism' – built on the development of domestic markets, mass production and the simultaneously dominant and determinant role of industrial capital – was the aberration. Then, what we are witnessing today is the realisation of the limit-possibility of finance capital in which banking capital (in the form of money) is not only dominant but also determinant. It is at least possible that the emergence of an international economy of debt financing and of the ecumenical flows of money begetting money, built on the spatial displacement of production and the increasing centrality of services (including cultural production), is not the sign of the failure of capitalism, but the beginning of a cycle of capital rejuvenation that promises the emergence of a new formation of capitalism. There is certainly no reason to assume that this formation would be any more benign than previous articulations of capitalism and globalisation; on the contrary, it shows every promise of becoming the most devastating and exploitative form of social power the world has ever seen, partly because of the second shift in the economy of globalisation which this machine produces.

If this were the only effect of this machine that the theory describes, what Deleuze and Guattari propose would be little more than another version of a postmodernising machine, comparable to Baudrillard, in which everything becomes the same, or in this case, money. But that is not the case, for their argument is that the first shift, operating as it were on one strata (the plane of content), is only possible because the machinery of globalisation is also operating simultaneously on a second strata (the plane of expression), and in fact the work of the machine is precisely to produce these strata together by articulating the relation between them.

Turning our attention to the second strata, then, we can remember Hall's claim that capitalism has to work with and across differences. Let us in fact accept this as true, at least in the past. Deleuze and Guattari explain this by arguing that traditionally capitalism attempted to refuse any coding (difference) which tied its productivity to an external code. Hence, they suggest, capitalism always moved ahead by producing decoded flows, but such decodings are never absolute for they are always limited by the recodings of capitalism's own 'axiomatics'. But perhaps this is no longer the case: just as the machine of contemporary global-isation has transformed the value of capitalism from capital to money, perhaps it has also changed the relationship of capitalism to difference. In fact, I would suggest that capitalism no longer works with and across difference but, rather, that it works to produce difference itself as the new form of expression. Unlike coding machines, it is not the particu-lar codes of difference that are important; it is not the content but the form of difference that is relevant. It is the form of difference that is being produced everywhere, on everything and that is articulated by the same machine to the production of money.[18] In other words, a new globalising machine is producing differences at the level of expression, as part of and in the service of both a newly emerging re-configuration of capitalism and a reorganization of the spatial economy of global power itself. This machine makes capitalism into a technology of dis-tribution rather than production, by producing a stratification in which differences proliferate in a highly re-territorialised world. Obviously, if this is the case, it makes the current faith in difference, as the site of resistance and agency, quite problematic. It is not merely a matter of claiming that this new globalising machine is reproducing itself across or even as space; rather, it attempts to produce space as differences and differences as space, a project which, as in all cases of machines of power, may never be entirely realisable.[19] But if difference has become the very geometrical mechanism of a new organisation of power, then the very possibility and meaning of social order is no less at stake than the meaning and possibility of social transformation, resistance and oppositional politics.[20]

I have described this third model as a stratifying machine, which operates by drawing lines, connecting events. It can be understood along the lines of Foucault's notion of a diagram which can be understood as schema for the organisation and exercise of power (Deleuze, 1988). In Foucault, the diagram stratifies or divides reality into the sayable and the visible or, more generally, into the knowable and the known. In more abstract terms, the stratifying machines organise events into two distinct populations or strata. Content describes a 'precise state of intermingling of bodies'; it is a non-passive assemblage of that which is acted upon. Expression describes the functional or transformational individualities which act upon content. Each plane, as well as the diagram itself, embodies a distinct principle of agency.[21] It is important to realise that there is nothing inherent or essential about particular events that guarantee in advance what strata they will be 'assigned' to, as it were. Rather it is by organising and connecting the events that the stratifying machine constructs every reality as the relation of these two strata. Each strata defines a range of possible events or actions, so that together they define a practiced and practice-able (at the organic level, a livable) reality. Moreover each strata has both a form (on which coding machines operate to establish homologies within a strata) and a substance (on which territorialising machines operate). Thus, the stratifying machine (or diagram) is the condition of possibility – in spatial rather than temporal terms – for both coding and territorialising machines.

I have not attempted to adjudicate between these three machines as models of contemporary globalisation, although I have made some observations along the way which certainly suggest my own suspicions. It will be, in the end, impossible to describe the contemporary spatial economy of power without taking all three machines into account, but that still does not solve the problem: insofar as there is something new and specific about that economy, within which of these three models must it be located? In some sense, this is obviously an empirical question – not one to be answered out of an already defined theoretical position – but it is also a question that cannot begin to be answered unless we are willing to rethink the philosophical foundations of cultural studies, and to challenge its continued articulation within modern structures of thought.

Conclusion

I want to end by returning to the question of how to do cultural studies in the age of contemporary globalisation, for it is, I believe, necessary to rethink the task of cultural studies. That is, as cultural studies is re-articulated into and by the logics of productivity and spatiality, the very ways it describes its tasks and practices will have to be rethought as well. I want to take a brief stab at that now, although it is obviously premature. It will be easier to start with those ways of describing cultural studies that are clearly inappropriate within a productive and spatial logic, even though some of them may describe things that cultural studies is already in danger of becoming. Cultural studies is not about mapping the aesthetic onto the social, or the theoretical onto the textual, or the social onto the aesthetic. It is not about tracing the trajectories of desire and power, or the inscriptions of the social in the text. It is not about treating theory as a metaphor for social or textual processes, nor treating social and textual processes as metaphors for theory. It is not about rediscovering what we already know – whether about domination or the possibilities of resistance – anywhere in the relations among texts, subjects, and the social. It cannot be described simply in terms of the relations between the production of culture, cultural texts and the consumption of culture, as if merely reproducing Marx's circuit of production. Nor is it exclusively about the relations of ideology, desire and pleasure. It is not the ethnographic documentation of the local. It is not, at least in the first instance, the embodiment of a grand epistemological revolution, although it may be built on one, and it certainly does challenge traditional notions of 'rigorous methodologies'. It is not simply a theory of the textual production and/or communication of meaning, or the construction of subject-positions within systems of difference, or the politics of representation. Cultural studies may use all of these things but it will always be on its way to somewhere else.

I think that cultural studies, as it moves outside the determinations of modern thought, is about the relations on articulations between discursive alliances, everyday life and the machineries of power. Discursive alliances are, I believe, the 'object' of cultural studies. A discursive alliance is always more than *texts* and always more than *a* discursive practice; it is an articulated configuration of practices, a piece of the context as it were, constructed by the critic in his or her attempt to map the real effectivities of cultural relations.[22] Such alliances define not only where and how people 'live' specific practices, but also provide cultural studies' way into the lived experience of power, reality, etc. By everyday life, I want to signal that the ways we live are themselves configurations or structures of power. Here we can, for example, distinguish, with Foucault, between regimes of sovereignty, of discipline, of governmentality and, I might add, of disciplined mobilisation. And finally, by the machineries of power, I mean the apparatuses that mobilise different parameters and aspects of power to organise space and thus, among other things, to produce the possibilities of alliances.[23] What I am proposing then, finally, is that cultural studies must escape culture. It may start with culture, it may construct culture as its object, but its real task is to describe, understand and project the possibilities of lived material contexts as organisations of power. Its task is to understand the operations of power in the lived reality of human beings, and to help all of us imagine new alternatives for the becoming of that reality. Culture is both its site and its weapon, but it is not the limits of cultural studies' world. In the end, I am trying to disarticulate cultural studies from the modern 'discovery' of the social construction of reality, to find a way, not to get rid of discourse and culture, but to de-imperialise them by bringing back notions of space and material reality.

Notes

1 This chapter draws upon and revises ideas first presented in Grossberg (1996a). It is part of a larger project on the philosophical foundations of cultural studies and the critique of modern thought.

2 For an elaboration of this description, see Grossberg (1995a). Certainly the most common definition of cultural studies at the moment would seem to equate it with theories of power organised around structures of identity and difference: gender, sexuality, race, nationality, ethnicity, etc.

3 See Chen (1996).

4 I am grateful to Doreen Massey (personal conversation) for making this clear. See Massey (1994).

5 For an elaboration of the place of economics in cultural studies, see Grossberg (1995b); McRobbie (1996) and Clarke (1991).

6 For an elaboration of this critique of the centrality of the politics of identity and difference in cultural studies, see Grossberg (1996b). For the critique of the privileging of marginality, see Tony Bennett (1993) on charismatic closure.

7 My own work draws upon a line of philosophy that can be traced back to the premodern philosophy of Spinoza. However, Spinoza's has to be contextualised as part of a regional history of the Mediterranean/Middle East which includes Jewish (e.g. Maimonides) and Arab (Ibn Sina) thinkers. See Alcalay (1993).

8 See Grossberg (forthcoming).

9 Of course, this is a crucial problem with broad implications. Does one need such a position in order to define and mobilise political opposition? Must such a position equate the political and the ethical? How is one to respond to a postmodern relativism which would seem to undermine not only the possibility of such a position, but the possibility of politics itself? What is the relation between ethical and political positions, especially in the context of the United States where ethics tends to dominate politics, even in political discourses?

10 But this emphasis on mobility and marginality is certainly characteristic of a much broader range of discourses within cultural studies, especially postcolonial theory.

11 Obviously, this would seem to raise serious epistemological issues – about how we know, how we constitute the object (event) and the subject. I am reluctant to take these issues up, partly because I think the priority of epistemology is a function of the logics of modern thought.

12 In fact, such notions preceded the emergence of modern thought.

13 I am aware of a certain rhetorical excess here. While it would certainly be reasonable to refer here to a logic of space-time rather than simply space, there are at least two reasons which favour the latter strategy. First, because of the central place of temporality in modernity, space-time is likely to quickly become time or at least, and this is the second reason, the relation between space and time is likely to be conceptualised dimensionally, thus enabling space and time to be radically separated and opening the possibility of a reprivileging of time.

14 There is an obvious implicit reference to Marx here. And after all, Marx as much as Deleuze and Guattari (or Spinoza) can be read as a critique of

Kantian modernism. But Marx's critique of Kant was limited: while he made the space of culture into the site of power, he could not problematise that space. He could not recognise that the production of this space itself (in the logic of mediation) was a product/production of power. At the same time, he obviously could neither account for, nor escape the privileging of temporality and history. At the same time, I do not see my position as 'post-Marxist' except in the weakest sense: I am trying to take account of the limitations of Marxism as articulated by Marx produced by the articulation of the apparatuses of modernity and a particular formation of capitalism.

15 One might think here of the work of Homi Bhabha and, as well, of Gauri Viswanathan.

16 One can also question why ethnoscapes are given so much prominence across so many discourses. The answer seems to have to do with the centrality of post-colonial critics in current work, and the fact that the politics of identity and difference is still often taken for granted within the continuing space of both poststructuralism and cultural studies.

17 Another way of viewing this would be to say that fictitious capital has become real and determinant if not dominant.

18 This is connected in powerful ways to the decline of private property, even in the advanced capitalism world: e.g. the collapse of the dream of owning a house and the rise of leasing agreements.

19 Consider here the current celebrations of the exotic.

20 One possible misreading of this argument (globalisation as stratification) is that it basically reproduces a base-superstructure model. This is not correct: first, because the present argument is specific to a particular formation rather than a general theory; and second, because it claims that the relation between expression and content is not expressive since it is produced elsewhere (by the diagram as it were). Thus it is not that content produces expression, but that the stratifying machine (or what Deleuze and Guattari call the abstract machine) produces both always in relationship.

21 This is distinguished from pragmatism which generally assumes the same machines operating on every strata and in every stratification.

22 Obviously, I am questioning the role of the category of text in cultural studies. I would argue that texts have to be reconceived as a particular construction of certain events within discursive alliances.

23 From the perspective of the producers of an apparatus, what is produced is the audience-context relation; from the perspective of the audience, what is produced is the audience-text relation; and from the perspective of cultural studies, what is produced is the space of context.

References

Alcalay, Ammiel (1993) *After Jews and Arabs: Remaking Levantine Culture*, Minneapolis: University of Minnesota Press.

Appadurai, Arjun (1990) 'Disjuncture and difference in the global cultural economy', *Public Culture* 2.

Bauman, Zygmunt (1990) *Legislators and Interpreters*, Cambridge: Polity.

Bennett, Tony (1993) 'Being "in the true" of cultural studies', *Southern Review* 26:2.

Chen, Kuan-Hsing (1996) 'Not yet the postcolonial era: the (super) nation-state and the trans*nationalism* of cultural studies', *Cultural Studies* 10:1.

Clarke, John (1991) *Old Times New Enemies*, New York: Routledge.

Clifford, James (1988) *The Predicament of Culture: Twentieth Century Ethnography, Literature and Art*, Cambridge: Harvard University Press.

Deleuze, Gilles (1988) *Foucault*, trans. Sean Hand, Minneapolis: University of Minnesota Press.

Deleuze, Gilles and Guattari, Felix (1987) *Anti-Oedipus: Capitalism and Schizophrenia*, trans. R. Hurley, M. Seem and H. Lane, Minneapolis: University of Minnesota Press.

Foucault, Michel (1981) 'Questions of method: an interview', *I & C* 8, pp. 3–14.

Frow, John and Morris, Meaghan (1993) 'Introduction' to *Australian Cultural Studies: A Reader*, Urbana: University of Illinois Press.

Gilroy, Paul (1993) *The Black Atlantic: Modernity and Double Consciousness*, Cambridge: Harvard University Press.

Grossberg, Lawrence (1995a) 'Cultural studies: what's in a name (one more time)', *Taboo*, 1.

Grossberg, Lawrence, (1995b) 'Cultural studies vs political economy: is anybody else bored with this debate?', *Critical Studies in Mass Communication* 12, pp. 72–81.

Grossberg, Lawrence (1996a) 'The space of culture, the power of space: cultural studies and globalization', in Iain Chambers and Liddia Curti (eds) *The Postcolonial Question*, London: Routledge.

Grossberg, Lawrence (1996b) 'Identity and cultural studies: is that all there is?', in Stuart Hall and Paul de Gay (eds) *Cultural Studies and Identity*, London: Sage.

Grossberg, Lawrence (forthcoming) 'Space and cultural studies'.

Grossberg, Lawrence, Nelson, Cary and Treichler, Paula (eds) (1992) *Questions of Cultural Identity*, New York: Routledge.

Hall, Stuart (1991) 'The local and the global', in Anthony D. King (ed.) *Culture Globalization and the World System*, London: Macmillan.

Hunter, Ian (1988) *Culture and Government: The Emergence of Literary Education*, London: Macmillan.

Kellert, Stephen H. (1993) *In The Wake of Chaos*, Chicago: University of Chicago Press.

Massey, Doreen (1994) *Space, Place and Gender*, Cambridge: Polity.

McRobbie, Angela (1996) 'Looking back at New Times and its critics', in David Morley and Kuan-Hsing Chen (eds) *Stuart Hall: Critical Dialogues in Cultural Studies*, London: Routledge.

Morris, Meaghan (1988) 'Tooth and claw: Tales of survival and *Crocodile Dundee*', in *The Pirate's Fiancee: Feminism Reading Postmodernism*, London: Verso.

Morris, Meaghan (1992) 'On the beach', in Grossberg *et al.* (eds) *Cultural Studies*, New York: Routledge.

O'Hanlon, Rosalind (1988) 'Recovering the subject: subaltern studies and histories of resistance in colonial South Asia', *Modern Asian Studies* 22.

Robbins, Bruce (1993) *Secular Vocations: Intellectuals, Professionalism, Culture*, London: Verso.

Rosaldo, Renato (1989) *Culture and Truth: the Remaking of Social Analysis*, Boston: Beacon.

Wachtel, Howard (1986) *The Money Mandarins*, New York: Pantheon Books.

Wheelwright, Ted (1994) 'Futures, markets, . . .' *Arena Magazine* February–March.

Williams, Raymond (1958) *Culture and Society 1780–1950*, New York: Harper and Row.

A question of cultural studies

When asked to describe the pedagogical project of their work, scholars in cultural studies are fond of citing the lesson that Raymond Williams drew from his experience of extramural teaching in postwar Britain: 'the real power in a classroom is the power to define the questions, and, by asking questions, to challenge the comfortable boundaries of the teacher's own disciplinary competencies'.[1] However, when I was recently asked to address the topic 'A question of cultural studies' the title had me wondering for weeks, 'which question?'.[2]

Any academic author will ask, as a matter of course, which questions she should address, and most wonder what expectations an audience will bring to a topic. To discuss cultural studies, however, is to face special difficulties. Take my title, for example. We rarely come across texts called 'A question of history' or 'A question of English', and when we do it is understood that they are likely to be using the names of the disciplines in a limited rather than a global sense; in practice, 'English' or 'history' rarely refers to the geographically dispersed and institutionally diverse history of an entire academic enterprise. No one familiar with academic work expects 'English' or 'history' to be encompassed by a single question, and practitioners can normally take it for granted that they will share with most audiences at least some understanding, however basic, of what it is that these disciplines do.

Cultural studies, in contrast, is a relatively recent, minor and still, perhaps, unfamiliar development in the humanities. So it is all too easily assumed, especially by its critics, that the whole of cultural studies can be dealt with in summary fashion (reading one or two articles or authors suffices to form an opinion), and that the only serious question that it raises is the question of its very legitimacy not just as a discipline – a question much debated in cultural studies itself – but as any kind of scholarly endeavour. In part, this assumption derives from the relative newness of cultural studies as a project merely thirty years old, and from a real uncertainty, shared by its exponents as well as its critics, about its institutional place. It is also a product of the intensely reductive polemic that has attended the recent emergence of 'cultural studies' as an object of fanciful and sometimes derisive media commentary. So I have to wonder whether there is likely to be any congruence, at the moment, between the questions that a diverse group of humanists may bring to a discussion of cultural studies, or any congruence between those questions and my own.

Should I begin, once again, with a question of definition – what *is* cultural studies?[3] I'd rather not, since there are many treatments of this question and I believe that it is high time for more Australian practitioners to put their heads down, ignore the flak, and start producing the substantive accounts of cultural life, past and present, that we claim that our field can generate and that would clarify our project. On the other hand, cultural studies is nothing if not 'public' in its sense of intellectual vocation. So is it reasonable to ask whether cultural studies is really – as Don Anderson so vividly explained in the *Sydney Morning Herald* – a form of 'Paterson's Curse' spreading through our universities and replacing the study of literature with studies of *Middlemarch* as television soap?[4] Or is cultural studies rather, as Beatrice Faust suggests in one of the strangest polemics I have read, 'a Swiss army knife made in China'?[5] – a cheap, inauthentic reproduction (as my parents used to say about those Japanese cars and television sets) of a 'real thing' fabricated somewhere else?

Published as a column in the *Weekend Australian*, Faust's article is a good example of the weird and wonderful mythology now flourishing around cultural studies. Faust is not alone in believing that 'Cultural studies rejects the traditional . . . arts that constitute high culture and need a modicum of background, taste and critical aptitude before they become pleasurable'. Nor is she the only critic to proceed from this false premise to assume that she herself can dispense with acquiring 'a modicum of background' in cultural studies before declaring it bunk. What does surprise me is that a reputable author should so confidently rebuke cultural studies for not doing 'until recently' the very things that one of its major strands has long been famous for doing, namely asking consumers of culture to evaluate their own activities, finding out 'who goes to Madonna concerts', and producing 'specific or quantitative' studies of the results. Faust also informs her readers that 'cultural students' will only discuss Barbara Cartland 'the better to attack her' in sermons against capitalism, sexism and racism. In fact, leading figures in British and US cultural studies have for years been under attack from other practitioners (including me) for espousing an anaesthetic optimism about Madonna and Barbara Cartland that renders *criticism* of their work illegitimate.[6]

If 'cultural studies' is becoming a media *topos* allowing otherwise sensible scholars to talk wildly through their hats, Lawrence Grossberg, one of the foremost US practitioners of cultural studies, may be right to suggest, however humorously he does so, that his field is in fact 'the Generation X of the academic world':

> Like the post baby-boom generation that is referenced in this odd phrase . . . everyone is talking about it but no one seems to know what it is. Lots of people are suddenly claiming to do it while others, nervous about its rather sudden success, are attacking it.[7]

Perhaps the 'question of cultural studies' raised here is why the academy should need an X factor at this time. An X factor is an empty but structurally necessary form that operates independently of the contents attributed to it. Twenty-five years ago, the catalyst for nervousness in the humanities was structuralism; fifteen years ago, semiotics and post-structuralism; ten years ago, postmodernism; five years ago, deconstruction; last year, 'political correctness'; this year, cultural studies. If a sense of crisis is endemic to our modern conception of the humanities as entailing a 'critical' practice, the more specific need for a portent of disaster that is also a symbol of insane success has become a relatively stable feature of debate *about* the humanities during the past two decades – a time of immense upheaval in the funding, organisation and legitimation of our whole education systems.

All the more reason, then, to ask, in a mundane and unrepentantly academic spirit, not what cultural studies 'is' but what it does, and does not, claim *to do* as a working project in the humanities. This is the question that I want to consider in the rest of this chapter. However, in order to proceed in an orderly fashion, I shall begin with another question of definition: am I posing my question of cultural studies in the role of a critic of the canon? If so, which canon?

'*The* canon' is a phrase primarily associated for me with the discipline of English, in which I trained at Sydney University twenty years ago but which I don't professionally practise. But since I am a feminist rhetorician who works on Australian cinema and television, with sidelines in the study of travel writing and commercial public space, the sensible answer seems to be, yes, of course I'm a critic of the canon. If I am not directly involved in changing what Eve Sedgwick calls the 'one overarching master-canon of literature', I am engaged in some of my work – for example, on the Australian journalist and popular novelist Ernestine Hill – in contributing to the proliferation of the 'potentially infinite plurality of mini-canons' that follows from 'fracturing' (in Sedgwick's phrase) the master-canon. Moreover, all my work in cultural studies is connected with those projects *in* literature that have, as she argues, most effectively challenged not the 'empirical centrality' of the master-canon in the English curriculum, but its 'conceptual anonymity'. I, too, would like to think with Sedgwick that, 'never again need women – need, one hopes, anybody – feel greeted by the Norton Anthology of mostly white men's Literature with the implied insolent salutation, "I'm nobody. Who are you?"'.[8]

In my case, this sense of a connection between counter-canonical work in literature and some areas of work in cultural studies comes from a long association with the transdisciplinary project of feminist criticism. However, it is also nicely encompassed by the most relaxed general definition that I know of 'cultural studies', proposed by Tony Bennett. For Bennett, our current usage of the term is necessarily elastic:

> It now functions largely as a term of convenience for a fairly dispersed array of theoretical and political positions which, however widely divergent they might be in other respects, share a commitment to examining cultural practices from the point of their intrication with, and within, relations of power.[9]

Nevertheless, there are definite constraints on this usage. Let me emphasise Bennett's insistence on locating cultural practices 'with and *within* relations of power'. As my mention of feminism will suggest, academic cultural studies does sustain a socially critical, even a reforming vocation for intellectuals – although the forms this vocation may take and the scope of the claims made in its name may be as varied as the commitments and inclinations of any group of professional people. Generally, work in cultural studies *is* profoundly concerned, as Faust says, with 'capitalism, elitism, racism, sexism' and with imperialism and colonialism as well. (This is hardly a scandal; after all, what area of the humanities capable of sustaining a skerrick of interest in the great human conflicts of our time is not deeply concerned with these things?)

Cultural studies does *not*, however, treat power relations as intrinsically or uniformly bad, and it does not construe power only as an oppressive property that *other* people 'have'. Power is not necessarily a bleak and paranoid concept, and cultural studies is not a discourse of powerlessness. Power is understood positively as a productive and consequential capacity to act, and power relations are defined not only in terms of a distribution of boundaries, prohibitions, and constraints, but also in terms of the processes of empowerment and disempowerment involved in even the most ordinary forms of engagement with a specific power structure.

Clearly, the critique, defence and reconstruction of literary and other canons is one such form of engagement – a specialised form, no doubt, but none the less productive and, I think, consequential. People working in cultural studies are often accused of cultural 'levelling'; it is said that we reject all systems of value and the very idea of standards. Yet I could hardly claim to speak as an enemy of canonisation. With John Frow, I am co-editor of a Reader called *Australian Cultural Studies*; I am professionally engaged in creating 'mini-canons' for cultural studies itself.[10] So are many other people. Indeed, it would be true to say that one of the burning issues for cultural studies internationally, involving scholars in Taiwan, Canada, Hong Kong, the United States and Finland quite as intensely as in Australia, is what to do with 'the' cultural studies master-canon – of which there is already more than one. For many of us, 'the canon' is the tradition of British cultural studies from Richard Hoggart and Raymond Williams to Stuart Hall; for some, it is the Chicago School of social thought and its twentieth-century legacies; for others (among whom I am one), the Western European surrealist tradition of analysing everyday life, sometimes inflected by Eastern European schools of semiotics.

Noting, in passing, the Euro-American and predominantly masculine cast of these canons, I think it is a fair working generalisation to say that there is more making than breaking of canons going on in cultural studies around the world at the moment – at a national level, certainly, but also in the terms of gender, ethnicity, class, sexuality, and experience of colonialism. To stress this is to rejoin Eve Sedgwick when she distinguishes between 'those of us for whom relations within and among canons are *active relations of thought*' (those for whom questions of canonicity are alive, pressing, culturally and politically consequential) and those who conduct themselves as merely 'keepers of a dead canon'.

All this examining of cultural practices inevitably entails a critical dialogue and some tension, even competition, between the disciplines (cultural practices that they are). I work in a zone of cultural studies emerging between history and communications; I am, for example, interested in the ways in which Australian cinema and television have not only reworked the narrative materials of a national past but shaped the formation (as I do believe they have) of new practices of historiography and a different, more cosmopolitan sense of what 'nationality' may come to mean in an age of global satellite transmission. As a media scholar, then, I am most uncomfortable with the idea that cultural studies simply involves, as the stereotype has it, replacing or (let's be serious) supplementing Shakespeare with Madonna in English departments.

Like Graeme Turner and Ann Curthoys, professors of English and history respectively, I disagree not only with Don Anderson's comic jeremiad but with Simon During's more ambivalent account of cultural studies as a market-driven expansion of the English curriculum.[11] I don't deny that this is happening; I don't *think* it's a bad thing; and I certainly do not say that English professors can't do cultural studies. I would say that when and if they turn Madonna or a shopping mall or a TV talk show into an ersatz literary text, they may be doing something interesting but it isn't cultural studies. I must also disagree with Donna C. Stanton's astounding claim, made recently in her capacity as editor of the influential journal *PMLA*, that a new 'receptiveness to work in cultural studies' does not require literary scholars to distinguish between 'literature' and 'culture', because 'literature . . . can and should be construed broadly enough to include culture'.[12] In my view, to refuse to construe significant differences between literary and other cultural practices is to refuse to 'receive' cultural studies.

So let me shift the focus of my questioning a little in order to ask of this disciplinary turbulence: what *kind* of question does the emergence of cultural studies pose for the humanities today? Why are some people, for no apparent good reason, beginning to use the term 'cultural studies' as a synonym for the humanities? Here I do tend to agree with Simon During that the question of cultural studies is in part a question of 'the deep economic transformation we call globalisation' (to use a sweeping, impossible term), and therefore also a question of what may become of the humanities, or, more positively, of what the humanities may *become* in an education system which remains, as the Australian one does, 'future-directed' in a classically modern way[13] – while confronting a future in which the category of 'culture' is perhaps not really proliferating like Paterson's Curse but rather collapsing, relatively slowly but inexorably, into the economic and the informatic.

In this context, cultural studies can work as a space where disciplines talk to each other, question each other, tread on each other's toes, with a view to redefining a shared, if not common, sense of purpose. This kind of engagement has to be serious. It involves hard work, not just adding a couple of prestigious books from another discipline on to one's usual bibliography, or pepping up one's objects with a dash of pop contemporaneity. Cultural studies also involves comparative work rather than a loose 'interdisciplinarity'. A literary reading of a shopping mall that does not seriously engage with questions that arise in history, sociology and economics remains – however productive a transformation of 'the' canon of English it may enable – a literary reading, not cultural studies.

I also want to ask whether this question of the future of the humanities occurs as the same question from discipline to discipline, and in different national, institutional and educational contexts. I tend to think not. To indicate why not, I want to consider in detail some recent programmatic statements about cultural studies by Lawrence Grossberg. Since I am largely in sympathy with his approach, his admirably clear and definite propositions will serve as a useful guide to a way of thinking about cultural studies. Since Grossberg writes as an American scholar, and as a professor of communications (rather than English) who has written extensively about the differences as well as the links between British and US practices of cultural studies, I also want to ask how his arguments relate to current contexts of debate in Australia.[14]

In two related essays, 'Cultural studies: what's in a name?' and 'Cultural studies: what's in a name (one more time)', Grossberg puts forward a set of strong 'not statements'[15] in order to limit what cultural studies can claim to be able to do.[16] This is a fairly contentious gesture; it contests the infinitely vague expansive power ascribed by *PMLA* to 'literature', and it goes against the romantic grain of those who desire to see in cultural studies a pure source of raw, undisciplined energy. However, it is also an affirmative gesture in the spirit of Stuart Hall's insistence that cultural studies 'does have some will to connect; it does have some stake in the choices it makes. It does matter whether cultural studies is that or that.'[17]

For Grossberg, cultural studies is NOT '*merely an excuse for disci-*

plines to take on new, usually popular, cultural objects'.[18] Cultural studies is not defined by particular materials, objects or topics. In contrast to what Don Anderson believes, to practise cultural studies does not automatically entail teaching television soap instead of or even alongside literary texts; when departments of English choose to do this, they do so for their own institutional reasons. In fact, and in contrast to what Beatrice Faust believes, 'you can', says Grossberg, 'do cultural studies of almost anything' – including the formation of literary canons, and/or the master-canon produced by any evaluative professional practice.

It follows that cultural studies is NOT *a theory of popular culture.* In cultural studies, the concept of the popular does not directly refer to the commodities produced by rapid-turnover cultural industries, still less to folkloric traditions. Rather, 'the popular refers to a specific view of the relationship between people and power, to a view of where and how power is located in their lives'; the popular is in fact a 'field of questions' that demands that we examine how power works where people live their lives.[19] So cultural studies involves what Henri Lefebvre once called a critique of everyday life: that is, an investigation of particular ways of using 'culture', of what is available *as* culture to people inhabiting particular social contexts, and of people's ways of *making* culture.[20] This field may include, once again, 'high culture', and the discriminations that using this concept may entail at a given historical moment for particular social groups (including academics).

It follows that cultural studies may include analysis of the formation and functioning of canons. More generally, cultural studies involves an active engagement with the social creation of 'standards', 'values' and 'taste'. In its mode of engagement, however, cultural studies is NOT *'equivalent to critical or cultural theory'.* For cultural studies, the theoretical is a response to (or, as Roland Barthes once put it, an 'outcome of'[21]) specific practices and contexts. To say that the relationship between people and power generates a field of questions is to say that the practice of cultural studies involves the production of theories; it is not a matter of 'applying' a pre-existing theory to a given empirical field, nor of 'doing theory' as a literary genre.

For Grossberg, 'if someone's theory tells them the answers in advance, because their theory travels with them across any and every context', they are not doing cultural studies – although their work may be interesting and important, and their answers may provide 'important truths'. It follows that cultural studies is *not* represented by 'the work of such important critics as Fred Jameson, discovering once again the class struggle (or the third world struggling against the colonisers)', or by 'identity critics discovering once again, apparently to their surprise, that the latest Hollywood production is sexist and racist'.[22]

This is the non-statement with which Grossberg most strongly differentiates between the practice of cultural studies and one of the major modes of critical reading now associated with cultural theory on the one hand, and 'political correctness' on the other. Cultural studies is a question-driven, not a doctrine or answer-driven, practice. So Don Anderson and Beatrice Faust are mistaken in conflating cultural studies with so-called 'PC' criticism, as they are in conflating cultural theory (so often held to be an elitist, hermetic and unsociably difficult discourse) with the very broad public debates about manners, morals, behaviours and (let's face it) 'work practices' that the paranoid myth of political correctness attempts to discredit.

Cultural studies certainly is, or at least aspires to be, a way of politicising intellectual practices. But doing cultural studies does not impose on practitioners a particular political agenda, and it does not entail any fixed positions or ready-made solutions to conflicts. To examine the 'relationship between' people and power, and to ask 'where and how' power is located in their lives, is to adopt a *contextual* or a pragmatic approach to politics. This stress on relations and locations also ensures, as Grossberg points out, that 'cultural studies does not reduce culture to power, nor does it claim that particular relations of power are somehow inherent in, or intrinsic to, specific cultural texts, practices, or relations'.[23] For the same reasons, of course, cultural studies does not reduce power to culture; rather, 'it believes that culture can only be understood in terms of its relations to everything that is not culture'.[24]

If we can agree that cultural studies is a pragmatic and materialist practice, the question of what it *does* claim to be able to do, in what kinds of association with other academic disciplines, can be posed in a more positive spirit. From Grossberg's supple and intricate exposition of aims, objects and methods in cultural studies, I can discuss only two major points that arise from the preceding discussion and bear directly on the theme of the canon and its critics.

The first point, simply put, is that *cultural studies is a political theory of contexts, and its method can be defined as 'articulation'*.[25] Let me take each of these terms, 'context' and 'articulation', in turn. For Grossberg, contexts might best be thought of as 'specific bits of everyday life' positioned between culture, understood as 'a specific body of practices', and particular social forces, institutions, relations of power. Cultural studies, then, works to understand how contexts are 'made, unmade, and remade', and how contexts change the meaning and the *value* of cultural practices (in some instances, their varying 'canonical' force); one of the characteristic assumptions of cultural studies is that contexts are always dynamic, and are usually open to change.

This is why cultural studies is not a utopian field in which value is abolished and everything made equal and interchangeable with everything else. On the other hand, this is also why cultural studies does not lend itself to a dystopian repetition of verities about the eternal and ubiquitous evils of capitalism, racism, colonialism and patriarchy. In between these two extreme and rigid positions – both of which are attributed to cultural studies by its critics with no apparent sense of contradiction – cultural studies operates in the 'human milieu' of culture. In doing so, cultural studies does take an interventionist approach to the milieux it inhabits; as Grossberg says, it attempts 'to enable people to act more strategically in order to change their context for the better'.

The form of Grossberg's insistence that cultural studies is radically contextualist in part derives from a rejection of the 'encoding and decoding' model that for so long dominated research and thinking about communications. (This model is still active in, for example, the 'answer-retrieval' forms of ideology critique whereby sexism and racism are deemed to be encoded in messages, from which their presence is decoded by the ever-surprised critic.) To reject this model in favour of the radical contextualism outlined above – that is, in favour of a relational understanding of 'specific bits of everyday life' – is also to reject the idea that a 'context' is just a more or less detachable environment casually surrounding a 'text'.[26] So while Grossberg's concern is not directly with the critique of 'the canon' that preoccupies scholars in English, his project can *connect with* the rethinking of the relationship between literary acts, critical institutions and social dynamics conducted by (for example) Eve Sedgwick.

Before turning to the mode of connection that Grossberg calls 'articulation', I want to note that the US literary critic and theorist Stanley Fish has offered an account of cultural studies that in some ways resonates with Grossberg's stress on contexts. In 'Being interdisciplinary is so very hard to do' (a powerful defence of disciplinarity that would make interdisciplinary work *impossible* to do), Fish argues, in effect, that the disciplines themselves are contexts in Grossberg's sense –

bounded fields of organised practice that are constructed and revisable, but real. For Fish, the fact that disciplinary boundaries may shift does not mean that they are illusory. On this basis, he allows two ways of framing the emergence of cultural studies:

> Either the vaunted 'blurring of genres' (Clifford Geertz's now famous phrase) means no more than that the property lines have been redrawn – so that, for example, Freud and Nietzsche have migrated respectively from psychology and philosophy to English and comparative literature – or the genres have been blurred only in the sense of having been reconfigured by the addition of a new one, of an emerging field populated by still another kind of mandarin, the 'specialist in contextual relations'.[27]

If we bring to bear on this alternative Grossberg's distinction between critical theory (produced in part by the disciplinary 'migrations' of Freud and Nietzsche) and cultural studies, the either/or structure of Fish's argument can be displaced by a recognition of two co-existing practices which may, but need not, be aligned, opposed or connected at different times in particular contexts. As a good critical theorist, Fish subsequently does this himself by approving both sides of his alternative: 'I find the imperialistic success of literary studies heartening and the emergence of cultural studies as a field of its own exhilarating'.[28]

For Grossberg, however, cultural studies is not an interdisciplinary project in Fish's sense; *articulation* is not the same as *interdisciplinarity*. If cultural studies draws on a variety of disciplinary methodologies – ethnography, textual analysis, survey research, archival investigations – its aim in doing so is not to 'blur' genres but rather to connect and remake practices (including genres), and the relations contextually holding between them, in precise and motivated ways. Nor does cultural studies aspire to achieve interdisciplinarity construed as a utopian condition, a borderless academic world. For cultural studies, articulation is not an ideal but a model; it is a model of the social formations of power, and also of its own practice or method. 'Articulation', says Grossberg, 'is the methodological face of radically contextualist theory.'[29]

Taken from the work of Antonio Gramsci and elaborately developed by subsequent work in political theory using Gramsci's theory of hegemony,[30] 'articulation' can most easily be grasped as a term referring to what joints and hinges do – joining while separating, simultaneously limiting and enabling movement – as well as to what happens when we speak. Used as a model of a practice, 'articulation' describes the process

whereby social forces are connected and disconnected, make alliances
and break them or reshape them, thus forming and transforming contexts. What makes this a powerful model for analysing 'specific bits of
everyday life' in highly mediated societies is its double reference to (or
its 'articulation of') rhetorical and irreducibly material orders of reality. Adroitly used, the concept of articulation allows us to bypass those
paralysing debates about the relative status of different practices construed as though they were competing realities (the 'discursive' and the
'non-discursive', for example), and to ask how these connect and interact in specific instances. For this reason, Grossberg insists that cultural
studies constitutes its object 'as an *alliance*, a set of relations among
practices (not all of which need be textual, symbolic, signifying nor even
discursive)', and that an alliance is understood as 'an *event*, always constituted with and constitutive of a larger context of relationships'.[31]

One of the best-known examples of British cultural studies conducted along these lines is *Policing the Crisis*, a collective work published in 1978 which created a framework predicting how Thatcher was
able to 'disarticulate' the interests of large sectors of the English
working class from the Labour Party and 'rearticulate' them not only to
the Conservative Party but, through the production of fantasies, dreams
and exemplary stories as well as through legislative and administrative
changes, to the cultural values of yuppies in the south.[32] While this
famous example of successful articulation comes from British political
culture, many Australian examples come to mind. Without using the
concept explicitly, Judith Brett covers comparable ground in her study
of *Robert Menzies' Forgotten People*;[33] we could also consider the ways
in which the Labor Party governed Australia from 1983 to 1996, and the
shift from the articulation of business and union interests to Labor
under Prime Minster Hawke (1983–91) to the more 'inclusive' politics
of the Keating period – including the articulation of the arts community and much of the intelligentsia to Labor with the *Creative Nation*
statement and the republicanism debate.[34]

While political examples are handy for clarifying the *term* 'articulation', there is no need to restrict the field of its application to political
culture narrowly defined, or to reduce its analytical power by using it to
declare that 'everything is political'. In some of my own research on
Ernestine Hill, for example, I have examined how the discipline of
English reshaped itself in Australia during the 1950s and 1960s not only
by 'disarticulating' a great deal of Australian writing from the field of
literature, but by re-articulating much of that writing – travel books,

landscape writing, documentary social realism, romantic historical
fiction – to the field of popular culture, then newly expanding under the
influence of radio, cinema and television.[35] It is pertinent to the question of canons to note that this change of status entailed, for works like
Hill's *The Great Australian Loneliness* (1937) and *My Love Must Wait*
(1941), not only a fall from a classic to a non-canonical condition, but,
more precisely, consignment to a region of culture deemed ephemeral
and thus outside the domain of great and lasting works to which the
concept of 'the canon' might apply.

However, a practitioner of cultural studies does not immediately
proceed to rage against canonicity or to denounce the cultural politics
of English in the 1950s and 1960s. Instead, she can formulate, in a
mundane scholarly way, further questions: did this fairly recent division
of Australian writing help to form our present understanding of
popular culture? If so, how? What associations between otherwise differing media are enabled by the distinction between the ephemeral and
the durable, and what effects do these associations have? Is this essentially temporal distinction still a useful one, and, if so, in which contexts
of usage and analysis, and for whom? How else might the relationship
between literature and popular culture be understood? Should we
retrieve travel-writing and popular romance for literature, or should we
be forming canons specifically for use in the criticism and the teaching
of popular culture's history? Or is this question itself badly posed, inviting an anachronistic imposition of modernist literary values (prizing
uniqueness, originality, singularity) on cultural practices characterised
by mass production, seriality, and repetition? Depending on how we
answer these questions, what relations can be made or unmade between
projects in English and projects in communications and history?

If it is easy to point to examples of articulation at work as a *process*
in the world around us, and then to show what it means to call articulation a *method* of analysing this process, it is crucial to stress that
articulation, in Grossberg's framework, is also a *model* of practice in a
very strong sense. To say that articulation is the 'methodological face'
of a discipline of contextuality is to say that making, unmaking and
remaking contexts is also something that we – intellectuals, humanists
– can actually *do* in our everyday work; we can use this model to remake
the role of the humanities in the academy as well as to reshape the relations between the disciplines. This is why articulation is a way of dis-
tinguishing as well as connecting specific projects, not a way of blurring
them in an inchoate interdisciplinarity. This is also, of course, why the

theory and method of articulation have had such influence on recent thinking about multiculturalism and 'globalisation' in Simon During's sense.

The second positive statement that I borrow from Grossberg's discussion follows from his account of contexts and his stress on the different modes of connection that different contexts may require: *cultural studies is 'a practice which attempts to maintain the discipline of authority in the face of relativism'.* This point bears directly on the issue of canon-critique and canon-formation, and it directly contradicts the confused notion circulated by recent polemics that cultural studies is at once an indulgence in unconstrained relativism and an authoritarian practice of 'correction'. It should be clear by now that in cultural studies it is axiomatic that culture *matters*; culture is a productive site of transformation and conflict as well as of pleasure, desire and consumption. Therefore, standards and values *matter* to practitioners of cultural studies. So does involvement in ongoing social debates about standards and values, and about how competing or incompatible values may adjust to each other in multicultural societies. As Bruce Robbins puts it:

> Whatever else PC may be, to the extent that it is real, it involves not the neglect of all standards but the creation and imposition of new standards . . . Far from institutionalizing relativism, professional scholars have been in the business of fashioning and refashioning standards, norms, values. As of course they have been in the business of producing individuals who hold ethical, epistemological, aesthetic, and political beliefs, and whose attachment to their work is inextricable from those beliefs – in short, who have a sense of vocation.[36]

If this argument broadly explains *why* cultural studies is an attempt to maintain 'authority' in the face of relativism, *how* it does so is, once again, a matter of articulation. As Grossberg points out, the model of articulation commits cultural studies to a position that is neither 'essentialist' nor 'anti-essentialist' in its approach to social experience. Unlike essentialist philosophies, cultural studies 'locates everything in relations' rather than in the terms related, and it holds that specific historical relations are not necessary in the sense that they need not be the way they are. However, work in cultural studies does not proceed from this rejection of essentialism to a principled anti-essentialism: rather, it affirms the historical reality, though not the necessity, of those relations that actually hold.

In order to clarify this 'third' position, Grossberg turns to the long-running debate about indeterminacy in US literary theory. Very crudely, if we accept (for the sake of argument) that a text does not have to mean what 90 per cent of readers seem to think it means, we can see why some literary theorists put a lot of energy into elaborating possibilities for the other 10 per cent. Cultural studies – here including the activities of many students of literature[37] – is more likely to be interested in why 90 per cent of readers come to the conclusions that they do. In other words, cultural studies is interested in the historical and social constraints on interpretation and in the pressures that limit choices, constrain semiosis and shape experience – constraints and pressures that are produced by human institutions and that can, sometimes should, be changed.

The question then arises: what sort of authority is to be maintained and for whom? Obviously, a radically contextual discourse will refuse to offer a single answer to this question; it all depends. It is fair to say, however, that while authority for cultural studies is very much a matter of context – it is neither general in form nor universal in force across a given social formation – authority is also not totally 'relative' in the equalising sense. These two positions seem contradictory only if we assume, as some of the more idealist defences of an 'overarching master-canon', for example, commonly do, that authority has to be singular in form.

Plurality and relativity are often conflated by critics of cultural studies. But to say that authority is not singular in our society is not to say that all claims to authority are equally valid. To admit that modes of authority are plural and context-specific is simply to recognise the existence of competing as well as differing and sometimes incommensurable value systems, institutions, and human milieux in a given society. Given this recognition, cultural studies allows us to take the further step of insisting that authority is articulated in contexts which limit the possibilities for what authority can mean and who can be said, by whom, to exercise authority – and how, if necessary, those limits can be changed.

Three recent examples of a positive renegotiation, rather than the abolition, of 'the discipline of authority' in Australia must suffice to connect these rather abstract propositions to our everyday professional lives:

• the complex debates, now broadly familiar to a very large public, about who has the authority to invoke Aboriginal cultural traditions, and on what terms. The increasing recognition by non-Aboriginal

Australians that we do *not* have authority to use these traditions indiscriminately, or as we please, is the product of a political struggle by Aboriginal people to introduce new concepts of propriety and cultural property, and certainly not a rampant relativism, to white Australian culture.

• the efforts of feminist critics since the late 1960s to establish the authority of 'experience' as a way of legitimating particular speech genres and, subsequently, grounding new forms of academic research and writing. This is an example of the creation of a new mode of authority which has slowly transformed practices right across the humanities, from the re-evaluation of letters, diaries and autobiographies in literary studies to new methodologies in oral history, and on to the rethinking of the status and usage of 'case studies' in sociology and 'informants' in ethnography.[38]

• the conflict over 'authority' that is now underway between humanities academics and the print and radio journalists who increasingly report academics' activities without always sharing their disciplinary formations and commitments, or their collegial sense of what is appropriate to particular professional contexts, but who are authorised by journalistic codes to report experiences of academics' doings to particular audiences. In my view, this conflict has the potential, if handled more gracefully by academics, to generate an important new public dialogue about the circulation of knowledges (and the plurality of authorities) in contemporary Australian society.[39]

In a lengthier discussion, it would be useful at this point to connect my remarks about the value of 'articulation' as a way to think more strategically about changing particular contexts to an account of the problems of public image, and the problems of maintaining authority, now faced by the humanities in Australian universities. However, I must conclude with two brief points about why I see it as a mistake to take US debates about 'the (literary) canon' as emblematic either of the situation of English in Australia, or of a general 'crisis' of the humanities held to be the same all over the English-speaking world. The universality of both canon and crisis was taken for granted in most Australian reportage of the US 'political correctness' debates, and I believe that, wherever one stands on such debates, this assumption is mistaken. Similar debates do arise in Australian universities, but they are differently articulated; in our context, they have a different value.[40]

My first point is that 'English' in Australia is not central to the humanities as it has been, in differing ways, in Britain and the United States for half a century. English here is crucial, but not central. In British paradigms of the humanities, 'English' in the Arnoldian tradition managed to usurp some of history's claims to be the discipline of statecraft: the study of English could shape admirably equilibrated civil service personalities, forming, as During puts it, 'an autonomous, balanced personhood based on the reading of a traditional canon'[41] as well as elevating the critic, as Robbins points out, to the status of a 'self-appointed conscience of modern society'.[42] In the vastly complex context of US higher education, another version of English (associated with the so-called 'New York intellectuals') installed itself, roughly from the late 1920s to the early 1960s, as the core discipline of a patrician but *adversarial* culture.[43] Over much the same period in Australia, English was struggling merely to establish itself as a recognisable discipline – recognisable, that is, by the British and US versions of English that I've just outlined.

History, rather than English, has been 'central' to the humanities in Australia, and it seems clear that history in Australia is now fully reassuming its classical mantle as the nation-building discipline that most directly articulates the humanities to government. If we look beyond the syndicated polemics about political correctness and the assault on 'English' recycled in our media, and look instead to Australian debates in history, we can see not only conflicts and, yes, polemics (both of which are indispensable to intellectual life), but all the signs of a period of great creativity. In Australia today, Aboriginal histories, women's histories, settler and migrant histories, regional histories, are being re-articulated not only to each other and to new national narratives but also to comparable projects in other countries: in the Asia-Pacific region, as policy requires, but also in Europe, the Americas and Africa. The critique of the 'one overarching master-canon of literature', in other words, is coinciding here and now with a nation-forming moment in which, paradoxically, the classic understanding of 'nation' – one people, one language, one culture, one overarching master-canon – is, to put it bluntly, out of the question.

This same creativity is now visible in English, too: the past decade has seen the revival and transformation of literary history, an expansion and diversification of the literatures available for study, and a new interest in comparative ventures capable of articulating different literary practices, minority cultures, national traditions and distinct disciplinary projects. So I believe that Simon During is wrong to suggest, on the evidence of shrinking 'worldwide enrolments', that 'the heyday of academic English is over'.[44] Certainly, During's vision of 'the departure of English' is an ambivalent one, highlighting the necessary withdrawal, in an Australian context of globalisation, from an Anglocentric, monocultural understanding of what English can claim to do; in During's usage, a departure is also something positive, a setting off in new directions towards new goals.

Yet to declare the 'heyday' of English over concedes too much, in my view, to the monocultural version of English that dominated the discipline's past. Australian literature, on the whole, was not well served by that version of English; too much Australian writing, too much Australian experience as a colonial society in a particular part of the world, and, quite simply, too many Australian people, had to be excluded from the canonical field to make that version work. In my view, the heyday of academic English in Australia may be only just beginning with the 'departures' that During heralds – and this resurgence has very little to do with whether Madonna, bless her, is or is not accorded her hot-spot on the curriculum.

This brings me to my second and final point. Speaking to an American academic audience, Larry Grossberg insists that cultural studies 'begins by allowing the world outside the academy to ask the questions of us as intellectuals'.[45] Few Australian humanists, I would suggest, need such a reminder, working as we do in a public education system where many practical as well as theoretical and ethical problems derive from the intensity with which we are required to be accountable to worldly interests, social as well as national and governmental, that relentlessly question the value and the pertinence of everything that we do.

Anyone who doubts the 'radically contextual' difference between the United States and Australia in this respect might take another look at the funniest and, perhaps, the most culturally truthful US attack on political correctness: Roger Kimball's *Tenured Radicals*.[46] Kimball's book so viciously lumped together so many critical tendencies that heartily loathed each other (identity politics and deconstruction, for example) that it almost single-handedly prompted them to re-articulate their projects – no mean achievement for a polemic. Nowhere, however, in Kimball's comic soap opera about a rich, heroic, handsome mastercanon under assault from scruffy hordes of jargon-spouting tenured ratbags is there any place, or any hint of any need for a place, for the figure of a Whingeing Wendy saying to the keepers of the canon, as well as to their critics, 'where's the money coming from?' – as there is and

probably always will be, now, in the Australian academy.[47] The question
of where the money comes from, and what kinds of public accountability and responsiveness may be required of academics as a result, is no
more a real question for Kimball now than it was for Sydney University's
Professor John Anderson in 1943, when, in response to a previous Labor
government's reforming ambitions, he gave his great defence of university autonomy in 'The servile state' (an essay which would certainly
be canonical for any course I might teach on criticism and cultural
policy).[48]

In Australia today, hard questions are asked about 'the money' and
thus about the worldly sources of institutional authority and the duties
that may ensue. So what makes cultural studies distinctive in Australia
if it can't simply be its worldliness? I could add to what I've already said
that 'we're making it up as we go along' – a standard cultural studies
reply. I would also add that cultural studies is a project that enables us
to see Simon During's farewell to English not only as the partial,
ambiguous gesture that I think he intends, but as too negative, too
elegiac in force. I prefer to think that, far from ending the heyday of academic English in Australia (let alone killing history), cultural studies
engages English and history along with other disciplines in a conversation, perhaps even a think-tank, capable of producing answers to the
questions our world asks of us as intellectuals, and capable of developing the new kinds of authority that we will need to make our answers
matter, in this world, in future.

Notes

A first version of this chapter was published in *The Humanities and a Creative
Nation: Jubilee Essays*, ed. Deryck M. Schreuder (Canberra: Australian
Academy of the Humanities, 1995).

1 As cited in Lawrence Grossberg, 'Cultural studies: what's in a name?', B.
   Aubrey Fisher Memorial Lecture, October 1993, published by the
   Department of Communication, University of Utah, Salt Lake City, Utah,
   p. 1.
2 This paper was first commissioned by Margaret Clunies-Ross for 'The
   "Canon" and Its Critics', a session of the Jubiliee Symposium of The
   Australian Academy of the Humanities ('Celebrating the Humanities'),
   held at the State Library of New South Wales, Sydney, 2–5 November 1994.
3 See my '"On the beach"', in *Cultural Studies*, ed. Lawrence Grossberg, Cary
   Nelson and Paula Treichler (New York: Routledge, 1992), pp. 450–78;

'Cultural studies', in *Beyond the Disciplines: The New Humanities*, ed. K. K. Ruthven (Canberra: Australian Academy of the Humanities, 1992), pp. 1–22; and John Frow and Meaghan Morris, eds, *Australian Cultural Studies: A Reader* (Sydney and Chicago: Allen & Unwin and University of Illinois Press, 1993).

4 Don Anderson, 'Behind the lines', *Sydney Morning Herald*, 18 June 1994, p. 10a. Paterson's Curse is a non-indigenous, rapid-spreading and harmful pasture weed.

5 Beatrice Faust, 'Pop goes reasoned analysis', *Weekend Australian*, 1–2 October 1994, p. 26.

6 Meaghan Morris, 'Banality in cultural studies', in *Logics of Television: Essays in Cultural Criticism* ed. Patricia Mellencamp (Bloomington: Indiana University Press, 1990), pp. 14–43.

7 Grossberg, 'Cultural studies: what's in a name?', p. 1.

8 Eve Sedgwick, *Epistemology of the Closet* (Berkeley and Los Angeles: University of California Press, 1990), pp. 49, 50.

9 Tony Bennett, 'Putting policy into cultural studies', in *Cultural Studies*, ed. Grossberg, Nelson and Treichler, p. 23.

10 My thanks to David Bennett for reminding me of this point.

11 Simon During, 'Say goodbye to English', *Australian Higher Education Supplement*, 7 September 1994, p. 31. This text is a short excerpt from 'Writing, youth, universities: an inaugural lecture on taking up a professorship in English and cultural studies', University of Melbourne, September 1994. For responses to During, see 'Letters' of 14 September and 21 September.

12 Donna C. Stanton, 'Editor's column', *PMLA* 109:3 (1994), 362–3.

13 During, 'Writing, youth, universities', manuscript. My thanks to Professor During for showing me the full text of his lecture.

14 Lawrence Grossberg, *It's A Sin: Essays on Postmodernism, Politics and Culture* (Sydney: Power Publications, 1988), and *We Gotta Get Out Of This Place: Popular Conservatism and Postmodern Culture* (New York and London: Routledge, 1992).

15 I take this term from Anne Freadman and Amanda Macdonald, *What Is This Thing Called Genre?* (Mount Nebo: Boombana Publications, 1992).

16 Lawrence Grossberg, 'Cultural studies: what's in a name (one more time)', *Taboo*, 1 (1995). For 'Cultural studies: what's in a name?', see note 1 above.

17 Stuart Hall, 'Cultural studies and its theoretical legacies', in *Cultural Studies*, ed. Grossberg, Nelson and Treichler, p. 278.

18 Grossberg, 'Cultural studies: what's in a name?', p. 2.

19 *Ibid.*, pp. 9–10.

20 See Michael De Certeau, *The Practice of Everyday Life*, trans. Steven F. Rendall (Berkeley: University of California Press, 1984), and Henri Lefebvre, *Everyday Life in the Modern World*, trans. Sacha Rabinovitch (New Brunswick and London: Transaction Books, 1984).

21 Roland Barthes, 'Outcomes of the text', in *The Rustle of Language* (Oxford: Basil Blackwell, 1986), pp. 238–49.

22 Grossberg, 'Cultural studies: what's in a name?', p. 6 and note 17, p. 12.

23 Grossberg, 'Cultural studies: what's in a name (one more time)'.

24 *Ibid.*

25 Grossberg, 'Cultural studies: what's in a name?', p. 9.

26 On the text/context distinction, see my 'Introduction' to Paul Willemen, *Looks and Frictions: Essays in Cultural Studies and Film Theory* (Bloomington: Indiana University Press, 1994), pp. 1–23.

27 Stanley Fish, *There's No Such Thing as Free Speech* (New York and Oxford: Oxford University Press, 1994), p. 238. The phrase 'specialist in contextual relations' is cited from Alton Becker as cited in Clifford Geertz, 'Blurred genres: the refiguration of social thought', in *Critical Theory since 1965*, ed. Hazard Adams and Leroy Searle (Tallahassee: Florida State University Press, 1986), p. 521.

28 Fish, *There's No Such Thing as Free Speech*, p. 242. For a more nuanced discussion of the emergence of new disciplines, see Anne Freadman, 'Charles Peirce's "Philosophy of Notation"', *Southern Review*, 26:2 (1993), 186–203.

29 Grossberg, 'Cultural studies: what's in a name (one more time)'.

30 See Ernesto Laclau and Chantal Mouffe, *Hegemony and Socialist Strategy: Towards a Radical Democratic Politics* (London: Verso, 1985). For a full account of the concept of articulation in cultural studies, see Grossberg, *We Gotta Get Out of This Place*.

31 Grossberg, 'Cultural studies: what's in a name (one more time)', emphasis mine.

32 Stuart Hall, Chas Critcher, Tony Jefferson, John Clarke and Brian Roberts, *Policing the Crisis: Mugging, the State, and Law and Order* (New York: Holmes and Meier, 1978).

33 Judith Brett, *Robert Menzies' Forgotten People* (Sydney: Macmillan, 1992). Robert Menzies was Prime Minister of Australia from 1949 until his retirement in 1966, and his (conservative) Liberal Party remained in power, in coalition with the Country Party, until 1972.

34 Creative Nation was a national cultural policy released by the Commonwealth of Australia in October 1994. On Keating, see my *Ecstasy and Economics: American Essays for John Forbes* (Sydney: EmPress, 1992), and 'Lunching for the Republic: feminism, the media and identity politics in

the Australian Republicanism debate', in *Multicultural States: Identity and Difference*, ed. David Bennett (London: Routledge, forthcoming).

35 Meaghan Morris, 'Panorama: the live, the dead and the living' in *Island in the Stream: Myths of Place in Australian Culture*, ed. Paul Foss (Sydney: Pluto, 1988), pp. 160–87.

36 Bruce Robbins, *Secular Vocations: Intellectuals, Professionalism, Culture* (London: Verso, 1993), p. 23.

37 I am grateful to a question from the floor at the Jubilee Symposium for prompting me to clarify this point.

38 On this issue at the intersection of the humanities and social sciences, see *Handbook of Qualitative Research*, ed. Norman K. Denzin and Yvonna S. Lincoln (London: Sage, 1994).

39 On the US context, see Michael Berube, *Public Access: Literary Theory and American Cultural Politics* (London: Verso, 1994).

40 See the papers on 'Policing cultural identity: the "political correctness" debate' in *Cultural Studies: Pluralism and Theory*, ed. David Bennett, Melbourne University Literary and Cultural Studies, vol. 2 (1993), 183–210.

41 During, 'Say goodbye to English', p. 31. On the discipline of English and the cultivation of 'personhood', see Ian Hunter, *Culture and Government: The Emergence of Literary Education* (London: Macmillan, 1988).

42 Robbins, *Secular Vocations*, p. 60.

43 See Bruce Robbins, ed., *Intellectuals: Aesthetics, Politics, Academics* (Minneapolis: University of Minnesota Press, 1990) and Andrew Ross, *No Respect: Intellectuals and Popular Culture* (New York and London: Routledge, 1989).

44 During, 'Say goodbye to English', p. 31.

45 Grossberg, 'Cultural studies: what's in a name?', p. 6.

46 Roger Kimball, *Tenured Radicals* (New York: HarperPerennial, 1991).

47 'Whingeing [i.e. whining] Wendy' was the popular name given to a figure from Labor Party advertising in the late 1980s – a working-class woman who responded to the Liberal Party's electoral promises with the harshly-voiced question, 'Where's the money coming from, Mr Howard?'. A key element of Wendy's success was the way she embodied and *voiced* ('articulated') Labor's policies of economic rationalism – influenced by neo-conservative economics, and in most ways a radical break with Australian Labor tradition – by speaking for Labor as a typical, budget-conscious, housewife. This helped Labor to seize the Liberal party's high ground of 'responsible economic management', while reassuring its own electoral base.

48 John Anderson, 'The servile state', in *Studies in Empirical Philosophy* (Sydney: Angus and Robertson, 1962), pp. 328–39.

3 Graham Murdock

Cultural studies at the crossroads

It is a truism, but nonetheless true, that what you see depends on where you stand and which direction you look in. My own view of the present state of cultural studies and its prospects is inevitably coloured by my experience of Thatcherism and its aftermath, and of the ways in which it has reshaped the intellectual and political agenda in Britain. Those living and working elsewhere approach the future of the area with other preoccupations rooted in different experiences. But, underneath the variations of emphasis, I detect a common concern with where we go next and how we get there.

A set of broadly shared question marks is now beginning to form over the future of cultural studies, prompted by a general recognition that a crossroads has been reached and that it's time to take a long hard look at our central projects and preoccupations, at our dominant conceptualisations and preferred methodologies, and at the interventions we wish to make.

You don't have to subscribe to the more apocalyptic or fanciful visions of postmodern theory to accept that as we move towards the century's close we are faced with substantial realignments and changes in economic, political, and symbolic life, both within nation-states and within the world system as a whole. If cultural studies is going to have something distinctive and worthwhile to say about these shifts we will need to examine the intellectual baggage that we carry around with us and decide what to keep and what to throw away. To do this, we have to backtrack a little, and re-examine the projects, procedures, and politics which have shaped our practice up until now. I shall confine my remarks to work in Britain, not because I believe it is in any way privileged or paradigmatic, but because it highlights the conceptual and methodological issues we have to address particularly clearly.

British cultural studies' three projects

Cultural studies in Britain developed in reaction to the dominant definition of 'culture' bequeathed by the conservative tradition of cultural criticism, and sought to challenge it at two basic levels.

In opposition to the identification of 'culture' with a particular selection of canonised texts and legitimised practices, it reasserted the anthropological conception of culture as all the ways in which people make sense of their situation and express these understandings in their everyday lives. It was therefore as interested in the 'lived texts' of social rituals and social institutions as in artefacts. Where conservative cultural commentary saw only an absence of 'culture' within the working class, cultural studies set out to uncover the variety and vitality of situated practices and beliefs, and to demonstrate their authentic roots in popular experience.

At the same time, it was clear that resources for meaning construction were not generated entirely within particular situations. Key elements were provided by the products promoted by the commercial cultural industries, by the discourses of state agencies and political parties, and by the paternalistic rhetorics of the public institutions such as schools, museums, and public broadcasting, which actively promoted the 'selective tradition'. Consequently, cultural studies' second major project was to show how these top-down initiatives worked ideologically to mobilise popular understanding and practice in the service of the asymmetric power relations between producers and consumers, government and citizens, and intellectuals and publics.

These two projects converged to produce a third, which was expressly concerned with the interplay between situated cultures and ideological formations, and particularly with the ways in which the first provides resources for negotiating, refusing, and resisting the second.

There are a range of problems with each of these strands, but in the space available here I want to concentrate on the issues that seem to me to be most pressing.

Everyday culture and popular creativity

Cultural studies' concerns with the active audience for commercially provided culture and the dialectical relations between concrete experience and mediated meaning have been elaborated in a wide range of studies, from Richard Hoggart's portrait of working-class culture between the wars, through the successive waves of research on youth subcultures, popular decodings of televisual texts and women's pleasure, to the current vogue for studies of domestic consumption. Each of these literatures deserves detailed discussion, but for the moment I want to underline some basic problems with this whole tradition of work. The first has to do with the methods of inquiry employed.

Although cultural studies has taken over cultural anthropology's central focus on the making and taking of meaning in everyday life, it has not generally used properly ethnographic methods. There are some notable exceptions, such as Paul Willis, but, by and large, empirical evidence has been gathered through casual observation, one-off interviews, and single group discussions. This produces 'thin' rather than 'thick' descriptions (Geertz, 1973), and means that interpretations are insufficiently contextualised.

This problem is particularly acute in instances such as Dick Hebdige's influential (1979) reading of youth subcultural styles, where the interpretations on offer are detached almost completely from the situational dynamics being analysed and from the self-understandings of participants. As a reading of 'lived texts' it has great elegance and panache, but as an account of how working-class youth subcultures actually developed and what they meant to their supporters, it contains a number of errors and misunderstandings that better ethnography could have avoided (see Hobbs, 1988, Chapter 6).

Even where direct evidence is available, as in Dorothy Hobson's work on housewives watching soap operas or David Morley's research on decoding, insufficient knowledge about the life situation and beliefs of the subjects often forces the analyses to explain particular readings by resorting to the general structural categories of class, gender, and ethnicity. To avoid this and generate more complex accounts of the social basis of everyday cultural activity we need not only better ethnographies but also bridging concepts that can link situations and formations, practices, and structures. Lawrence Grossberg (1989) rightly calls for a theory which specifies the differential access which social groups have to particular clusters of practices and specific forms of agency, but as I have argued elsewhere (Murdock, 1989a), Pierre Bourdieu's work provides a more productive starting point for this enterprise than de Certeau's currently fashionable writings. Whereas de Certeau focuses on the ways in which the 'procedures and ruses of consumers compose the network of an antidiscipline' (de Certeau, 1988: xv). Bourdieu underscores the inertia exerted by the prevailing structures of economic

and symbolic capital and the ways they penetrate and organise everyday practice by regulating access to the competencies required for particular forms of consumption (Bourdieu, 1977, 1984).

From romanticism to populism

De Certeau's voluntaristic formulation reinforces the romanticism that
has underpinned a good deal of work in cultural studies. This stance
has fuelled a continual search for signs of popular resistance to set
against the regularities, routines, and ideologies of industrial capitalism. John Fiske, for example, is in no doubt at all that 'The culture of
everyday life is best described through metaphors of struggle or antagonism: strategies opposed to tactics, the bourgeoisie by the proletariat;
hegemony met by resistance, ideology countered or evaded; top-down
power opposed by bottom-up power, social discipline faced with disor-
der' (Fiske, 1989: 47). There are several problems with this preference
for refusal. Firstly, as Stanley Cohen has noted in relation to studies of
youth subcultures, 'the constant impulse to decode only in terms of
opposition and resistance means that instances are sometimes missed'
when interpretations and practices are 'taken over intact from dominant
commercial culture' (Cohen, 1980: xii). Secondly, and more importantly, the romantic celebration of consumer activity can easily support
a stance which colludes (however unwittingly) with the commercial
populism of the new conservatisim.

This is the case with John Fiske's view that because successful television programmes like *Dallas* have to connect with the lives and values
of a variety of social groups in order to retain a mass audience, there is
no need to press for a production system committed to defending and
extending a diversity of expressive forms. Indeed, in his view, 'diversity
of readings may best be stimulated by a greater homogeneity of programming' (Fiske, 1987: 319). This argument is fundamentally mistaken. Whilst it is self-evidently the case that prime-time programming
has to provide multiple points of pleasure for a socially differentiated
audience, the formats it employs clearly operate to regulate the range of
discourses and presentations called into play in important ways, pre-
ferring some whilst marginalising or excluding others. As a consequence there are identities, experiences, and forms of knowledge which
are consistently pushed to or off the edge of the schedules. To argue
otherwise is to accept commercial television's pat claim that it gives
people what they want and need, and to undermine the case for new

forms of public broadcasting that can address the full range of contemporary cultures. If John Fiske had been sitting in 10 Downing Street
when the relevant legislation was going through Parliament, Britain
would never have launched Channel 4 with its statutory obligation to
extend programme diversity, and the country would have missed the
most extensive contemporary attempt to engage with cultural plurality.

The view of audience members as first and foremost active consumers also helps to reinforce the new conservatives' promotion of the
marketplace as the fundamental sphere of liberty and of the freedom to
choose between competing products as the core of individual rights.
This conception operates to displace the alternative view of audience
members as citizens with other entitlements, including rights of access
to the full range of information, argument, and interpretation they need
in order to understand their situation and to intervene to change it if
they so choose (see Murdock and Golding, 1989). The question of
citizenship – its nature and future – is one of the key contemporary
issues. If cultural studies is to make an effective intervention in this
debate, it needs to recover its commitment to 'a more dense and partic-
ipatory culture (and) not merely endorse the goals of greater individual
freedom to choose' between cultural commodities and to develop
counter interpretations and uses (Rustin, 1989: 68).

To accomplish this we must continue to 'tune our ears to voices that
have not yet been heard' (MacCabe, 1995: 13) but we must also look for
ways of respecting difference without lapsing into a happy relativism in
which anything goes. The entitlements to representation, access and
expression that constitute the cultural rights of citizenship are coupled
with a responsibility to participate in reconstructing a workable
common culture that can underwrite a renewed notion of the common
good. Not by advancing some 'imagined consensus, which we are all
supposed to share' (Eldridge and Eldridge, 1994: 110). Nor by rebuild-
ing established hierarchies of value against which all cultural activities
are measured, and most found wanting. Cultural studies has been at the
forefront of toppling these edifices and exposing their deployment as
instruments of symbolic violence. In their place it has demonstrated
that culture is both ordinary and extraordinary, mundane in its permea-
tion of everyday life but often exceptional as a context for ingenuity and
improvisation. But celebrating the plurality and specificity of lived cultures poses problems for any attempt at 'critical movement across the
spaces between incommensurate evaluative regimes' (Frow, 1995: 134).
In taking the dismissed, despised and demonised seriously, cultural

studies has tended to elevate separation at the expense of solidarity. We are left with a medieval landscape dotted with cultural encampments flying their own colours. To move beyond this we need to draw up a new cultural contract that defines the cultural rights and responsibilities required for full citizenship in a complexly stratified society.

This involves a move away from the expressive individualism of some recent work on audiences and consumption back towards a more thorough engagement with the ways that meanings and identities are negotiated socially, and with the ways that these grounded processes are structured by wider economic and ideological formations.

Critical pluralism and the contest of discourse

Recent work on ideology has been marked by a decisive and irreversible rejection of the 'dominant ideology' thesis in all its forms, and the development of what we can call 'critical pluralism'. From this new perspective the cultural field appears as the site of a continual struggle between competing discourses, each offering a particular way of looking at or speaking about the social world (or particular segments of it), and engaged in a contest for visibility and legitimacy across a range of social institutions. Whilst it accepts the pluralist stress on competition, it retains critical theory's insistence on the radically unequal nature of discursive struggles arising from the fact that some discourses are backed by greater material resources and have preferential access to the major means of publicity and policy-making. Consequently, to talk about the cultural field is to speak of a field of relations structured by power and difference in which some discourses are more central and dominant than others, but where these 'positions are never permanently fixed' (Hall, 1989: 51). In a number of late capitalist societies, the commercial speech of the consumer system and the discourses of neo-conservatism enjoy a number of advantages. However, their command of popular consciousness cannot be guaranteed simply by their present ubiquity and centrality; it has to be constantly worked and struggled for.

Their success will largely depend on their ability to 'articulate' common sense, in the double sense of linking its separate and contradictory elements together in a functioning whole (in the same way that an articulated lorry is made up of a cab and a trailer that can be uncoupled), and of finding forms of rhetoric and signification that anchor this discursive formation convincingly in everyday experience

(Grossberg, 1986: 53). Since the rise of Thatcherism provides a particularly rich instance of this process of 'articulation' in action, it has, not surprisingly, become a major focus of debate in Britain, and one in which Stuart Hall has played a leading role (see Hall and Jacques, 1983; Hall, 1988; Gamble, 1988). Underlying this discussion is an essentially simple question: how had Mrs Thatcher managed to get away with it for so long?

Stuart Hall's work illustrates the strengths and weaknesses of approaching this question from within a cultural studies framework. The strengths are in the analysis of Thatcherism as a new discursive formation which combines the 'liberal discourses of the "free market" and economic man and the organic conservative themes of tradition, family and nation, respectability, patriarchalism and order' (Hall, 1988: 2). The problems lie in the evaluation of its popular impact and Hall's relative lack of interest in the available empirical evidence. Despite Thatcherism's acute orchestration of key themes in commonsense thinking, there is a good deal of evidence to suggest that it has been rather less successful in achieving hegemony in Hall's sense of the term (see Hall, 1988: 7) than his analysis would predict. Not only are Mrs Thatcher's electoral successes more plausibly explained as the outcome of pragmatic choices and the absence of a credible alternative government rather than as indications of popular support for Thatcherism (Hirst, 1989, Chapter 1), but studies indicated that collectivist values more than held their ground during the Thatcher years (Rentoul, 1989).

Hall's work on Thatcherism also points to another, deeper problem with cultural studies as it is currently constituted. This has to do with its tendency to privilege questions around the state of the nation.

Cultural studies and the condition of England

The British tradition of cultural criticism was always strongly linked to what came to be known as 'the condition of England question'. The question was this: how was it possible to construct a common culture in a situation where the uneven growth of industrial capitalism was creating deep class divisions and where organised religion was losing its always slim hold over the popular imagination? The conservative response was to embark on a general 'invention of tradition' (Hobsbawm and Ranger, 1983) designed to provide new symbols and rituals of nationhood that would bind the country together in an imagined community, strong enough to displace the solidarities of class, region, and locality. The construction of a selective cultural tradition which embodied the essential qualities of 'Englishness' in their 'highest' form was an integral part of this project (Dodd, 1986).

Although cultural studies expressly set out to deconstruct this formation of nation and people, it has ended up working within its general framework. Indeed, a good deal of work in British cultural studies can be read as a series of meditations on 'the condition of England' devoted to interrogating national ideologies and exploring the counterformations of class, and to a lesser extent region. As a consequence it has so far had little to say about the explosive growth of transnational culture. However, there is little doubt that questions about the shifting relation between national, sub-national, and supranational cultural formations are central to any proper understanding of the contemporary world.

Coming to terms with the multinationals and multiculturalism

Interest in the transnational circulation of representations has grown over the last decade as a result of three main factors. Firstly, the spread of new communications technologies, particularly video cassette recorders and satellite television, has enabled the Hollywood studios, the major advertising agencies, and the multinational entrepreneurs of the moving image to get around many of the regulations governing national broadcasting and cinema systems and open up new markets for their products. Secondly, this process has been given an added boost in many countries by the enthusiasm for privatisation policies (Murdock, 1989b). Thirdly, there is now considerable interest in exploring the cultural implications of economic groupings such as the European Community and the Pacific Rim.

The dynamics of contemporary globalisation are of course more complex than the cruder characterisations of 'cultural imperialism' allow for. To argue that they impose alien cultures on indigenous peoples simply revives the 'dominant ideology' thesis. Nor is Marshall McLuhan's metaphor of the 'global village' much help. It is tempting to see satellite relays of rock concerts or royal weddings as a transnational village fete, a fluid mingling of rich and poor, celebrities and fans, residents and visitors: tempting but misleading. More useful is the notion of the 'global shopping mall' (Barnet and Cavanagh, 1994, Part Two), an imaginary galleria that accommodates boutiques, craft shops, thrift stores and pavement stalls alongside supermarket outlets and chain stores, but suffuses everything with the glamour of commodities. They speak seductively of the intimate relations between ownership and identity, possession and expression. Prompted by the opening of previously closed or protected consumer markets around the world, and vigorously promoted by the ubiquitous advertising carried by the new satellite channels, consumerism has emerged as one of the main contemporary cultural systems. It introduces new discourses and ways of looking and new nomadic identities and pleasures into countries whose recent cultural history has been dominated by the politics of nation-building. Unpicking the shifting relations between the national and the global, the state and the market, citizen and consumer, is one of the central tasks for cultural studies. This will certainly require fine-grained research on particular local dynamics to set alongside Daniel Miller's path-breaking work on Trinidad (Miller, 1994). Case studies are essential, as a basis for puzzling out the complexities and nuances of current cultural collisions and encounters and as an antidote to facile generalisations and comparisons.

At the same time, in an era when every country is locked into an emerging world cultural system, knowledge of how that system works provides an indispensable context for interpreting and explaining situated activity. We must learn how to think globally while acting locally, and put some energy into developing concepts and forms of writing which will explicate the links between knowable communities and larger formations (see Marcus and Fischer, 1986, Chapter 4).

One powerful experiential connection between national conditions and the world system operates through exile, migration, and resettlement. These movements have assumed particular significance in the post-colonial era and have made multiculturalism a key issue for a growing number of societies, including Britain.

Within cultural studies writings Britain's black population has frequently been celebrated as a source of white style or empathised with as victims of racism, but until comparatively recently their own cultural strategies remained mostly uncharted. Consequently, black students coming to the area often experienced its analyses of the national condition as a 'morbid celebration of England and Englishness from which blacks (were) systematically excluded' (Gilroy, 1987: 12). Nor was this simply a British problem. Although it expressly set out to challenge the prevailing belief in 'a monolithic Australian culture' by revealing the 'richness and diversity' of the country's lived cultures, Fiske, Hodge and

Turner's book, *Myths of Oz* (1987), offers no sustained analysis of the new ethnic communities and their complex relations to white Australia. Nor does it engage with Aboriginal cultures. Yet here, as everywhere else in the post-colonial world, questions of national culture and identity can only be properly posed, let alone answered, if the legacies of dispossession, forced settlement and migration and the emergent dynamics of diaspora and multiculturalism are taken fully into account.

This requires new points of contact and exchange between cultural studies and other areas of analysis. It also requires new accounts of diaspora, written from the inside, out. That such work is now beginning to appear is one of the most positive signs of cultural studies' continuing vitality. In Britain a new generation of intellectuals is speaking from within black British experience and interrogating the legacies of empire from the other end of the colonial chain. This effort is bringing new insights and histories to bear on 'the state of the nation' and introducing new, transnational categories into cultural studies, most notably Paul Gilroy's notion of 'The Black Atlantic', a double cultural formation 'originated by, but no longer the exclusive property of, blacks dispersed within the structures of feeling, producing, communicating, and remembering' in the world forged by the shifting relations between Europe, Africa, the Caribbean and the United States (Gilroy, 1993). The cultural dynamics of diasporas and multiculturalism and their intersections with transnational realignments in economic and political formations (see, for example, Appadurai, 1990; Walters, 1995) are a major area for future research in cultural studies.

Coming to terms with political economy

The other major problem with contemporary cultural studies is its continuing refusal to incorporate a critical political economy of culture. True, there have been some recent moves in this direction, but as recent writings on postmodernism show all too clearly, there is still some way to go before a theoretical synthesis is achieved. At the moment, work on the postmodern condition falls into two broad categories. There is a burgeoning literature on the emergence of postmodernist forms of representation and aesthetics. There is also a growing volume of commentary on the transition from a Fordist economic regime to one organised around flexible accumulation, in which information and communication systems come to play a central role as factors of production. As yet, however, there have been few attempts to theorise the possible linkages between these two movements, and most of these have come from social scientists, rather than from cultural studies (Lash and Urry, 1987; Harvey, 1989).

The need for cultural studies to take the insights of critical political economy seriously is clearly signalled by the popularity of the notion of 'cultural industries' which is now to be found peppering the speeches and reports of politicians and policy-makers as well as academics. Its currency points to a growing awareness that the cultural industries are both similar to and different from other industries. On the one hand, they are clearly organised industrially in specifiable ways and are part of the general productive system. On the other hand, the goods they manufacture – the movies, advertisements, magazines and TV shows – are unlike the products of other industries in that they play a pivotal role in organising the images and discourses through which we make sense of the world. They do not simply make commodities; they make available the repertoire of meanings through which the social world, including the world of commodities, is understood and acted on. It is not enough simply to acknowledge this duality (see Fiske, 1989, Chapter 2), we need to conceptualise the relations between the material and discursive organisation of culture without reducing one to the other.

It is precisely this focus on the *interplay* between the symbolic and the economic which distinguishes a political economy approach from one grounded solely in academic economics. Where economists are primarily interested in how the cultural industries work as part of the bounded domain of 'the economy', political economy is concerned to show how different ways of financing and organising cultural production (and production in general) have traceable consequences for the range of discourses and representations in the public domain and their accessibility to audiences. Neo-conservatives see markets as the best guarantor of diverse production and consumer choice. Those like myself, in the critical camp, point to the distorting effects of inequalities in the distribution of wealth and income and argue for positive public intervention to underwrite expressive diversity and public access.

The need to retain a countervailing force to the onward march of cultural commodification has become ever more pressing with the global rise of neo-liberal economic policies over the last fifteen years. The romance of the 'free' market has been successfully exported from the heartlands of mature capitalism to the fragments of the former Soviet Empire, to an increasing number of Third World countries, and, most significantly of all, to China. The result is a profound tightening of the ties binding culture to economy. The complex of policies bundled together as 'privatisation' has enlarged the scope of market dynamics at the expense of the public sphere and ensured that the digital convergence of old and new media is taking place under the corporate logos of the leading communications conglomerates (Murdock, 1994b). At the same time, the transition to information capitalism is producing high levels of structural unemployment which combine with the erosion of welfare to create new and expanding patterns of poverty. The new times we are living in are hard times for many (Murdock, 1994a).

Cultural studies has had a great deal to say about the distinctiveness and novelty of the contemporary situation, celebrating the unfixing of familiar categories and the liberating shocks of the new. But it has paid far less attention than it should to the inertia and injury of inequality and the consolidated reach of the capitalist captains of culture.

In principle, many of those working in cultural studies accept the need for a critical political economy, but stop short of integrating its insights into their own analytical practice. Stuart Hall, for example, has recently argued that, although the structure of ownership and control within the cultural industries is not 'a sufficient explanation of the way the ideological universe is structured, it is a *necessary starting point*' (Hall, 1986: 11, my italics). Yet in another recent piece, he castigates critical political economists for having 'no conception of the struggle for meaning' and dismisses their analyses as crude and reductionist (Hall, 1989: 50). This may be true of some variants (e.g. Herman and Chomsky, 1988, Chapter 1), but it is not a necessary consequence of pursuing critical political economy's core project. The sticking point is the vexed question of 'determination'.

Instead of persisting with Marx's original proposition that the economic determines 'in the last instance', with its implication that there is always a direct link between economic organisation and cultural activity (however attenuated) we can adopt Stuart Hall's own very useful suggestion to think of the economic as determining in the 'first instance' (Hall, 1983). This immediately opens up the possibility of combining recent work in critical political economy with advances in the analyses of discourse and visuality. In my own work, for example, I have sought to argue, firstly, that the changing economies of cultural production promote certain cultural forms and practices at the expense of others (e.g. Murdock, 1989c), and secondly, that once in play, these cultural forms play a key role in organising the contest of discourse on their own account by granting or withholding visibility and legitimacy (e.g. Schlesinger, Murdock and Elliott, 1983). A parallel argument can be made for cultural consumption (see Murdock 1989a).

Back to the future

If cultural studies is to maintain its intellectual vitality and its relevance to contemporary conditions and political debates, it needs to broaden its core concerns and establish new points of connection with work at the cutting edge of the social sciences. There are a number of areas where social scientists are developing ideas which are directly relevant to cultural studies' main projects. Instances include sociological work on how the contest of discourses around key issues is organised (e.g. Hilgartner and Bosk, 1988; Gamson and Modigliani, 1989), and research in social psychology on the role of discourse and texts in the social constitution of identity (e.g. Shotter and Gergen, 1989). Cultural studies' relative isolation from these initiatives is one of the penalties of its emergence as a self-sustaining area of academic study with its own selective tradition of canonised texts. To counter this we need to recover the original interdisciplinary impetus and be more adventurous in crossing intellectual check-points.

We also need to restore cultural studies' commitment to making practical as well as academic interventions. This certainly involves arguing with policy-makers and contributing to debates on the funding and organisation of cultural activity, but it also means renewing and developing the dialogue with the subjects of our inquiries, through adult and continuing education, public speeches, journalism, and programme making. The barriers to this enterprise arise not only from the crises of intellectual practice and representation, but also from the institutional crisis of the public sphere. If cultural studies is to contribute in a central way to current debates, we will need to fight long and hard to defend and extend the spaces and resources that allow intellectual work and political argument to proceed independently of commercial pressures and the encroachments of state and government. If a decade of Thatcherism taught us in Britain anything, it was this.

References

Appadurai, A. (1990) 'Disjuncture and difference in the global cultural economy', in M. Featherstone (ed.), *Global Culture*, London: Sage, 295–310.

Barnet, R. J. and Cavanagh, J. (1994) *Global Dreams: Imperial Corporations and The New World Order*, New York: Simon and Schuster.

Bourdieu, P. (1977) *Outline of a Theory of Practice*, Cambridge: Cambridge University Press.

Bourdieu, P. (1984) *Distinction: A Social Critique of the Judgement of Taste*, London: Routledge and Kegan Paul.

Cohen, S. (1980) *Folk Devils and Moral Panics: The Creation of the Mods and Rockers*, Oxford: Martin Robertson.

de Certeau, M. (1988) *The Practice of Everyday Life*, Berkeley: University of California Press.

Dodd, P. (1986) 'Englishness and national culture', in R. Colls and P. Dodd (eds), *Englishness: Politics and Culture 1880–1920*, Beckenham: Croom Helm Ltd.

Eldridge, J. and Eldridge, L. (1994) *Raymond Williams: Making Connections*, London: Routledge.

Fiske, J. (1987) *Television Culture*, London: Methuen.

Fiske, J. (1989) *Understanding Popular Culture*, London: Unwin Hyman Ltd.

Fiske, J., Hodge, B. and Turner, G. (1987) *Myths of Oz: Reading Australian Popular Culture*, Sydney: Allen and Unwin.

Frow, J. (1995) *Cultural Studies and Cultural Value*, Oxford: Clarendon Press.

Gamble, A. (1988) *The Free Economy and the Strong State: The Politics of Thatcherism*, London: Macmillan.

Gamson, V. A. and Modigliani, A. (1989) 'Media discourse and public opinion on nuclear power: A constructionist approach', *American Journal of Sociology*, Vol. 95, No. 1, 1–37.

Geertz, C. (1973) *The Interpretation of Cultures*, New York: Basic Books Inc.

Gilroy, P. (1987) *There Ain't no Black in the Union Jack: The Cultural Politics of Race and Nation*, London: Hutchinson.

Gilroy, P. (1993) *The Black Atlantic: Modernity and Double Consciousness*, London: Verso.

Grossberg, L. (1986). 'On postmodernism and articulation: An interview with Stuart Hall', *Journal of Communication Inquiry*, Vol. 10, No. 2, 45–60.

Grossberg, L. (1989) 'The context of audiences and the politics of difference', *Australian Journal of Communication*, No. 16, 13–36.

Hall, S. (1983) 'The problem of ideology: Marxism without Guarantees', in B. Matthews (ed.), *Marx: A Hundred Years On*, London: Lawrence and Wishart, 57–85.

Hall, S. (1986) 'Media power and class power', in J. Curran *et al.* (eds), *Bending Reality: The State of the Media*, London: Pluto Press, 5–14.

Hall, S. (1988) *The Hard Road to Renewal: Thatcherism and the Crisis of the Left*, London: Verso.

Hall, S. (1989) 'Ideology and communication theory', in B. Dervin *et al.* (eds), *Rethinking Communication, Volume One: Paradigm Issues*, London: Sage Publications, 40–52.

Hall, S. and Jacques, K. (eds), (1983) *The Politics of Thatcherism*, London: Lawrence and Wishart.

Harvey, D. (1989) *The Condition of Postmodernity*, Oxford: Basil Blackwell.

Hebdige, D. (1979) *Subculture: The Meaning of Style*, London: Methuen.

Herman, E. and Chomsky, N. (1988) *Manufacturing Consent: The Political Economy of the Mass Media*, New York: Pantheon.

Hilgartner, S. and Bosk, C. L. (1988) 'The rise and fall of social problems: A public arenas model', *American Journal of Sociology*, Vol. 94, No. 1, 53–78.

Hirst, P. (1989) *After Thatcher*, London: Collins.

Hobbs, D. (1988) *Doing the Business: Entrepreneurship, the Working Class, and Detectives in the East End of London*, Oxford: Oxford University Press.

Hobsbawm, E. and Ranger, T. (eds), (1983) *The Invention of Tradition*, Cambridge: Cambridge University Press.

Lash, S. and Urry, J. (1987) *The End of Organised Capitalism*, Cambridge: Polity Press.

MacCabe, C. (1995) 'Tradition too has its place in cultural studies', *Times Literary Supplement*, 26 May, 13.

Marcus, G. E. and Fischer, M. (1986) *Anthropology as Cultural Critique: An Experimental Movement in the Human Sciences*, Chicago: University of Chicago Press.

Miller, D. (1994) *Modernity – An Ethnographic Approach; Dualism and Mass Consumption in Trinidad*, Oxford: Berg.

Murdock, G. (1989a) 'Critical inquiry and audience activity', in B. Dervin *et al.* (eds), *Rethinking Communication, Volume Two: Paradigm Exemplars*, London: Sage Publications, 226–49.

Murdock, G. (1989b) 'Redrawing the map of the communications industries: concentration and ownership in the era of privatisation', in M. Ferguson, *Public Communication: The New Imperatives*, London: Sage Publications.

Murdock, G. (1989c) 'Televisual tourism: National image-making and international markets', in C. W. Thomsen (ed.), *Cultural Transfer or Electronic Imperialism?* Heidelberg: Carl Winter Universitatsverlag, 171–184.

Murdock, G. (1994a) 'New times/hard times: leisure, participation and the common good', *Leisure Studies*, Vol. 13, 239–48.

Murdock, G. (1994b) 'The new mogul empires: media concentration and control in the age of convergence', *Media Development* Vol. XLI, No. 4, 3–6.

Murdock, G. and Golding, P. (1989) 'Information poverty and political inequality: citizenship in the age of privatised communication', *Journal of Communication*.

Rentoul, J. (1989) *Me and Mine: The Triumph of the New Individualism?* London: Unwin Hyman.

Rustin, M. (1989) 'The politics of post-Fordism: or, the trouble with new times', *New Left Review*, No. 175, 54–77.

Schlesinger, P., Murdock, G. and Elliott, P. (1983) *Televising 'Terrorism': Political Violence in Popular Culture*, London: Comedia.

Shotter, J. and Gergen, K. J. (1989) *The Texts of Identity*, London: Sage Publications.

Walters, M. (1995) *Globalisation*, London: Routledge.

Eros, eroticism, and the pedagogical process

As professors we rarely speak of the place of eros or the erotic in our classrooms. Trained in the philosophical context of Western metaphysical dualism, many of us have accepted the notion that there is a split between the body and the mind. Believing this, individuals enter the classroom to teach as though only the mind is present and not the body. To call attention to the body is to betray the legacy of repression and denial that has been handed down to us by our professional elders, who have usually been white and male. But our non-white elders were just as eager to deny the body. The predominantly black college has always been a bastion of repression. The public world of institutional learning was a site where the body had to be erased, go unnoticed. When I first became a teacher and needed to use the restroom in the middle of class, I had no clue as to what my elders did in such situations. No one talked about the body in relation to teaching. What did one do with the body in the classroom? Trying to remember the bodies of my professors, I find myself unable to recall them. I hear voices, remember fragmented details but very few whole bodies.

Entering the classroom determined to erase the body and give ourselves over more fully to the mind, we show by our beings how deeply we have accepted the assumption that passion has no place in the classroom. Repression and denial make it possible for us to forget and then desperately seek to recover ourselves, our feelings, our passions in some private place – after class. I remember reading an article in *Psychology Today* years ago when I was still an undergraduate, reporting a study which revealed that every so many seconds while giving lectures many male professors were thinking about sexuality – were even having lustful thoughts about students. I was amazed. After reading this article, which as I recall was shared and talked about endlessly in the dormitory, I watched male professors differently, trying to connect the fantasies I imagined them having in their minds with lectures, with their bodies which I had so faithfully learned to pretend I did not see. During my first semester of college teaching, there was a male student in my class whom I always seemed to see and not see at the same time. At one point in the middle of the semester, I received a call from a school therapist who wanted to speak with me about the way I treated this student in the class. The therapist told me that the student had said I was unusually gruff, rude, and downright mean when I related to him. I did not know exactly who the student was, could not put a face or body with his name, but later when he identified himself in class, I realised that I was erotically drawn to this student. And that my naive way of coping with feelings in the classroom that I had been taught never to have was to deflect (hence my harsh treatment of him), repress, and deny. Overly conscious then about ways such repression and denial could lead to the 'wounding' of a student, I was determined to face whatever passions were aroused in the classroom setting and deal with them.

Writing about Adrienne Rich's work, connecting it to the work of men who thought critically about the body, in her introduction to *Thinking through the Body* Jane Gallop comments:

> Men who do find themselves in some way thinking through the body are more likely to be recognized as serious thinkers and heard. Women have first to prove that we are thinkers, which is easier when we conform to the protocol that deems serious thought separate from an embodied subject in history. Rich is asking women to enter the realms of critical thought and knowledge without becoming disembodied spirit, universal man (Gallop, 1988: 7).

Beyond the realm of critical thought, it is equally crucial that we learn to enter the classroom 'whole' and not as 'disembodied spirit'. In the heady early days of women's studies classes at Stanford University, I learned by the example of daring, courageous women professors (particularly Diane Middlebrook) that there was a place for passion in the classroom, that eros and the erotic did not need to be denied for learning to take place. One of the central tenets of feminist critical pedagogy has been the insistence on not engaging the mind/body split. This is one of the underlying beliefs that has made women's studies a subversive location in the academy. While women's studies over the years has had to fight to be taken seriously by academics in traditional disciplines, those of us who have been intimately engaged as students and/or teachers with feminist thinking have always recognised the legitimacy of a pedagogy that dares to subvert the mind/body split and allow us to be whole in the classroom, and, as a consequence, wholehearted.

Recently, Susan B., a colleague and friend, whom I taught in a women's studies class when she was an undergraduate, stated in conversation that she felt she was having so much trouble with her graduate courses because she has come to expect a quality of passionate teaching that is not present where she is studying. Her comments made me think anew about the place of passion, of erotic recognition in the classroom setting because I believe that the energy she felt in our women's studies classes was there because of the extent to which the women professors teaching those courses dared to give fully of ourselves, going beyond the mere transmission of information in lectures. Feminist education for critical consciousness is rooted in the assumption that knowledge and critical thought engaged with in the classroom should inform our habits of being and ways of living outside the classroom. Since so many of our early classes were taken almost exclusively by female students, it was easier for us not to be disembodied spirits in the classroom. Concurrently, it was expected that we would bring a quality of care and even 'love' to our students. Eros, as a motivating force, was present in our classrooms. As critical pedagogues we were teaching students ways to think differently about gender, understanding fully that this knowledge would also lead them to live differently.

To understand the place of eros and eroticism in the classroom we must move beyond thinking of these forces solely in terms of the sexual, though that dimension need not be denied. Sam Keen, in his book *The Passionate Life*, urges readers to remember that in its earliest conception 'erotic potency was not confined to sexual power but included the moving force that propelled every life-form from a state of mere potentiality to actuality' (Keen, 1983: 5). Given that critical pedagogy seeks to transform consciousness, to provide students with ways of knowing that enable them to know themselves better and live in the world more fully, to some extent it must rely on the presence of the erotic in the classroom to aid the learning process. Keen continues:

> When we limit 'erotic' to its sexual meaning, we betray our alienation from the rest of nature. We confess that we are not motivated by anything like the mysterious force that moves birds to migrate or dandelions to spring. Furthermore, we imply that the fulfillment or potential toward which we strive is sexual – the romantic-genital connection between two persons. (1983: 5)

Understanding that eros is a force that enhances our overall effort to be self-actualising, that it can provide an epistemological grounding informing how we know what we know, enables both professors and students to use such energy in a classroom setting in ways that invigorate discussion and excite the critical imagination.

Suggesting that this culture lacks a 'vision or science of hygeology' (health and well-being) Keen asks, 'What forms of passion might make us whole? To what passions may we surrender with the assurance that we will expand rather than diminish the promise of our lives?' (1983: 19). The quest for knowledge that enables us to unite theory and practice is one such passion. To the extent that professors bring this passion, which has to be fundamentally rooted in a love for ideas, we are able to inspire. The classroom becomes a dynamic place where transformation in social relations is concretely actualised and the false dichotomy between the world outside and the inside world of the academy disappears. In many ways this is frightening. Nothing about the way I was trained as a teacher really prepared me to witness my students transforming themselves.

It was during the years that I taught in the African-American studies department at Yale, a course on black women writers, that I witnessed the way education for critical consciousness can fundamentally alter our perceptions of reality and our actions. During one course we collectively explored in fiction the power of internalised racism, seeing how it was described in the literature as well as critically interrogating our experiences. However, one of the black female students, who had always straightened her hair because she felt deep down that she would not look good if it were not processed, changed. She came to class after a break and told everyone that this class had deeply affected her, so much so that when she went to get her usual 'perm' some force within said no. I still remember the fear I felt when she testified that the class had changed her. Though I believed deeply in the philosophy of education for critical consciousness that empowers, I had not yet comfortably united theory with practice. Some small part of me still wanted us to remain disembodied spirits. And her body, her presence, her changed look was a direct challenge that I had to face and affirm. She was teaching me. Now, years later, I read again her final words to the class and recognise the passion and beauty of her will to know and to act:

I am a black woman. I grew up in Shaker Heights, Ohio. I cannot go back and change years of believing that I could never be quite as pretty or intelligent as many of my white friends – but I can go forward learning pride in who I am . . . I cannot go back and change years of believing that the most wonderful thing in the world would be to be Martin Luther King, Jr.'s wife – but I can go on and find the strength I need to be the revolutionary for myself rather than the companion and help for someone else. So no, I don't belive that we change what has already been done but we can change the future and so I am reclaiming and learning more of who I am so that I can be whole.

Attempting to gather my thoughts on eroticism and pedagogy, I have re-read student journals covering a span of ten years. Again and again I read notes that could easily be considered 'romantic' as students express their love for me, our class. Hear an Asian student offer her thoughts about a class:

> White people have never understood the beauty of silence, of connection and reflection. You teach us to speak, and to listen for the signs in the wind. Like a guide, you walk silently through the forest ahead of us. In the forest everything has sound, speaks . . . You too teach us to talk, where all life speaks in the forest, not just the white man's. Isn't that part of feeling whole – the ability to be able to talk, to not have to be silent or performing all the time, to be able to be critical and honest – openly? This is the truth you have taught us: all people deserve to speak.

Or a black male student writing that he will 'love me now and always' because our class has been a dance, and he loves to dance:

> I love to dance. When I was a child, I danced everywhere. Why walk there when you can shuffle-ball-change all the way? When I danced my soul ran free. I was poetry. On my Saturday grocery excursions with my mother, I would flap, flap, flap, ball change the shopping cart through the aisles. Mama would turn to me and say, 'boy stop that dancing. White people think that's all we can do anyway.' I would stop but when she wasn't looking I would do a quick high bell kick or two. I didn't care what white people thought, I just loved to dance – dance – dance. I still dance and I still don't care what people think white or black. When I dance my soul is free. It is sad to read about men who stop dancing, who stop being foolish, who·stop letting their souls fly free . . . I guess for me, surviving whole means never to stop dancing.

These words were written by O'Neal LaRone Clark in 1987. We had a passionate teacher/student relationship. He was taller than six feet and I remember the day he came to class late and came right up to the front, picked me up and whirled me around. The class laughed. I called him 'fool' and laughed. It was by way of apology for being late, for missing any moment of classroom passion. And so he brought his own moment. I too love to dance. And so we danced our way into the future as comrades and friends bound by all we had learned in class together. Those who knew him remember the times he came to class early to do funny imitations of the teacher. He died unexpectedly last year – still dancing, still loving me now and always.

When eros is present in the classroom setting then love is bound to flourish. Well-learned distinctions between public and private make us believe that love has no place in the classroom. Even though many viewers could applaud a movie like *The Dead Poet's Society*, possibly identifying with the passion of the professor and his students, rarely is such passion institutionally affirmed. As professors we are expected to publish, but no one really expects or demands of us that we really care about teaching in uniquely passionate and different ways. Teachers who love students and are loved by them are still 'suspect' in the academy. Some of the suspicion is that the presence of feelings, of passions, may not allow for objective consideration of each student's merit. But this very notion is based on the false assumption that education is neutral, that there is some 'even' emotional ground we stand on that enables us to treat everyone equally dispassionately. In reality, special bonds between professors and students have always existed but traditionally they have been exclusive rather than inclusive. To allow one's feeling of care and one's will to nurture particular individuals in the classroom to expand and embrace everyone goes against the notion of privatised passion. In student journals from various classes I have taught there would always be complaints about the perceived special bonding between myself and particular students. Realising that my students were uncertain about expressions of care and love in the classroom, I found it necessary to teach on the subject. I asked students once: 'Why do you feel that the regard I extend to a particular student cannot also be extended to each of you? Why do you think there is not enough love or care to go around?' To answer these questions they had to think deeply about the society we live in, how we are taught to compete with one another. They had to think about capitalism and how it informs the way we think about love and care, the way we live in our bodies, the way we try to separate mind from body.

There is not much passionate teaching or learning taking place in higher education today. Even when students are desperately yearning to be touched by knowledge, professors still fear the challenge, allow their worries about losing control to override their desires to teach. Concurrently, those of us who teach the same old subjects in the same old ways are often inwardly bored – unable to rekindle passions we may have once felt. If, as Thomas Merton suggests in his essay on pedagogy 'Learning to live', the purpose of education is to show students how to define themselves 'authentically and spontaneously in relation' to the world, then we can best teach if we are self-actualised. Merton reminds us that 'the original and authentic "paradise" idea, both in the monastery and in the university, implied not simply a celestial store of theoretic ideas to which the Magistri and Doctores held the key, but the inner self of the student' who would discover the ground of his or her being in relation to him- or herself, to higher powers, to community. That the 'fruit of education . . . was in the activation of that inmost center' (1949: 9). To restore passion to the classroom or to excite it in classrooms where it has never been, we must find again the place of eros within ourselves and together allow the mind and body to feel and know and desire.

References

Gallop, Jane (1988) *Thinking Through the Body*, New York: Columbia University Press.

Keen, Sam (1983) *The Passionate Life*, San Francisco: Harper & Row.

Merton, Thomas (1949) 'Learning to Live', In Naomi Burton Stone and Brother Patrick Hart (eds) *Love and Learning*, New York: Farrar, Strauss & Giroux, Inc. 3–14.

Part Two

Bodies, images and music

'After the love has gone': bio-politics and etho-poetics in the black public sphere

The biological, with the notion of inevitability it entails, becomes more than an *object* of spiritual life. It becomes its heart. The mysterious urgings of the blood, the appeals of heredity and the past for which the body serves as an enigmatic vehicle, lose the character of being problems that are subject to a solution put forward by a sovereignly free Self. Not only does the Self bring in the unknown elements of these problems in order to resolve them; the Self is also constituted by these elements. Man's escape no longer lies in freedom, but in a kind of bondage. To be truly oneself does not mean taking flight once more above contingent events that always remain foreign to the Self's freedom; on the contrary, it means becoming aware of the ineluctable original chain that is unique to our bodies, and above all accepting this chaining.

Emmanuel Levinas

A crowd of men and women moiled like nightmare figures in the smoke-green haze. The juke box was dinning and it was like looking into the depths of a murky cave. And now someone moved aside and looking down along the curve of the bar past the bobbing heads and shoulders I saw the juke box, lit up like a bad dream of the Fiery Furnace, shouting
Jelly, Jelly
Jelly,
All night long.

Ralph Ellison

In a preliminary discussion of some of the tropes of freedom that have occupied and been created by the black public sphere, I want to point to some of the key ethical and political questions that arise when critically inclined intellectuals discover the special potency of popular cultural styles. These are often outlaw forms that may demand an end to disinterested and contemplative criticism, but which pose even greater problems for politically engaged critics whose work − irrespective of their noblest motives − is revealed to be inadequate where it moves too swiftly and too simplistically to either condemn or celebrate. Where the unseasonal fruits of counter-culture become popular and the marginal moves into the mainstream, it would be absurd to expect to find politics programmatically constituted. It would also be mistaken and certainly immodest for hyper-privileged people to anticipate that these forms of consciousness are doomed by their unholy locations to remain forever merely pre-political.

A special version of these issues can be reconstructed where black vernacular forms have recently appeared as objects of serious academic scrutiny. It features strongly in discussions of hip hop and rap because of the way that these expressions precipitate and dramatise intra-communal conflicts over the meanings and forms of freedom and also because the extraordinary global transformation triggered by hip hop was wholly unanticipated. With this unforeseen planetary change on our side, black critics have displayed a special reluctance to give up the qualified axiological authority that we fought so hard to attain. However, I believe that we are still largely subject to a special condition of dependency upon the 'ethnic' authenticity that vernacular forms manifest and which critical discourses suggest only they can confer upon a range of other less obviously authentic cultural activities. These problems of value, of judgement and, of course, of politics have been compounded in a time of great uncertainty about the limits of racial particularity and racial solidarity. Though it has a wider currency, the special authority that authentic vernacular forms supposedly supply has been invoked by the critics who are most comfortable with absolutist definitions of culture. It specifies the elusive quality of racialised difference that they alone can claim to be able to comprehend and to paraphrase, if not exactly translate. The desire to monopolise the practice of these transcultural skills and engage in the varieties of social regulation that they sanction, endows some critics with an extra investment in the uniqueness, purity and power of the vernacular.[1] However, that inflated uniqueness is punctured when underground phenomena appear amidst the brightness and glamour of the cultural industries and their insatiable machinery of commodification. It is understandable why commentators, especially academics, should desire to enlist the ruthless alterity of hip hop as part of an argument for the legitimacy of our own interpretive activity. But what political and ethical issues arise when we do so? This question prompts a renewed engagement with questions of class and power that persistently disrupt the body-coded solidarities based on 'race' and gender. Following on from this, in what sense might hip hop be described as marginal today? Those who assert the marginality of hip hop should be obliged to say where they imagine the centre might now be. Hip hop's marginality is as official, as routinised, as its overblown defiance and yet it is still represented as an outlaw form. This is a mystery that aches to be solved. Further clues may be furnished by delving into uncomfortable issues like hip hop's corporate developmental association with the 'subcultures' that grow up around television, advertising and cartoons or by interrogating the revolutionary conservatism that constitutes its routine political focus but which is over-simplified or more usually ignored by its academic celebrants.

Professor Henry Louis Gates Jr.'s principled defence of Luther Campbell's 2 Live Crew is rightly remembered as an important historical moment in which these difficult issues were clarified. Four years later, the erasure of Campbell's Caribbean affiliations and his elective affinity for lily-white Luke Skywalker seem less problematic than his appetite for regionally-based conflictual dialogue with west coast rappers, his enthusiastic involvement in the class-coded world of celebrity golf, his reported eagerness to become involved in publishing soft-core pornographic magazines, and most interesting of all, his recently disclosed enthusiasm for the work of the infamous English comedian Benny Hill. The contribution that Hill's gurning techniques or anglo-vernacular characters like Ernie the milkman may have made to the multiplicity, impurity and hybridity that is hip hop surely provides the last nail in the coffin of ethnocentric accounts of its origins and development. 'The way that I get updated on my thing is I get different girls, and I ask them what they like to do. Playboy been around for years, and Penthouse. Benny Hill been around a long time here . . . maybe I'll start going off and doing more of the Benny Hill type thing, and being more funny.'[2] The Benny Hill effect dictates that syncretism is an unpredictable and surprising process. It also underlines the global reach of popular cultures as well as the complexity of their crossover dynamics. Crossing, like outer-national diaspora dispersal, is no longer something that can be conceptualised as a uni-directional or reversible process. The way back is barred. The very qualities in hip hop that have led to it being identified not as one black culture among many but as the very *blackest* culture – one that provides the scale on which all the others can be evaluated – have a complex relationship to the signs of pleasure and danger that solicit identification from white affiliates and practitioners. Squeamish 'insiderist' criticism cannot face either the extent to which white consumers currently support black culture[3] or the possible implications of transracial popularity for the political struggles against white supremacy that lie ahead. Neither can they accept the catholic tastes of the creators of the form whose loyalty to the phattest beats usually exceeds their commitment to imaginary racial purity and phenotypically-coded musical production.[4]

The quest for better accounts of the processes of popular-cultural syncretism and their changing political resonance demands several other urgent adjustments in the way that we approach the popular phenomena that are grouped together under the heading hip hop. The first involves querying the hold that this outlaw form itself exerts on critical writers thanks to its quiet endorsement of their own desire that the world can be readily transformed into text – that nothing resists the power of language. This is a familiar problem that Michel Foucault has stated succinctly in his famous cautioning against reducing the bloody 'open hazardous reality of conflict' to the 'calm Platonic form of language and dialogue'.[5] It bites sharply in this area, especially when the phenomenology of musical forms is dismissed in favour of analysing lyrics, the video images that supplement them and the technology of hip hop production. Secondly, we need far more patient and careful attention to the issues of gender and sexuality than critics have been inclined to engage in so far. These are the conduits of crossover potential as well as the unstable core of spuriously naturalised racial particularity. Thirdly, we will have to produce a better understanding of the relationship between hip hop and the other (sub)cultural styles with which it is in creative dialogue.

I propose to address these issues in what follows and to focus initially on the point where the eddies that hip hop has produced de-stabilise and flow back into more recognisably traditional and predictable currents. I want to start by acknowledging the possibility that hip hop has contributed to the reinvigoration of rhythm and blues and address the slow jams and swing beat that – in Britain at least – have an altogether different potential for crossover appeal to white listeners whose support they do not actively seek. I want to begin and end with musical articulations of the apparently sex-obsessed culture that defines a privileged point of entry into the subaltern public sphere and affords a key to the notions of freedom that unexpectedly thrive there.

There is a significant moment in the old-school re-mix of R. Kelly's number one hit 'Bump And Grind' which has been on top of the black music charts on both sides of the Atlantic. The singer recycles the famous hookline from the Five Stairsteps' 1969 hit 'Ooh Child'. Sticking closely to their melody and phrasing, he cautions or possibly promises the woman to whom his song of seduction is apparently addressed that 'things are gonna get freakier'. This transforms the relatively wholesome and optimistic spirit of the original which had comforted its listeners with the reassuring news that 'things are gonna be easier'. This is no longer plausible advice to the black listening public. R. Kelly remains more faithful to the profane muses of rhythm and blues than most of his fellow practitioners of 'swing'[6] – a hybrid offspring of soul and rap. However, his citation and adaptation of the earlier tune is not motivated by the desire to engage in the archaeology of living 'intertextual' tradition. It works like a stolen sample or a borrowed instrumental riff to index the inter-performative relationships that constitute a counter-cultural subculture. He makes the past audible in the here and now but *subserviently*. History is conscripted into the service of the present.[7] Kelly's subversive transformation of the older tune, cut in the year that he was born, betrays the oedipal impulses that are the cornerstone of this hidden modern tradition. In a small way, his gesture, which manages to be simultaneously both insubordinate and reverent, expresses the contraction of the black public sphere. This process has developed closely in step with what might be termed the narrative shrinkage of the rhythm and blues idiom: one of the more pernicious effects of the pre-eminence of a hip hop culture currently dominated by grim tales of sex, drugs and gun play. Kelly's cool pose is entirely complicit with what bell hooks has identified as the 'life threatening choke hold (that) patriarchal masculinity imposes on black men'.[8] It could be argued that the explicit repudiation of social amelioration which Kelly's words contain, conveys something important about the imploded contemporary character of black political culture which finds it progressively more and more difficult to be political at all. However, I want to suggest something different and slightly more complex, namely that it is the association of repudiating progress with the assertive pursuit of sexual pleasure that provides a distinctive historical embodiment of the dismal moment in which public politics becomes unspeakable and bio-politics[9] takes hold.

R. Kelly's popularity is one of many signs that the black body politic is now regularly represented internally and externally as an integral but 'freaky' body. Racialised sex is an ephemeral residue of political rebellion. The androcentric and phallocratic presentation and representation of heterosexual coupling at which he excels is both the sign and the limit of a different charisma and a different utopia than those that Kenny Burke and his siblings had in mind in Chicago twenty-five years ago.[10] Their choice of the name 'Stairsteps' for their pre-Jacksons family quintet suggested upward momentum, racial elevation and communal movement towards something 'brighter', something closer to the heavens if not to God. I want to explore the possibility that this goal, which was identifiable thanks to its illumination amidst the darkness of white supremacy that threatened to engulf it, was named freedom – a word that has been steadily disappearing from the political language of blacks in the west and which will be even more remote from their consciousness now that the liberation of South Africa has been formally accomplished. I want to mourn the disappearance of the pursuit of freedom as an element in black vernacular culture and to ask why it seems no longer appropriate or even plausible to speculate about the freedom of the subject of black politics in the overdeveloped countries. I also want to examine the effects on the public political world of transposing that yearning for freedom into a different mode. This is signalled by the growing centrality of what might be called a racialised bio-politics of fucking: a means of bonding freedom and life. This move towards bio-politics is best understood as an outgrowth of the pattern identified as 'identity politics' in earlier periods by a number of writers.[11] It is a mood in which the person is defined as the body and in which certain exemplary bodies, for example those of Mike Tyson and Michael Jordan, Naomi Campbell and Veronica Webb, become instantiations of community. This situation necessitates a different conception of freedom than those hitherto channelled into modern citizenship or developed in post-slave cultures where bodily and spiritual freedoms were sharply differentiated and freedom was more likely to be associated with death than life. Organic intellectuals on this historic frequency from Frederick Douglas to George Clinton suggested that the most valuable forms of freedom resided in the liberation of the mind. Dr Funkenstein's prescription was 'Free your mind and your ass will follow'. Racialised bio-politics operates from an altogether different premise that refuses this distinction. It uses a reversal of these historic priorities to establish the limits of the authentic racial community exclusively through the visual representation of racial bodies – engaged in characteristic activities, usually sexual or sporting – that ground and solicit identification if not solidarity. This development is problematic for several reasons. For one thing, it marks that racial community exclusively as a space of heterosexual activity and confirms the abandonment of any politics aside from the ongoing oppositional creativity of gendered self-cultivation: an activity that is endowed with almost sacred significance but undertaken in something of the same resolute spirit as working out with weights. If it survives, politics becomes an excusively aesthetic concern with all the perils that implies and the racial body, arranged suggestively with a precision that will be familiar to readers of de Sade, supplies its critical evaluative principle. Affiliates of the racialised collectivity are thereby led 'to focus their attention on themselves, to decipher, recognise and acknowledge themselves as subjects of desire, bringing into play between themselves a certain relationship that allows them to discover, in desire, the truth of their being'.[12]

The termination of talk about freedom and the proliferation of signs and talk about sexuality as racialised recreation have coincided. Together they point to a novel form of artistic production that goes beyond therapeutic cultures of compensation where simple sameness supplied the premise and the entry ticket, into an aesthetic sense of racial difference for which the sculpted male bodies that adorn albums by bands like Jodeci and crooners like R Aab, are a notable popular signifier.[13] These silences and embodied signs yield insights into the changing and embattled character of the black public sphere. They represent the end of older notions of public interaction that helped to create and were themselves created by the forms of densely coded, verbally mediated inter-subjective dialogue that nurtured racial solidarity and made the idea of an exclusive racialised identity a credible, operable one. The time-worn model of black publicity derived from sacred rituals and musical utility survives but in a vestigial and profane form. Its precious dialogical attributes retain a dwindling ethical significance even as this drains away and is replaced by morbid phenomena like the Americocentric image of the black public sphere as the inner city basketball court. This is an exclusively male stage for the theatre of power and kinship in which sound is displaced by vision and words are generally second to gestures. The natural aristocracy defined by means of bodily power and grace can announce its heroic godly presence there.[14] A hint of the significance of this location emerged in a recent interview with R. Kelly in *Vibe* magazine:

Robert Kelly grew up all over the South Side of Chicago. He and his boys are into basketball, and three or four mornings a week they show up at one of their favourite courts (18th, 47th, 63rd, 67th or 115th street). 'When I hit the court and people know me, it's "Hell, naw, that's that guy that be singin'". They don't realize I'm just a regular guy. I'm anxious to prove myself. I can ball just like you do. I'll take it to the hole just like you, if not better.'[15]

At present, the poetic topography of race and place centred on the basketball court has no equivalent in Britain's black cultures. However, some of these points about the relationship of identity, publicity and masculinity can be illustrated by the popular reception of the black basketball action movie *Above The Rim*. The soundtrack CD from this movie features material from eighteen different artists and it has been a powerful initial marketing tool for a film that promises to complete and extend the narrative of *White Men Can't Jump* in a more gritty mode that takes its reality effects from hip hop's masculinist lexicon. The soundtrack has displaced R. Kelly from the top of the album charts since I first sat down to try and write this piece.

The popularity of film-associated anthologies like the *Above The Rim* album offers important evidence that the independent power of music is waning while the authority of the image culture on which music has become increasingly parasitic grows steadily. It was, after all, a similar sound track album from the Bill Duke film *Deep Cover* that first unleashed the talent of Snoop Doggy Dogg, the young rapper from Long Beach who is the most successful artist in the history of the style and who is now the centre of the moral and political panics about gangsta rap. One track from the *Above The Rim* set features DJ Rogers, the greatest male gospel singer of his generation, who has been induced by producer Dr Dre to sing 'Doggie Style', a song that endorses and amplifies Snoop's historic call to cultivate a set of distinctive sexual habits that can bring certainty, confidence and resoluteness back to racialised being:

Let's do it doggie style
I really like to ride it doggie style . . .
baby come closer I want to undress you
I'm gonna give it to you baby until you can take no more . . .
you and I on the floor let's get freaky . . .
baby don't you move you'll disturb my groove . . .
turnover lay your head down so I can get freaky
please let me lick you in my favourite way
turnover baby and back up into me so let me love you down
there's no need to worry I'm your doggy style man.

A chorus of singers interposes appropriate exhortations. This is more than the pursuit of sexual pleasure as compensation for the wrongs wrought in the name of white supremacy. We shall discover below that it is more even than a dionysian alternative to the asceticism of figures like Ice Cube who have responded to contemporary uncertainties about racial identity and solidarity with an austerity programme that articulates some ancient priestly notions about the association of sexual abstention with the acquisition of knowledge and the forms of self-love necessitated by communal reconstruction.[16]

The changed composition and signification of the black body politic has been associated with a number of other social and technological shifts that cannot be explored in detail here, though they must be noted in passing. First, this transformation cannot be separated from the privatisation of both cultural production and use – a long-term trend that has important implications for attempts to defend the political significance of black popular culture. The basketball court configuration of the public sphere is suggestive here. It indicates that the vernacular forms that were once called street culture have largely left the public world of the streets which are no longer seen primarily as a privileged space for the elaboration of cultural authenticity but rather as the location of violence, crime and social pathology. The vital unfolding of racialised culture is now projected as taking place in discrete private, semi-private and private public settings that can be found, like the ball court, between the axes established by the bedroom and the car. Second, the family supplies the sole institutional site for bio-politics and, as I have pointed out elsewhere, a radical localism operating under the sign 'hood' projects community as a simple accumulation of symmetrical family units.[17] The family remains important because it narrows the horizons of any lingering aspiration towards social change. But as Jodeci make clear, the sanctity and integrity of the family can be readily sacrificed when more important hedonistic objectives come into view. The duty of parental care exists in opposition to the space of sexual intimacy where the most intense meanings of being black are established:

girl where is our child?
send it to your mother's for a while
all my friends are gone you know I sent them home
girl I live for you so I don't give a fuck about the news
so please turn off the TV

and if you give a damn about me I wanna hear you moan
let's be alone
what's better than you and me? you're better than a damn movie
our love is so much fun
let's do some freaky shit and then I'll make you come . . .

The gender-neutrality of the child in this torrid narrative suggests extreme paternal indifference rather than political correctness. It is clearly significant that on this scale of excitement it is cinema that provides the bench-mark. The fact that RAab's agenda for an evening at home is similar to that proposed by Devanté Swing and the boys can be gleaned from something as simple as the list of song titles on his album: 'Try My Love', 'Foreplay', 'Where She At?', 'Feel Me', 'Give In To Me', 'Give It A Try', 'You're The One', 'Close The Door', 'Can't Let Go', 'Good Lovin' and 'It's Just Like That'. His album jacket warns prospective purchasers that his bass-heavy music will destroy their audio systems unless they make technical adjustments. He then supplies what amounts to a moral health warning in case his paean to the joys of recreational sex is misunderstood.

This album is dedicated to all the brothers and sisters who believe monogamous relationships still work. The songs on this album are about one brother's involvement with one sister. We brothers have got to stop treatin' and callin' our sisters bitches and whores. They are true extensions of our existence. Sisters have got to wake up also – Stop competing with each other and respect your fellow sister and their situations, no matter what it is. We have got to turn this shit around and stop hurting one another. We are only destroying one another. Can't you see what's goin on? Can't you see it's wrong? Our ancestors are very disappointed. Peace.[18]

Third, the patterned use of black music reveals a lot about the changing quality of the subaltern public culture. The dominant place of radio in fixing the limits of the black public sphere as an interpretive community has been ceded to video in ways that compromise the power of sound and the dialogic principles on which the black vernacular was built in times past. It is interesting to note that Snoop Doggy Dogg has dramatised each medium's different claims for the right to represent the culture as a whole in the snippets of humour and drama inserted between his rapped contributions on his album (also entitled *Doggy Style*). The proliferation of jokes, sketches and other humorous material on recent black popular music recordings does more than try and fill up the enhanced playing time made possible by the CD format. This tactic is common to recent offerings by Snoop, DRS, 7669 and Xscape. It seems to be a bid to simulate and thus recover a variety of dialogical interaction that has been inhibited by the technology of production but is sought by underground users nonetheless. It may also provide carefully constructed cues to the crossover listenership that can attune them to the signs of pleasure and danger that they desire. The proliferation of these dramatic inserts is yet another indication that the foundational authority of the performance event has been undermined by the emergence of musical forms that cannot be faithfully or readily translated into concert settings as a result of their technological base. The impact of problems arising from the political economy of clubs and other venues should also be noted. Faced with these changes, street culture has become many things, most notably 'jeep culture' as cars have become larger-scale equivalents of the Walkman – a piece of technology named by a word which, by lacking a plural, signifies its association with the same sad process of social privatisation.

While everyone else was following NWA into naming their bands with mysterious sequences of initials or numbers that only initiates could de-code (UNV, POV, SWV, DRS, 7669, are the most obvious examples), R. Kelly called his musical back-up team Public Announcement, a name that bypassed the vogueish urge to encrypt. It openly acknowledged a different historic obligation to service the alternative, subaltern public spheres that have hosted the processes of vernacular identity formation through a variety of different communicative technologies (print, radio, audio, video) and in a wide range of settings at various distances from the core event of cultural performance.

These successive communicative technologies organise space and time in different ways and have solicited and fostered different kinds of identification. They create and manipulate memory in dissimilar ways and stage the corporeal and psychical enigmas of cultural identity in contrasting processes. Their political effects are various and contradictory but the long-term tendency for music, sound and text to give way to image cannot be dismissed. We must ask whether scopic identification and desire differ from what might be called the alternative 'orphic' configurations organised around music and hearing. Do the latter privilege the imaginary over the symbolic? The growing dominance of specularity over aurality contributes a special force to representations of the exemplary racial body arrested in the gaze of desiring and identifying subjects. Misrecognised, objectified and verified, these images have become the store houses of racial alterity now that the production of subjectivity operates through different sensory and technological mechanisms. We must be clear about what is gained and what may be being lost in the contemporary displacement of sound from the epicentre of black cultural production:

> In sound, and in the consciousness termed hearing, there is in fact a break with the self complete world of vision and art. In its entirety, sound is a ringing, clanging scandal. Whereas in vision, form is wedded to content in such a way as to appease it, in sound the perceptible quality overflows so that form can no longer contain its content. A real rent is produced in the world, through which the world that is *here* prolongs a dimension that cannot be converted into vision.[19]

The trials of freedom

> Knowledge is freedom and ignorance is slavery . . .
>
>   Miles Davis

Contemporary studies of black vernacular culture are just as silent as hip hop about the concept of freedom and its political and metaphysical significance. This is puzzling given the complex historical connections between slavery and freedom that are evident in the forms black culture assumes and the ways it is engaged by its producers and its users. Freedom has sometimes emerged as a theme in the writing of black history, and the dialectical interrelation of freedom and slavery has been addressed, but where this has happened, freedom has usually been presented as a solitary event: a break-point or rupture. It is seen as a threshold that was irrevocably crossed once slavery was formally declared to be over and populations of ex-slaves moved uneasily into the new spaces of enhanced autonomy – intimate, private, civic, economic – that the concept helped to define. The desire to acquire civic and economic freedoms and the pursuit of personal freedoms had been closely aligned during the period of struggles against slavery. Considerable tension between these different dynamics developed in the post-emancipation period. The fundamental shift represented by the Jubilee was felt to require the opening of a new chapter in the narrative of black history, even where the forms of civil society in which the newly-freed found themselves instituted noval unfreedoms that compounded powerlessness, immiseration and poverty or retained and modified patterns of racialised domination from the slave period.[20] Freedom was seen to be relevant primarily because it represented the termination of slavery rather than the beginning of a different sequence of struggles in which its own meanings would be established and its future limits identified. Once formal free status was gained it could appear that there was no further need to elaborate the distinctive meanings that freedom acquired among people radically estranged from the promise and practice of freedom by generations of servitude enforced by terror. The end of slavery produced several new 'technical' solutions to the problems of discovering and regulating free black selves.

> After the coming of freedom there were two points upon which practically all the people on our place were agreed, and I feel that this was generally true throughout the South: that they must change their names, and that they must leave the old plantation for at least a few days or weeks in order that they might feel really sure that they were free.[21]

It was only among blacks in the United States that ready access to political institutions defined freedom's post-slave boundaries. Even in that exceptional situation, the limits of freedom had to be first found and then tested. Leon Litwack[22] has pointed to the significant role of marriages in symbolising and demonstrating the free status of the freed slaves. The place of the family, the significance of domesticity and the need to acquire clearly demarcated spaces for intimate and private activity are all important issues in the technologies of the free self that have left lingering imprints upon today's libidinal economies and erotic allegories of political desire. The relatively limited role of obviously political institutions in establishing the history of those incomplete emancipations that did not straightforwardly deliver substantive freedom in the form of political rights is therefore something that needs to be explored carefully. If bell hooks is right, the compensatory take-up of patriarchal masculinity by ex-slaves and their descendants might be fruitfully linked to critical analysis of the development of democracy compromised by the imperatives of white supremacy. The coercive regimes that followed modern racial slavery under the banners of freedom were, just as that slavery had been, internal to western civilisation. Their histories complicate the history of democracy and the assumption of social and moral progress towards which that heroic tale is often directed. Under the guidance of ideologues who were self-consciously developing the arts of governing, disciplining and educating the post-slave self, the former slaves and their descendants gradually and unevenly acquired the freedoms to vote, associate, organise and communicate. They became bearers of rights and practitioners of skills that confirmed their equal value as free people in circumstances that made liberty and equality impracticable though not unthinkable. Their descendants continue to stretch the bounds of the civility that enclosed and promoted these rights. It would be mistaken to assume that the gap between formal, rhetorical declarations of black emancipation and the practical realisation of democratic hopes defines and exhausts the politics of being free. I want to suggest that, however important the relatively narrow understanding of freedom centred on political rights has been, it leaves vast areas of thinking about freedom and the desire to be seen to be free, untouched. A politics of freedom (and indeed of being free) needs to be addressed today with a special sensitivity because the meanings of freedom and the idioms through which it is apprehended have become extremely significant for interpretations of contemporary popular culture. Important work has already been undertaken in this area by the anthropologist Daniel Miller,[23] by historians of African-American religion such as Mechal Sobel[24] and Charles H. Long,[25] and in particular by Lawrence Levine whose invaluable study *Black Culture and Black Consciousness*[26] points to important historical connections between the subcultural reproduction of gender and mythic and heroic representations of freedom. Freedom has been less of an issue in broadly sociological studies of the utility and practice of black vernacular forms: sacred and profane.[27]

Rather than delve into the forms assumed and promoted by the protean consciousness of freedom, analysts have usually investigated the impact of becoming free on the slaves and on their patterns of cultural production. Exploring the transformations wrought by Jubilee and the effects of its ritual commemoration can however proceed without confronting either the value of freedom itself as an element in the lives of ex-slaves or the distinctive idiomatic practices through which they strove to represent the psychological, social and economic differences freedom made: to themselves, to their descendants and to the slave masters and mistresses who were themselves embarking on a journey out of slavery, ceasing to be oppressors and becoming exploiters. The memory of slavery is seldom addressed, though the silences and evasions around slavery that popular culture reveals make this more understandable. I have suggested that the dominance of love and loss stories in black popular musical forms embraces the condition of being in pain,[28] transcodes and interweaves the different yearnings for personal and civic freedoms, and preserves the memories of suffering and loss in a usable – irreducibly ethical – form. The incorporated memories[29] of unfreedom and terror are cultivated in commemorative practices. Song and the social rituals that surround it became a valuable means to cultivate a rapport with the presence of suffering and with death. Amidst the terror of slavery where bodily and spiritual freedoms were readily distinguished along lines suggested by Christianity – if not African cosmology – death was itself often understood as an escape. It offered the opportunity to acquire a higher, heteronymous freedom in which the mortal body – unshackled at last – would be cast aside as the newly liberated soul soared heavenward or took its place among the ancestral pantheon. Many practices that were forged in the habitus of slavery have lingered on. But today the social memory of slavery has itself been repressed or set aside and the traditon of dynamic remembrance it founded is being assaulted from all sides. The memory of slavery is seen as an encumbrance or an old skin that has to be shed before an authentic life of racialised self-love can be attained.[30]

The contemporary popular music of R. Kelly, Snoop Dogg, SWV and the rest registers these changes. The sharpest break between the older patterns and bio-politics is evident where love stories mutate into sex stories. Even when they were systematically profane, the modes of intersubjectivity described and sometimes practised in earlier stages in the unfolding of rhythm and blues were informed by the proximity of the sacred and the definitions of spiritual love that were cultivated there. Spirituality cast long shadows over emergent forms of secular and profane creativity in which songs of passion were often simultaneously songs of protest. Today, song is being relegated to the role of soundtrack for the expansion of the image world and the game of truth is updated. The new rules are fixed via a different, I am tempted to say postmodern, conception of mortality. The traditional cultivation of a rapport with the presence of death is recast because death is no longer a transition or release.[31] Dr Dre, the producer of Snoop's records, calls his label Death Row records. The changed value and understanding of death that has developed amidst the AIDS crisis, the drug economy and the militarisation of inner city life, is thus another factor re-shaping the black public sphere and its historicity:

> Daily life becomes a perpetual dress rehearsal for death. What is being rehearsed . . . is *ephemerality* and *evanescence* of things that humans may acquire and bonds that humans may weave. The impact of such daily

rehearsal seems to be similar to one achieved by some preventive inocula-
tions: if taken in daily, in partly detoxicated and thus non-deadly doses,
the awesome poison seems to lose its venom. Instead, it prompts immunity
and indifference to the toxin in the inoculated organism.[32]

It bears repetition that bio-politics specifies that the person is identified
only in terms of their body. The very best that this change precipitates
is a principled anti-Christian confrontation with the idea that life continues after death. It is the refusal of these religious antidotes to death
that is often described as nihilism.[33] In these circumstances, the desire
to be free is closely linked with the desire to be seen to be free and with
the pursuit of an individual and embodied intensity of experience that
contrasts sharply with the collective and spiritual forms of immortality
esteemed in times gone by. Jean Luc Nancy has emphasised how
freedom is linked to a politics of representation.[34] This relationship
accumulates special significance where 'race' becomes the rationality
for denying and withholding liberty and where studied indifference to
the death and suffering of others provides a short cut to the enduring
notoriety and celebrity associated with gangsterdom. This is now a
social phenomenon by virtue of its anti-sociality.

As old certainties about the fixed limits of racial identity have lost
their power to convince, ontological security capable of answering a
radically reduced sense of the value of life has been sought in the
naturalising power of gender difference and sex, as well as in the ability
to cheat death and take life. Sex and gender are experienced – lived con-
flictually – at a heightened pitch that somehow connotes 'race'. Gender
difference and racialised gender codes provide a special cipher for a
mode of racial authenticity that is as evasive as it is desirable. In these
circumstances, the iterative representation of gender, gender conflicts
and sexualities contributes a supple confidence and stability to
essentialist absolute notions of racial particularity. These may, like
Onyx and other homophobic ragga stars such as Buju Banton, demand
the death of all 'batty bwoy' as the price of their reproduction over time.
They may, like Jodeci, perform highly stylised ritual celebrations of
heterosexual intimacy that suspend and transcend the everyday incoher-
ence and disymmetry of gender, turning them into an ordered narrative
of racial being and becoming. With these specific examples in mind, it
is necessary to acknowledge that the centrality of gender to black
popular cultures can also be analysed as an alternative articulation of
freedom that associates autonomous agency with sexual desire and pro-

motes the symbolic exercise of power in the special domain that sexuality provides. In this crepuscular space, Bell Biv Devoe, a group who have taken the basketball tropes considerably further than anyone else, use them to provide a coy invitation to practice anal intercourse, DRS (Dirty Rotten Scoundrels) issue their female associates with the simple command to 'strip' and SWV (Sisters With Voices) urge their partners to go 'Downtown' and discover a way to their heart between their thighs.

> . . . You've been wondering how you can make it better
> baby its easy to turn my world inside out
> your discovery will take us to another place
> baby of that there is no doubt
> I've been waiting for the special moment, anticipating all the things
> you'll do to me
> make the first step to release my emotions and take the road to ecstasy
> you've got to go downtown . . . to taste the sweetness will be enough
> keep on doing doing what you're doing
> 'til you feel the passion burning up inside of me
> if you do me right we'll be making love all through the night
> when you uncover the mystery
> take it nice and slow baby don't rush the feeling . . .[35]

This is the context in which the allure and the etho-poetics of doing it doggy style should be situated. These are far from novel themes in black popular culture, but their significance has been transformed by the silencing of other racialised discourses that would qualify and therefore contest their representative status, by their increasing distance from sacred and spiritual concerns and by the bio-political focus that terminates the vernacular conception of the mind/body dualism as well as the modernist aspirations towards racial uplift that were once figured through the language of public-political citizenship.

Nihilism and pseudo-freedom

> an AK talks and bullshit runs
> I wish I had time to count all my guns . . .
> so get the fuck out the way when I spray
> freedom got an AK . . .
> don't come to me with no petition
> come to me with ammunition . . .
>
>   Da Lench Mob

As I have said, the theme of freedom remains important because it relates to contemporary debates about the anti-social consequences of black nihilism.[36] Influential interpretations of contemporary black politics have stressed the meaninglessness, lovelessness and hopelessness of black metropolitan life and argued that the chronic ethical crisis from which they apparently stem generates further symptoms of black misery in the homophobia, misogyny, anti-Semitism and fundamentalist nationalisms currently being affirmed in black political cultures. This corrosive power of their vernacular nihilism is traced to a variety of different causal mechanisms. Sometimes it is seen as a capitulation to the market views – individualism, ruthlessness and indifference to others – that dominate the mainstream corporate world and its popular cultural commodities. Alternatively, it has been interpreted as a set of 'ethnic' habits peculiar to blacks. Whether it is a mechanistic response to racism and material privation or a more creative 'ethnic' trait, it has been readily linked to the patterns of household organisation, kinship and community that supposedly distinguish black social life. Lastly, it is viewed as a structural feature of de-industrialised capitalism which no longer has need for the living labour of terminally broken black communities that are marginal to the ongoing practice of flexible accumulation and may be contemptuous of the limited economic opportunities offered to them by neo-slave employment in what is termed the service sector.

The concept of the underclass mediates these different accounts of black nihilism. Each explanation offers a tiny rational kernel in a large mystical shell, but even when taken together they do not satisfy. The nexus of consciousness and behaviour that is reduced to the pejorative term nihilism is associated with idiomatic representations of freedom. Its main contemporary genres and styles are property, sex and the means of violence. From this perspective, 'nihilism' ceases to be anti-social and becomes social in the obvious sense of the term: it generates community and specifies the fortified boundaries of racial particularity. Once again, the mediated, sedimented memory of slavery provides a valuable starting point in understanding the development of this vernacular pattern. For example, it directs attention towards the complex symbolism of wealth in black popular culture. The visual culture of hip hop pivoted briefly on the alchemical transformation of iron shackles into gold chains.[37] Racialised by Mr T whose bold exploits live on in the lost valley of cable TV, gold chains externalised the changing price of the (wage) slave's labour power – calculated on the basis of exchange

value. The gold in the chains expressed the limits of the money
economy in which they circulated but which they were also able to transcend, especially in times of crisis. The free humanity formerly
bestowed by God could now be conveyed in displays of wealth that far
exceeded the value of a person, of a body. The same sort of ostentation
can be detected in some contemporary hip hoppers' appetite for cars as
symbols of status, wealth and masculine power: 'Dre boasts a collection
of cars: a white Chevy Blazer, a convertible 300 sec Benz, a 735 BMW
two 64s and a Nissan Pathfinder (My mom's jacked my Pathfinder, she's
like my sister, she looks young. She's flossing in my shit so I guess I only
have five cars)'[38] Moving towards a consideration of the forms that the
relationship between civic and personal freedoms might take in the
post-liberal age, we must cultivate the ability to disentangle the ludic
from the programmatic and find any threads of politics that run
between them. One may appreciate that the problems displayed in these
attempts to reckon with freedom were born from slavery but the civic
freedoms of the modern west which constitute the privileged object of
these enquiries were not antithetical to slavery and other forms of legal
and legitimate bondage.

The enduring effects of slavery are most evident in the oft-stated
desires for freedom from the servitude of work and freedom from
oppressive, unjust law. They can also be felt in the identification of
freedom with death that marks some versions of black Christianity very
deeply and defers emancipation and the possibility of redemption to a
better, future world. Equipped, among other things, with the living
traces of an African onto-theology, slaves in the western hemisphere
neither sought nor anticipated that mode of dominating the external
world which provided Europeans with an essential precondition for
development of a consciousness of freedom. This process has been well
described by Murray Bookchin: 'Domination and freedom become
interchangeable terms in a common project of subjugating nature *and*
humanity – each of which is used as the excuse to validate control of
one by the other. The reasoning involved is strictly circular. The
machine has not only run away without the driver, but the driver has
become a mere part of the machine.'[39] Because it was so reliant on the
institutionalisation of their unfree labour, the slaves viewed the civil-
ising process[40] with scepticism and its ethical claims with extreme suspicion. Their hermeneutic agency grounded a vernacular culture
premised on the possibility that freedom should be pursued outside of
the rules, codes and expectations of colour-coded civilisation. The

transgression of those codes was itself a sign that freedom was being claimed. It presented the possibility of an (anti)politics animated by the desire of violation – a negation of unjust, oppressive and therefore illegitimate authority. By breaking these rules in small, though ritualised ways it was possible to deface the clean edifice of white supremacy that fortified tainted and therefore inauthentic freedoms. Cultures of insubordination located more substantive and worthwhile freedoms in the capacity to follow moral imperatives in restricted circumstances. They were elaborated through the media of music and dance as well as through writing. Music expressed and confirmed unfreedom while evolving in complex patterns that pointed beyond misery towards reciprocity and prefigured the democracy yet to come in their antiphonic forms. Dance refined the exercise of autonomous power in the body by claiming it back from the absolute sovereignty of work. It produced the alternative 'natural' hierarchy wholly antithetical to the order required by the institutions of white supremacy which today forms the basis of black sports cultures.

Words, texts and freedoms

The connection between writing and the consciousness of freedom has been carefully established in recent accounts of black cultural production. William L. Andrews[41] is the most prominent among a group of critics who have focused upon the significance of this relationship for students of black literature and culture. In particular, attention has been directed towards the importance of autobiography for slaves and ex-slaves. It has been recognised as a special location in which writing could stage the trial of merely formal freedoms. It provided an opportunity to elaborate a 'free' self created in the intimate, private process of writing but which could then be projected outwards into the public world. These tactics have carried a powerful political charge. While slavery endured, they amounted to calculated insubordination. When it was declared over, they helped to articulate important challenges to the racialised structures of domination that replaced and modified it.

Though less closely associated with writing in contemporary culture, the affirmation of black autonomy and the creativity that celebrates it still provide unpalatable fare to those reared on the bland diet of white supremacy. Even now, the amplified assertion of black freedom and the public exploration of the outer-limits of the autonomous black individual retain the power to provoke and enrage. I want to endorse the suggestion that the conjunction of freedom and writing constituted an important portal through which black intellectuals first glimpsed and then entered the assumptions and conventions of literary and philosophical modernity. However, I want to embellish the concern with black freedom within and sometimes against modernity differently. This means emphasising that writing is not the only, and may not even be the most important, vernacular idiom in which the consciousness of freedom was registered, possessed and displayed. To put it another way, the consciousness of freedom seems to me to have been even more important than solidly literary studies can indicate. There is certainly more to it than a politics of articulation in which language is claimed as the essential medium of black being in the world. Language, spoken and written, has not dominated modern black cultural creativity in any simple way. Its dense utility does not supply a set of privileged interpretive devices appropriate to the whole medley of vernacular cultures that are in some sense premised upon the incapacity of language to communicate diverse feelings, truths and desires that are barely unified by their common will to unsayability. The tension between writing and other expressive media has deep roots and complex contemporary manifestations. Literacy no longer monopolises the irreducible autonomy of the spirit.

The language used to 'stage' the acquisition and trial of fragile freedoms in what Houston A. Baker Jr has identified as interplay between the mastery of form and the deformation of mastery,[42] was the language of the slaveholder or of slavery. There was bound to be some degree of discomfort involved in its possession. The value of that tongue in providing the means through which the slaves might enunciate the fact and the comprehension of their freedom had to be an ambivalent one. It is also important that those who were most skilled in the manipulation of the language provided by masters and mistresses were viewed with scepticism and suspicion for that very reason. This was something that complicated the idea of representativeness. It circumscribed the political role of black intellectuals who were sometimes revealed to be inauthentic, not because in turning to the written word they abandon the homiletic, but because their education and elevation rendered them indifferent to the power of communicative forms that might be considered anterior to the workings of language.

A warning is being sounded here against using the capacity to manipulate language as the best measure of black autonomy. In the strange circumstances of black cultural production, the resort to the slaveholders' language – written or spoken – can be understood as a capitulation or even a betrayal. The choice of the 'nonsense' word hip hop as the proper name for this cultural revolution should underline that other forms of comprehension are in play. They work by means of non-sensical communicative strategies that are as much anti-linguistic as linguistic, anti-discursive as discursive. Making these anti-languages into ciphers for black authenticity carries a host of different dangers. However, something of the deep ambivalence towards speaking and writing in the tongue of bondage probably lingers on today, providing energy for the foundational anti-intellectualism on which black vernacular cultures have been re-built and legitimising their distinctive pattern of class antagonisms. The freedom to use the languages of slavery to construct and project a free self can be viewed as a defeat – a pseudo-autonomy – that signifies complete cultural submission to the power of the slaveholders which endures long after their transformation into employers. It is also the confirmation of an estrangement from the world prior to bondage. Individual writers were able to use this tainted tongue to announce their escapes from the order of white supremacy, but however liberating it may have been, their command of that idiom confirmed that the journey back was impossible. The language of the oppressor supplied a labyrinth in which the consciousness of oppression was doomed to wander.

It is possible and valuable to arrange these textual escape attempts socially and historically into traditions, genres and genealogies, but the textual mode of conjuring up freedom was also linked by its radical individualism. The relationships established between authors and reading publics were complex but there are, for example, important links between freedom and other varieties of cultural creativity that operated by a different dialogic principle that still has ethical and political significance.

I have suggested elsewhere,[43] in a reading of anti-capitalism in some African diaspora cultures, that these communicative patterns come together to found an alternative public sphere subordinated to and wholly discontinuous with the patterns of communal life enjoyed by the slaveholders and by the dominant groups in racially hierarchical societies. I have suggested that the fascination with names, re-naming and multiple naming that occurs routinely and consistently in the black popular cultures of the western hemisphere and the overdeveloped countries provide a useful preliminary means with which to identify the limits of the communities of interpretation which those public spheres help to construct. Feral, invisible and untameable forms – music, dance and gesture – help to configure notions of self and autonomy in a public sphere very different from that which has attracted the attention of commentators so far.

Freedom has been discussed in some thoughtful commentaries on post-slavery black cultures and social movements. These discussions of its philosophical and spiritual inflection or its role in adding to the moral authority of the civil rights movements by mobilising the memories of slavery are interesting but they have minimised the problems involved in its recognition, manifestation and possession. The consciousness of freedom has not been treated extensively in the analysis of black *popular* cultures. The relationship between consciousness of freedom and musical production and use remains particularly obscure, partly because those forms of expressive culture were tainted by their association with the terrors and humiliations of the slave period: gifts grudgingly given or enthusiastically promoted as a means to make the intolerable tolerable. They transcended and confirmed the condition of slavery. They were implicated in its functioning: a means to make the unbearable bearable. I am especially interested in the ways that patterns of signification are condensed in musical performances that may or may not involve the authority and authenticity of musicians playing or singing live. In this subaltern soundscape, phantasmagoric combinations of music and sound can join with other expressive anti-linguistic and a-linguistic forms to position and racialise their subjects. Acting on the body through specific mechanisms of identification and recognition, the drama of identification and desire generates the imaginary effect of an internal racial core or essence.

Today technology suffuses the public sphere that is produced in and through the intimate interactions of performers and crowds. But this potentially democratic and reciprocal relationship can still serve as an ideal communicative situation even when the original producers of the music and its eventual consumers are separated in space and time or divided by the technologies of sound reproduction and the commodity form which their art has sought in vain to resist. In the disreputable setting where the night time is the right time, breaking open the closed logic of the commodity necessitates a direct confrontation with the reification upon which the magical system of capitalism is based. This applies not just to dreams of liberating oppositional culture from these oppressive and constricting forms and formats, but to the liberation of individuality so that brittle relations between people gain a chance to acquire once more the evasive supple quality of relationships between human beings rather than objects. The living memory of slavery endows this redemptive practice with a melancholy mood. The idea of humanity that governs these possibilities is a misanthropic one, minimally defined via its counterfactual elements, radically sceptical and systematically profane in its assumptions and combativity.

While recognising the force of lingering ambivalence towards language, it is an important part of the argument here that song and the distinctive social relations that contextualise and support it are not just an integral component of the cultures of compensation provided by the slaveholders to their bondspeople for unfreedoms of slavery, but rather a premonition of the world beyond that condition, something like a tantalising prefiguration of other possibilities that was intermittently able to suspend the coercion and containment that characterised slavery and dispel them in the name of a different moral economy premised on the reconciliation of personal autonomy and social justice. A view of black public spheres as places in which freedom can be enacted emerges from this observation.

The return of the moral agent . . . in canine form?

> One cannot entirely refuse the face of an animal. It is via the face that one understands, for example, a dog. Yet the priority here is not found in the animal but in the human face . . . The phenomenon of the face is not in its purest form in the dog. In the dog, in the animal there are other phenomena. For example, the force of nature is pure vitality. It is more this which characterises the dog. But it also has a face.
>
> Emmanuel Levinas

Before I can conclude, I must raise, even if only to set aside, the question of whether Snoop Doggy Dogg's best-known oral trademark, '1-8-7 on an undercover cop', might simply be an idiomatic re-statement of some very well-known modernist anxieties over the limits of existential agency, autonomy and subjectivity in particular, about the relationship between self-making and deliberately taking the life of the other.[44] Snoop's music and rapping remain doggedly faithful to the antiphonic forms that link new world black styles to their African antecedents. The fading public sphere is configured negatively but it is still just about recognisable as a profane trans-coding of the black Christian congregation. Snoop's instructions to his audience – 'If you don't give a shit like

I don't give a shit wave your mother-fuckin' fingers in the air' – aren't very far from the cry of the old school rappers whose crossover ambitions required that they curse less or even from preachers who sought similar gestures of solidarity from their audiences.[45] In any form, these are gestures that enforce the priority of the saying over the said. We must remember that in this vernacular, dog is a verb as well as a noun.

The sleeve of Snoop's album *Doggy Style* is printed on recycled paper. He uses it to send out extra special thanks to, among other people, Golgatha Community Baptist Church (presumably the place where his career as a performer started as a chorister and pianist). The G side of Snoop's album begins with his best-known track. Its title is formed by two foundational questions. They arise like siblings at the heart of the historic dialogue that demands completion of the special ontological inquiries in which newly freed slaves engaged as they strove to define and clarify the boundaries of their new status as free modern individuals: 'WHO AM I (WHAT'S MY NAME)?'.

Understandably Snoop asserts that his work has no political significance whatsoever. When pressed to operate in that restricted mode, his rather conventional opinions seem to be a long way from anything that could reasonably be called nihilist.

As far as me being political, the only thing I can say is the muthafuckin' U.S. can start giving money to the 'hood, giving opportunity and starting businesses, something to make niggas not want to kill each another. Give them some kind of job and finances 'cos the killin ain't over love nor money. They are killin and jackin one another 'cos there ain't no opportunity. As long as it's black on black or black-on-brown it's cool – they don't like black on white. They send national guards like when we took off on their ass in 4.29.92, armed forces and army muthafuckas with big ass machine guns – on account of niggas stealing . . .[46]

Is the cartoon on the cover presenting Snoop as a dog a more reliable guide to the nihilism and anti-social qualities of his work? Why would a young African American choose, at this point, to present himself to the world with the features, with the identity, of a dog?[47] How does Snoop's manipulation of the dog mask that he did not invent but which he has used so creatively facilitate his crossover celebrity? Is he locating and testing out the limits of a plausible humanity or creating a new and sustainable relationship with nature within and without? Does the cat-chasing, dog-catcher-outwitting dog persona simply seek to make a virtue out of immiseration and insult in the familiar process of semiotic inversion capable of changing curse words into words of praise, of revalorising the word nigger? Is there a sense in which calling himself a dog expresses an accurate evaluation of the social status of young black men? What comment on the meaning of humanity does Snoop's movement between bodies – between identities – express?

A dog is not a fox, a lion, a rabbit or a signifyin' monkey. Snoop is not a dog. His filling the mask of undifferentiated racialised otherness with quizzical canine features reveals something about the operation of white supremacy and the cultures of compensation that answer it. It is a political and, I believe, a moral gesture. Choosing to be a low down dirty dog values the sub-human rather than the hyper-humanity promoted through bio-politics and its visible signatures. It would be missing the main point to over-emphasise that the dog is a sign for Snoop's victim status as well as his sexual habits or that it sometimes requires the techno-scientific resources of a firearm before it can interact with humans on equal terms. In opting to be seen as a dog he refuses identification with the perfected, invulnerable male body that has become the standard currency of black popular culture, cementing the dangerous link between bodily health and racial purity, dissolving the boundary line between singers and athletes and producing strange phenomena like R. Kelly's eroticised appropriation of Michael Jordan's divine masculinity and Shaquille O'Neal's career as a singer and rapper. Snoop's 'morphing' between the human and the canine displays those elements of identity that are not reducible to the six foot four inch body of his sometime owner 'Calvin Broadus'. There is something left over when that operation is performed. The metamorphosis requires that we confront Snoop's reflexive capacities. His stylised portrayal of the gangsta self as protean, shape-shifting and multiple is probably less significant than the full, vulgar, anti-bourgois force of the black vernacular that crouches behind it.[48] His low down dirty self directs public attention to the difficult zones where people become less than human. In a capitalist society things regularly take on the social characteristics of people. Emmanuel Levinas has reminded us that the fate and the role of animals can be quite different.[49]

' The other side of *Doggy Style* commences with a bathroom scenario that gives the proceedings a 'private' framing moment. It is a throwback to a previous era in the odyssey of rhythm and blues when the discourse of racial authenticity called for the removal of clothing rather than the exchange of human skin for canine fur. This little drama presents Snoop in conversation with a girlfriend. He is resenting the intrusion of the public world into their space of intimacy. Their conversation makes no mention of soul, but it is the bond between them. They stick closely to a script refined on hundreds of 'turn out the lights and light a candle' soul records. However their moves are not legitimated by references to any notion of love. The dog and the bitch belong together. They are a couple but their association does not bring about sexual healing. There is no healing in their encounter for the power of sex is not at work here as a means of naturalising racial difference. Nor is the unhappy union of bodily health and racial purity being celebrated. In this bathtub, cleanliness is not next to godliness though funkiness may be. Their funky, bestial sex is not about authenticity and offers no moment of communal redemption nor any private means to stabilise the reconstructed racial self – male or female. Snoop's work exceeds the masculinist erasure of the sexual agency of black women that it does undoubtedly contain.[50]

We have seen that doggy style *style* is part of a public conversation about sex, and intimacy, power, powerlessness and bodily pleasure that can be reconstructed even from the fragments of antiphonal communication that have been captured in commodity form and circulated multinationally on that basis. I want to end by suggesting that the ethical and political significance of Snoop's affirmation of blackness in dog-face has one more important layer. Its simultaneous questioning of humanity and proximity can be used not only to reinterpret what passes as 'nihilism' but to construct an argument about the positive value of intersubjectivity in black political cultures which are now subject-centred to the point of solipsism. Snoop's dog may also point to an escape route out of the current impasse in thinking about racialised identity. Arguing against those who would deny black popular culture any philosophical and metaphysical currency, we can bring the ethopoetical qualities in his call to do it doggy style into focus by inquiring why individuals should recognise themselves as subjects of freaky sexuality and asking about the premium that this talk about sex places on touch and the moral proximity of the other. Without wanting to supply a couple of esoteric 'ethnic' footnotes in the history of the desiring subject, it seems worthwhile to try and situate Snoop's dog and the chain of equivalences in which it appears somewhere in the genealogy of techniques of the black self. The radically alienated eroticism towards which he and his canine-identified peers direct our attention might perversely contribute some desirable ethical grounding to the debased black public sphere. We need to talk more, not less, about sex.

The 'dual solitude' transmitted and celebrated in the popular trope of doing it doggy style is not about a naive or pastoral mutuality. It breaks with the monadological structure that has been instituted under the stern discipline of racial authenticity and proposes another mode of intimacy that might help to recreate a link between moral stances and vernacular metaphors of erotic, worldly love. A periodisation of the subaltern modernity which encompasses this possibility is established in the movement from 'domestic allegories of political desire'[51] towards political allegories of private desire. Perhaps this conversation about sex can also rehabilitate the untimely issues of intersubjective responsibility and accountability that have been expelled from the interpretive community during the reign of ethnic absolutism and its bodily signs. The sociality established by talk about sex culminates in an invitation to acknowledge what Zygmunt Bauman, again citing Levinas, describes as the pre-ontological space of ethics.[52] In this setting we can call it a being *for* the other or non-being that exists prior to the racial metaphysics that currently dominates hip hop's revolutionary conservatism. This ethical core was central to the musical cultures of the new world as they adapted sacred patterns to secular exigencies. It was undervalued and then sacrificed. Snoop, R. Kelly, SWV and the rest are already playing their parts in its revitalisation. My anxiety is that the revolutionary conservatism that dominates hip hop is likely to have limited patience with them. Revolutionary conservatism's enthusiasm for the market means that commercial achievements will be respected. However, impurity and profanity cannot be tolerated in the long run because they contribute nothing to the heroics of racial reconstruction. Authoritarians and censors can play the authenticity card too. Revolutionary conservatism. This formulation takes us immediately to the limits of our available political vocabulary. There is something explicitly revolutionary in the presentation of violence as the key principle of social and political interaction and perhaps also in the hatreds of democracy, academicism, decadence, tepidity, weakness and softness in general that are regularly rehearsed. Conservatism is signalled loud and clear in the joyless rigidity of the gender roles that are specified in an absolutist approach to both ethics and racial particularity and, above all, in a gloomy presentation of black humanity composed of limited creatures who require tradition, pedagogy and organisation. This seems to go hand in hand with a fear and contempt of the masses. Ice Cube has reported this revealing conversation with Minister Farakhan: 'Mentally he told me, the people are babies. They are addicted to sex and violence. So if you've got medicine to give them, then put the medicine inside some soda so they get both and it won't be hard for them to digest'.[53]

It is important to remember that the dangers deriving from the fusion of bio-politics and revolutionary conservatism are not to be found in hip hop alone. Yet the conflict between them and other more democratic and emancipatory possibilities is readily visible there. Market-driven black popular culture is making politics aesthetic usually as a precondition for marketing hollow defiance. It is no longer communism that responds immodestly to this grave danger by imagining that it can politicise art but rather an insurgent intellectual practice that reacts to these fascistic perils by revealing the extent to which popular art has already been politicised in unforeseen ways.

Notes

1 Recent work by African-American academics, Tricia Rose and Michael Eric Dyson shares this quality in spite of their obvious political differences. See Tricia Rose, *Black Noise: Rap Music and Black Culture in Contemporary Ameria*, Wesleyan University Press, 1994, and Michael Eric Dyson, *Reflecting Black: African American Cultural Criticism*, Minnesota University Press, 1993.

2 Luther 'Luke Skywalker' Campbell interview by Joseph Gallivan in the *Independent*, 13 January 1994, p. 26.

3 Tricia Rose's assertions that hip hop is reducible to a core of invariant exclusively African American 'black practices' that permanently resist both commodification and white appropriation typifies this mode of denial (see Rose, *Black Noise*, pp. 7, 80–4).

4 A good example of this is the use of Leiber and Stoller's 'I Keep Forgettin'' as recorded by Michael MacDonald in the track 'Regulate' by Nate Dogg and Warren G. This can also be found on the Deathrow/Atlantic records soundtrack album to *Above The Rim*.

5 Michel Foucault, 'Truth And Power', in *Power Knowledge*, ed. Colin Gordon, Pantheon, 1980, p. 115.

6 Check out 'Sadie' the song dedicated to his mother on the Jive Records 1993 album *12 play*.

7 This type of citation does not take the form of parody or pastiche. Its intentions are disciplinary and it is best understood as a creative ordering that does not always serve progressive impulses. It does not play with the gap between then and now but rather uses it to assert a spurious continuity that adds legitimacy and gravity to the contemporary. A second example of the

shifting political resonance between these different periods in popular politics is provided by the way that the group Arrested Development borrowed parts of Sly and The Family Stone's 'Everyday People' and changed it into 'People Everyday'. The earlier song was an affirmation of pluralism that pivoted on the chorus:

> There is a blue one who can't accept the green one
> For living with a fat one trying to be a skinny one
> And different strokes for different folks . . .
> I am no better and neither are you
> We are the same whatever we do
> You love me – you hate me you know me and then
> You can't figure out the bag I'm in
> I am everyday people.

The decisive line of antagonism between different 'races' that the earlier song located and then erased is moved in the later one and is seen to operate within the racial group around the disrespectful drunken conduct of 'brothers' towards the singer's 'black queen'.

 8 bell hooks, 'Reconstructing black masculinity', in *Black Looks*, South End Press, 1993, p. 113.

 9 See Ferenc Fehér and Agnes Heller, *Biopolitics*, Avebury, 1994.

10 'I know this might sound funny coming out of my mouth but I do try to be different, I try to hit on a romantic sexual level, leaving just a touch to the imagination', R. Kelly interviewed in *Pride*, May/June 1994, p. 35.

11 An insightful version of this is outlined by June Jordan in 'Waiting For A Taxi', in *Technical Difficulties*, Pantheon, 1992.

12 Michel Foucault, *The Use Of Pleasure*, Viking, 1986, p. 5.

13 See also Michael Jordan, *Rare Air Michael on Michael*, ed. Mark Vancil, Harper Collins, 1993.

14 George L. Mosse, *Nationalism And Sexuality*, Madison, University of Wisconsin Press, 1985, esp. Chapter 3; Michael Jordan, *Rare Air Michael on Michael*.

15 *Vibe*, Vol. 2, No. 4, May 1994, p. 72. The same article offers these interesting observations about Kelly's living space: 'He lives downtown on the Loop, in a sparsely decorated one-bedroom apartment. "Where I live it's like Batman in Gotham City. No one knows where I live. If you come to my crib, you have to be blindfolded . . . It's not just an apartment to me. I hear my music in there. I never have any company because that's my solitude. My being silent about my personal life allows me to express it in the studio."'

16 See his discussion with Angela Davis in *Transition*, 58, 1992. It includes the following exchange:

> Ice Cube [I.C.] Did anyone in the Black Panther organization smoke?
> Angela Davis [A.D.] I'm sure they did.
> I.C. Did anybody drink?
> A.D. I'm sure they did.
> I.C. That ain't loving yourself . . . To me the best organisation for black people is the Nation of Islam. It is the best organisation: brothers don't drink, don't smoke, ain't chasin' women. They have one job . . .

17 Paul Gilroy, 'It's a family affair: black culture and the trope of kinship', in *Small Acts*, London and New York, Serpent's Tail, 1994.

18 RAab, 'You're The One', Rip It records 1002–2 (Florida), 1993, available from the Independent Label Coalition.

19 Emmanuel Levinas, 'The transcendence of words', in *The Levinas Reader*, ed. Sean Hand, Blackwell, 1989, p. 147.

20 Eric Foner, *Nothing But Freedom*, Baton Rouge and London, Louisiana State University Press, 1983.

21 Booker T. Washington, *Up From Slavery*, New York, Airmont Books, 1967, p. 27.

22 'No sooner had emancipation been acknowledged than thousands of "married" couples, with the encouragement of black preachers and northern white missionaries, hastened to secure their marital vows, both legally and spiritually . . . The insistence of teachers, missionaries and Freedmen's Bureau officers that blacks formalize their marriages stemmed from the notion that legal sanction was necessary for sexual and moral restraint and that ex-slaves had to be inculcated with "the obligations of the married state in civilized life"'. Leon F. Litwack, *Been In The Storm So Long: The Aftermath of Slavery*, Athlone Press, 1980, p. 240. See Chapter 5 'How Free IS Free?'.

23 D. Miller, 'Absolute freedom in Trinidad', *Man*, 26, 1991, pp. 323–41.

24 *Trabelin' On: The Slave Journey To An Afro-Baptist Faith*, Princeton University Press, 1988.

25 *Significations*, Fortress Press, 1986.

26 Oxford University Press, 1977.

27 Michael Eric Dyson is again typical of these problems. He notes (in *Reflecting Black*, p. 279) that in the black vernacular 'personal freedom often is envisioned through tropes of sexual release' but takes this observation no further. It is not solely a matter of 'release' though this choice of words has the virtue of making a connection with slavery explicit.

28 Paul Gilroy, *The Black Atlantic*, Harvard University Press, 1993, Chapter 6.

29 On this concept see Paul Connerton's useful book *How Societies Remember*, Cambridge University Press, 1989, Section 3 'Bodily Practices'.

30 Shahrazad Ali, *Are You Still A Slave?*, Civilized Publications (undated).

31 This is powerfully transmitted and its relationship to the problematics of freedom illuminated by several tracks by Ice Cube's crew Da Lench Mob. See for example, 'Capital Punishment In America' and 'Freedom Got an A.K.' both from their album *Guerrillas In The Mist*, Street Knowledge 7–92206–2.

32 Zygmunt Bauman, *Mortality, Immortality & Other Life Strategies*, Polity, 1993, p. 187–8. See also Ernst Bloch and Theodor W. Adorno, 'Something's missing', in Ernst Bloch, *The Utopian Function Of Art And Literature*, MIT Press, 1988, pp. 5–8.

33 Nas, 'Life's A Bitch' from the CD *Illmatic*, Colombia, CK 57684, 1994.

34 Jean Luc Nancy, *The Experience of Freedom*, Stanford University Press, 1993.

35 SWV, *It's About Time*, RCA 07863 66074–2, 1992. See also SWV, *The Remixes*, RCA 07863–66401–2, 1994.

36 Cornel West, 'Nihilism in black America', *Race Matters*, Beacon Press, 1993. See also Ishmael Reed, 'Airing dirty laundry' in the book of the same name, Addison Wesley, 1993.

37 The actor Mr T anticipated the views of a generation of old school hip hoppers when in 1985 he gave this explanation of his flashy taste in jewellery: 'The gold chains are a symbol that reminds me of my great African ancestors, who were brought over here as slaves with iron chains on their ankles, on their wrists, their necks and sometimes around their waists. I turned my chains into gold, so my statement is this: the fact that I wear gold chains instead of iron chains is because I am still a slave, only my price tag is higher now. I am still bought and sold by the powers that be in this society, white people, but this time they pay me on demand, millions and millions of dollars for my services. I demand it and they pay it . . . Yes, I am still a slave in this society, but I am still free by God. "How are you still a slave Mr T?" You see the only thing that interests this society is money. And the only thing that it fears and respects is more money. 'Mr T, *An Autobiography by Mr T*, W. H. Allen, 1984, p. 4. This account of the connection between slavery and identity links personal autonomy with the signs of wealth and the memory of terror. The condition of slavery persists but is changed by divine grace and the very worldly capacity to hire oneself out to others.

38 dream hampton, 'G down', *The Source*, September, 1993, p. 68.

39 Murray Bookchin, *The Ecology of Freedom*, Palo Alto, Cheshire Books, p. 272.

40 Frederick Douglass, *My Bondage My Freedom*, Miller, Orton & Mulligan, 1855, p. 50.

41 *To Tell A Free Story*, University of Illinois Press, 1986.

42 *Modernism and The Harlem Renaissance*, University of Chicago Press, 1987.

43 Paul Gilroy, '*There Ain't No Black In The Union Jack*', University of Chicago Press, 1991, Chapter 5.

44 See June Jordan, 'Beyond Apocalypse Now', in *Civil Wars*, Beacon Press, 1981, esp. p. 171. Robert C. Solomon, *From Rationalism To Existentialism*, Harvester, Chapter 7; see also the discussion of Albert Camus' *L'Etranger* in Edward Said's *Culture And Imperialism*, Chatto & Windus, 1993.

45 Reporting his recent performances in London *Hip Hop Connection* p. 14, noted this dynamic in operation: 'At times this gig resembled a game of Snoop Says . . . "Throw ya hands in the air," he'd yell and the audience dutifully obeyed. They were strangely content. It didn't occur to them that Doggy style's instrumental backing is ideally suited to a live concert. Dre's tuneful production means Snoop's performance should entail musicians, not a cheap impersonal DAT. Unperturbed by this glaring omission, fans avidly sang along to Snoop's casual patter.' See also Walter F. Pitts Jr, *Old Ship of Zion The Afro-Baptist Baptist Ritual in the African Diaspora*, Oxford University Press, 1993.

46 *Hip Hop Connection* 62, April 1994, p. 31.

47 Edmund Leach, 'Anthropological aspects of language: animal categories and verbal abuse', in E. H. Lenneberg (ed.), *New Directions in The Study of Language*, MIT Press 1964, pp. 23–63. See also Yi Fu Tuan, *Dominance and Affection: The Making of Pets*, Yale University Press, 1984.

48 Peter Stallybrass & Allon White, *The Politics & Poetics Of Transgression*, Methuen, 1986.

49 Emmanuel Levinas, 'The Name of A Dog, or Natural Rights', in *Difficult Freedom Essays on Judaism*, Athlone, 1990.

50 It is useful to compare *Doggy Style* with the out and out misogyny of DRS and other spokesmen for gangsterdom.

51 Claudia Tate, *Domestic Allegories of Political Desire*, Oxford, 1992, esp. Chapters 3 and 7.

52 Zygmunt Bauman, *Postmodern Ethics*, Blackwell, 1993, pp. 92–8.

53 Interviewed by Ekow Eshun in *The Face*, No. 65, February 1994, p. 91.

Rock anxieties and new music networks

Missing, presumed dead

For more than two decades, popular music studies and the higher journalism of record and concert reviewing have been dominated by an all-embracing discursive pattern that has coiled itself around a single four letter word: rock. Like all the great ideological figures 'rock' has proved to be extremely resistant to definition, placing or deconstruction. The term has tenacious roots, as I found when I trawled the first edition of one of the Ur-Texts, *The Rolling Stone Record Guide* (Marsh and Swenson, 1979) in search of the 'truth' of rock. I soon found myself chasing forlornly from put-down of artist A (as 'not remotely rock') to praise of group B ('perfect rock') in search of what distinguished rock from non-rock. But the deferral was not quite endless. At the end of my search stood a single figure, described by *Rolling Stone*'s then chief reviewer Dave Marsh as 'so much the fulfillment of the hopes and dreams of the rock tradition as handed down from Presley' and 'much more than any post-folkie word wizard' – Bruce Springsteen. The tautological circle closed: Springsteen was rock and non-rock (especially post-folkie word wizardry) was non-Springsteen.

Since that time, I have come to feel that the evocation of this master signifier is more of an obstacle than an aid to the development of the study of how popular music is produced and how it works. In my own work I've attempted to by-pass the term, though not always with success. But more recently, it seems to me that some major changes working through popular music seen in a global perspective make it easier to avoid the lure of 'rock' and make more apparent the historical and ideological relativity of the word and what it evokes.

In the second part of this chapter I describe some of the changes and the musical networks associated with them, focusing in particular on

European dance music. To begin with, however, I want to try to unravel the 'rock' discourse primarily through a symptomatic reading of one of the most cogent and systematic recent articulations of 'rock'. This text is Lawrence Grossberg's intervention at a conference held in Princeton University in 1992, later published as 'Is anybody listening? Does anybody care?: on talking about "the state of rock"' (Grossberg, 1994). This is an opportune time to attempt such a commentary because several of the leading rock critics have in the past few years expressed the view that all is not well with 'rock' and that it may be seriously ill if not actually defunct. Grossberg's text notes this trend and offers a classification of these anxieties about rock. He finds four 'rhetorical strategies or organising figures' in play. These are indifference (the collapse of the difference between 'rock' and 'pop'), fragmentation (the loss of an organising principle which can bind music fans together in a 'unity of rock'), Babel (the collapse of rock as a pop *lingua franca*) and loss of significance (as a cultural force, rock and roll no longer seems to mean anything). None of the critics from whom Grossberg quotes offers a definition of 'rock'. But by reading off what has been lost in the demise of 'rock' from the 'organising figures', we can discover that 'rock' represents something superior to pop, something full of meaning and something unifying for audiences. As a whole, 'Is anybody listening?' offers a schematic summary of the view of 'rock' that Grossberg has been developing for some time, and in what follows I try to respect the schematic character of the text while also attending to its exclusions and its asides as well as its positive formulations. Indeed, as I hope to show, there is value in the observations made in the text as 'asides'.

My starting point is the writer's own response to the 'death of rock' issue. While adopting an agnostic attitude towards this issue as it is presented in the rhetorical strategies he has listed, Grossberg admits the possibility that what he calls the 'rock formation' may also become extinct, or, as he prefers to express it, the formation may have a 'trajectory of disappearance'. The difference between this view and that of the rhetoricians is that Grossberg argues from a set of events which have affected what he calls the 'historical conditions of rock's possibility'. Grossberg's concept of 'rock formation' (which is broadly equivalent to the four-letter word as used by rock critics) is produced by the combined effects of four conditions of possibility which he locates in the post-World War II period in the United States. These conditions are socio-economic/political (affluence, Cold War), demographic/sociological (the large teenage population), cultural/technological (images of rebellion, indie record companies, 45 rpm discs, radio) and a fourth level which seems to be that of Raymond Williams's 'structure of feeling' where a 'postmodern' structure of feeling emerged amongst young people in the 1950s as the 'disarticulation' of a unity between affect and ideology which had provided an identity for the previous generation. What is striking about these 'conditions of possibility' is the absence of music itself as an active element in the process. It is almost as if we have returned to an antique Marxism in which music plays the part of the superstructure which is a ghostly epiphenomenon of the all-powerful base, represented here by those four conditions. At the beginning of his essay Grossberg makes clear that his term 'rock' is not genre-specific but refers to the 'entire range of post-war, youth-oriented . . . musical practices and styles'. This seems reasonable since his 'rock formation' has a life-span of over thirty-five years. However, the conditions of possibility do not seem to admit that the specific character of the ensemble of 1950s plebeian musics which Charlie Gillett defined as the five styles of rock 'n' roll (Gillett, 1970) had an active part in the consolidation of the 'rock formation'. The only hint of the specific contribution of music to the 'rock formation' comes in the discussion of the cultural importance of the figure of the American black within the images of rebellion available to the 'baby boomers'. This, says Grossberg, may help to explain the 'unique relation between rock and Afro-American sounds and rhythms'. But for the popular music scholar, this is hardly enough. Surely the 'youth-oriented musical practices and styles' were the focus around which the rock formation cohered? What specific colouring, weight or shape did these styles give the formation? In order to determine this, perhaps we would need to undertake what structural linguistics calls a commutation test: to replace music by, say, comic-books, pin-ball or movies as the focal point of the rock formation and then discover how different the formation would have been.

Discussions of pop within cultural studies, and in particular that corner of the field where youth subcultures were identified, have generally been characterised by a similar 'invisible presence' of the music itself. That is, the primarily sociological discourses of both subcultures and formations have tended to locate music almost always as a symptom or a sign of the essence or the consciousness of a youth group or generational group. When Grossberg says 'Rock is more than just a conjuncture of musical and lyrical practices', it is, by itself, an unexceptional statement. However, rock is also that 'conjuncture of musical and lyrical practices' with its own forms of materiality and efficacy which are not fully reducible only to a homology or a rallying cry. Without retaining, and at some stage foregrounding, the specificity of music as organised sound, analysis focused on the uses made of music by listeners risks becoming a bizarre variant of ideas about the sovereignty of the consumer. Particularly in the theory of subcultures, there is a sense in which music is made equivalent to clothing, shoes or hairstyles in a pattern of rational, orderly consumption – something chosen by the wearer rather than choosing him or her. As John Clarke wrote in one of the classic texts of subcultural theory, styles are constructed through the discovery of 'homologies between the group's self-consciousness and the possible meanings of the available objects' (Clarke, 1975).

In the case of music, at least, I want to suggest that such notions of homological matchings between 'self-consciousness' and object-meanings are too rationalist and voluntarist and that the primary process of listening to music involves the experience of being 'chosen' by a song, of being interpellated by it. Interestingly, this process has been acknowledged frequently by songwriters, most recently by Hugh Prestwood in 'The Song Remembers When', the leading country song of 1994 recorded by Tricia Yearwood. The lyric succinctly captures the experience of being taken by surprise by re-hearing unexpectedly an old song with significant emotional associations: 'When the whole world has forgotten / The song remembers when'. But the process has been little explored by writers on popular music. Amongst those writers who have provided some insights into the issue are Sean Cubitt (1984), Barbara Bradby and Brian Torode (1984) and Dave Laing (1985). In different ways, each of these texts draws on concepts from psychoanalysis or linguistics. If this interpellation is the most fundamental element in the consumption of music, it is also an experience common to members and non-members of subcultures and to those outside as well as within the 'rock formation'. Lawrence Grossberg's article acknowledges this experience but he tends to discount it as one which provides unwelcome interference to a notion of an individual's musical taste as defined by 'genre'. He illustrates the point with a comment from the eminent *Village Voice* critic Robert Christgau, who writes that 'we were committed to rock 'n' roll but that doesn't mean that we tuned out the opposition – what makes a hit a hit is that it penetrates your defenses' (Grossberg, 1994: 45). Christgau's choice of metaphor is telling. For rock critics and rock theorists, the repetitious, unforgettable or sexy dross of AM pop hits is a dangerous and unruly element liable at any time to disrupt the boundaries between the rock formation and 'the opposition'. Here the excluded opposition 'penetrates the defences' of the rock formation and operates a 'return of the repressed' into rock consciousness.

And that consciousness, as Barbara Bradby has pointed out, is historically located in the white, male baby-boomer generation of the United States and Britain. In discussing the anxieties expressed by participants in the 'death of rock' debate, she writes:

> what has 'died' is the ability of the discourse of 'rock' to impose a unity in the form of the white, male subject/author upon the heterogeneity of 'other' racial, sexual and gendered identities and musics on which rock music itself fed. This must make one suspicious about the anxiety around the absence of a centre and of opposition in these debates and the way they avoid discussion of the sexuality of rock. (Bradby, 1993: 163)

We left the main line of Grossberg's argument at the point where he, too, confronts the possibility of the death of rock. He rejects this outcome, however, in favour of an analysis which suggests that the 'rock formation' is undergoing a transformation (or even a resurrection) as each of its four conditions of existence more or less simultaneously mutates in the late 1980s and early 1990s. During these years, Grossberg seems to be suggesting, the American nation-state has entered a new phase. At the level of socio-politics, the United States is gripped by conservatism while demographically a new youth grouping, the so-called Generation X, has emerged and this generation embraces a fully postmodern structure of feeling. At the level of culture and technology, digital electronics has revolutionised sound recording and listening, while amongst media radio has given way to music television.

Why should the passing of the 'rock formation' matter to Grossberg or the *grands maitres* of newspaper criticism? We have encountered one answer, that sardonically posed by Barbara Bradby – the loss of control by the white male subject of the heterogeneity of popular cultural practice, a control symbolised by and embodied in the hitherto unchallengeable superiority of 'rock' to other musical life-forms. Unsurprisingly perhaps, 'Is anybody listening?' offers a more objectified and conventionally politicised answer to the question. Grossberg writes of the rock formation's ability to facilitate resistance to the power which organises 'everyday life' (the echo of subcultural theory in the word 'resistance' is significant): 'If it cannot offer transcendence, it can at least promise a kind of salvation. If it does not define resistance, it does at least offer a kind of empowerment, allowing people to navigate their way through, and even to respond to their lived context. It is a way of making it through the day' (Grossberg, 1994: 52). With this passionate, almost poetic outburst we are brought on to the terrain of what Grossberg calls the 'operational logic' of the rock formation. This terrain seems to exist alongside the two other logics, of production and commercialisation (apparatuses) and consumption (scenes). While the latter is the site of what Grossberg calls 'taste cultures', the region of operational logic appears to take us to a deeper level to describe the 'place of musical practices and relations in people's lived realities *understood socially . . . rather than psychologically'*. Grossberg explains this exclusion of the 'psychological' level by stating that is the realm of mere 'experience' as opposed to the social which is where 'determination and power' are situated. This is surely too simple a polarisation and one which again denies the importance of the subject and the subjective, and of the psychoanalytical, in the processes of power as well as those of responding to music.

At his level of the social, Grossberg argues that there is an operational logic specific to the rock formation defined by its ability to differentiate between Us and Them (those in the secret and those left outside) and by its activity as a 'de-territorialising machine'. The terms 'navigation' and 'empowerment' in Grossberg's text, on the other hand, could equally have been used by an advocate of the effect of religion or drugs in helping to 'make it through the day'. However, the statement gets a political edge from the use of the phrases 'everyday life' and 'de-territorialising machine', terminology attributed respectively to Gilles Deleuze and to Henri Lefebrve, the theorist of 'everyday life' whose work had some influence on the more politicised work of the Situationist International, notably through Guy Debord's *Society Of The Spectacle*.

In the post-rock formation inhabited by Generation X, Grossberg sees a slackening of the all-important distinction between Us and Them, so that (he adds wryly or wistfully) 'the only exclusionary function seems to be to exclude those for whom the music matters too much (those still in the rock formation?)'. Similarly, he writes with disapproval of a situation where fun has become 'depoliticised' since it is no longer defined by its antagonism to boredom while 'rather than dancing to the music you like, you like the music you dance to'. However, Grossberg adds that this new formation and its music provides a 'moment of optimism' even though it does not generate utopian music and lyrics which seek to 'de-territorialize the spaces of everyday life'. Instead the newer music 'keeps trying to name the power', presumably a reference to the ghetto naturalism in gangsta rap and the intense nihilism in grunge (Grossberg, 1994: 56–7). Although from its title onwards the article contains an element of unsureness about some of the propositions it puts forward, it ends on a cautiously upbeat note – perhaps the 'rock formation' will survive, but if it does, it will be under another name and in another body.

It seems to me that this reincarnation is unlikely to take place, or rather that if a new discursive formation of the 'rock' type did arise it would have equally to deny or control heterogeneous forces in the global musical field. I hope by now it is clear that 'rock' has a mono-lithic character that acts either to efface differences in the musical field or to categorically exclude a large amount of musical practice. Some of these areas of effacement and exclusion have already been mentioned. As Barbara Bradby points out in her important article, the practical operation of the 'rock' system tends to subordinate or domesticate the 'other' in terms of gender, sexuality, race, rhythms (Bradby, 1993). This exclusion is usually carried out in the name of resistance (the music of the subculture, of Us not Them) where what is excluded are the hits which appear to be complicit with commercialism or show a 'bad faith' in their willingness to provide fleeting pleasures for the mass of youth not capable of forming or joining a youth subculture.

Perhaps ironically, the ability of 'rock' to retain a certain hegemony within popular music and youth culture has been greatly enhanced by the commercial success of the musical form at regular intervals over the past thirty-five years. Thus, the principal allies of the cultural critics who have cleaved to the idea of 'rock' as a unifying force have been the major record companies and their multinational parents which have dominated the distribution of music over the same period. In his valu-able study of the practices and working ideologies of these companies, Keith Negus notes that despite the proliferation of other popular styles, during the late 1980s and after most A&R (artist and repertoire) departments in London gave priority in their talent-spotting activities to guitar-based rock groups with self-composed songs (Negus, 1992). The models were such earlier performers as the Beatles, Rolling Stones, Queen, Dire Straits or U2.

Although Lawrence Grossberg is careful to define his use of the term 'rock' to include a wide range of musics, the conventional uses of the words 'rock and roll' or 'rock' indicate a sense of a globally distributed style or group of styles of music deriving from an Anglophone diaspora which covers what I shall call the platinum triangle of North America, Britain and Australia. Although not exclusively so, the overwhelming majority of the creators of this globally dominant form are white and male. There are, of course, debates about who is rock and who isn't. 'Is anybody listening?' points out that the 'rock formation' sometimes excludes black music, sometimes lets some in. But the almost subliminal factors which are common criteria for every version of the 'rock pantheon' are geographical or ethnic origins (rock 'n' roll from Memphis, British beat from Liverpool, grunge from Seattle?) and 'mother tongue', English of course. Anything else – French rock 'n' roll, German heavy metal, Japanese beat – must be ersatz. And when the rock hegemony is disturbed by the popularity of irruptions from outside, the axes of the platinum triangle are bracketed off as Anglophonics in drag (Abba), or as non-rock – the electronics of Can and Tangerine Dream (too cerebral), the 1970s disco-music of Silver Machine or Boney M (too brainless).

Global, local, regional

Within the bold new discourse of the 'global and the local' increasingly shared by cultural analysts and speechwriters for multinational corporation presidents, platinum triangle rock has glided easily into a global role. The high point was Michael Jackson's *Thriller*, that triumphant pot-pourri of the 'entire range of postwar, youth-oriented' music. Since 1982 CBS Records and its successor Sony Music have sold almost fifty million copies around the world with many millions more of pirate cassettes and home-made tapes in circulation. Meanwhile, Jackson, Dire Straits, Pink Floyd and others regularly undertake two-year world tours to perform live in over thirty countries to total audiences of five million or more. But below the 'global' horizon, the 'local' co-exists more easily with the Anglophone in music than in most other cultural forms. Compared with films or television programmes, the costs of production for a sound recording are minimal. Sophisticated technologies are increasingly cheap to acquire and easy to manipulate without formal training. Partly for these reasons, 'local' (read national) musical modes, forms and traditions are tenacious and provide a resource of themes, rhythms, tunes for young musicians.

With that resource, numerous hybrid forms have been produced, mixing and matching elements from platinum triangle rock with indigenous elements from the cultures of Europe, Africa, Asia and Latin

America. While the domestication of rock 'n' roll outside the Anglophone territories in the 1950s was seldom an artistic success, there have been three later great waves which generated much vibrant own-language music across the globe. From the early 1970s there has been a range of so-called folk-rock or electric folk styles which continue into the present merging traditional tunes, words and instrumentation with the current beats and instruments of rock or electronic music. Secondly there was a series of national punk-rocks, notably in Europe inspired by but different from the British movement of 1976–78. Finally, the successes of American rap have in the 1990s inspired own-language rapping across the globe from Italy to Japan.

While the existence of this complex of musical activity at a national level away from the platinum triangle has served to temper ideas of a simple cultural imperialism in popular music, it did not undermine the prestige or centrality of Anglophone 'rock'. This was because for the most part it remained within national music cultures and could not compete at the 'transnational' level where *Thriller* seemed part of a global youth culture alongside cola and burgers. However, the past five years or so have seen the emergence of another level of musical practice, apparatus and scene, situated between the 'global' and the 'local'. This level is a 'regional' one, working through a mix of geopolitical and linguistic spaces. These networks are based in other language-groups (Chinese, Spanish), other geographical regions (Europe) and perhaps also amongst 'internally exiled' cultures within the platinum triangle itself (notably rap in the United States). The existence of these networks, each with its own structure of musical genres, modes of distribution and forms of relationship between performer and audience, will have the effect of de-centring the 'rock formation' and indeed of redrawing the musical boundaries and lines of force in what we are being told is a global cultural system.

The regional blocs and 'popularity'

There are three principal regional or linguistic-based production centres which now offer a significant counterweight to the English-language music of the platinum triangle. These are the songs of Mandarin and Cantonese Chinese language speakers in Asia, the music of the Spanish-speaking regions of the Americas and Europe, and the increasing amount of internationally successful music emanating from continental Europe, notably in the 'dance music' field.

To justify my contention that these blocs have established a comparable presence to that of Anglophone pop means finding some criteria for defining and judging the 'popularity' of musical forms. The discursive machines of the music industry and associated media have a simple answer to the question of 'popularity' – the sales of their products as ranked in charts or hit parades. Although these lists simply equate popularity with amounts of expenditure, this solution, and its implied corollary that greater sales equals greater importance or even higher quality, has frequently been adopted without question by 'independent' commentators. Both the economic logic of hit parades and what might be called their mass psychology remain an under-researched area. Jean Paul Sartre's masterly few pages in *The Critique of Dialectical Reason* remain an essential starting point (Sartre, 1976).

Because less than half of all discs and tapes purchased are represented in the hit parades, a more satisfactory source of information about musical preferences or tastes would be the total purchases of recorded music. In many parts of the world, this would also have to include 'pirate' tapes as well. Record industry organisations use the total market data to determine the relative sales of different musical genres or, more pertinent to this discussion, the sources of those sales. In the industry jargon, these sources are divided between classical repertoire, 'domestic' (i.e. national) pop and 'international pop' which originates abroad. However, those who purchase records represent only a minority of the population. Singles buyers in most countries are only a tiny minority of radio listeners. Therefore, a better measure of the popularity of certain songs could be the size of the audiences for the radio stations which feature those songs. Such a measure would be based on the assumption that to listen to a radio station is to assent to, or to like, the music played there. A further source of quantitative data on popularity would be a survey of musical tastes or preferences undertaken independently of the music industry, perhaps in conjunction with an inventory of the personal record collections of those contributing to the survey.

Since about 1992, the various data from record sales and radio station audiences tend to show a shift away from Anglo-American music and towards local or regional popular styles and recordings, notably in countries of Asia and Europe. Amongst the recent statistics are these: twenty-nine of the top hundred best-selling singles in the Netherlands in 1994 were of Dutch origin, the highest number since 1982; local (national) songwriters and performers had 40 per cent of the hit records in Germany in the same year. In Hong Kong, for example, English-language music's share of record sales fell from 30–40 per cent in the mid-1980s to 15 per cent in the early 1990s.

According to most Asian music industry experts, so-called 'Cantopop' and Mandarin-language songs are the most listened to by young people throughout Taiwan, Hong Kong, Singapore, Malaysia and within China itself. The leading figure in Cantopop, Jacky Cheung, sold over three million copies of his most recent album whose title translates as *Kiss and Goodbye*. Equally significant is the proliferation of styles of Chinese-language music, not least in the People's Republic of China. A report of a New Year 1995 concert given in Hong Kong by four PRC-based artists noted how each differed from Cantopop and from each other. Their own styles ranged from folk to hard rock via punk (Levin, 1995). This has occurred in a region whose overall economies, including the media and culture industries, have been growing faster than those of any other continent. The cultural and economic weight of this music has been recognised even by the international satellite broadcasters, News International and Viacom, which both operate pan-Asian programming. Both Channel V of Murdoch's Star TV network and MTV Asia are dedicating the majority of their 24-hour music channels to Chinese music.

Spanish is the first language of over 200 million people and the operations of major television production companies and multinational record companies in particular have made this into a 'single market' for popular cultural material. In particular there are increasing cultural flows between Southern Europe and Latin America. The fastest growing Hispanic population is in the United States where there are growing networks of Spanish-language radio and television stations and music industry institutions. The newest Hispanic superstar is Mexican-born Luis Miguel whose last album of ballads sold seven million copies. Miguel has so far resisted the wishes of his record company, a subsidiary of Time Warner, to record and perform in English. The past decade has also seen a proliferation of new Hispanic musical forms, often grafting elements from American rock on to rhythms or lyrical figures drawn from existing Latin styles.

The new European pop

Language is the principal unifying factor for these Asian and Hispanic regional music blocs. The unity of the new music bloc in Europe is more complex. To begin with, the most common language used for lyrics is probably English, although Italian, French, German and Dutch are sometimes in evidence. The bloc involves forms and methods of production and 'spaces' as well as certain formal features associated with contemporary dance music genres.

As in Asia and the Hispanic space, a range of musical styles operates within the bloc. In an article completed at the start of 1992 (Laing, 1992), I described a range of musical works emanating from continental Europe which were to some extent achieving an international impact, attracting audiences from outside the domestic culture or home language community of the musician or producer. At that stage, the significance of this work was in some doubt. It might have been some kind of 'blip' in a 'never-ending story' of an Anglo-American hegemony in popular music since the 1950s, as, in retrospect, was the success of Abba in the 1970s or Julio Iglesias a decade later. Or it might have represented the beginnings of a structural change in the geopolitics of contemporary pop. Three years further on, the quantity of continental European music in circulation throughout the continent and beyond has grown. On a simple statistical level, the number of best-selling records created in Europe which have become international best-sellers has increased. In 1994, for instance, the Dutch-based pop-dance group Ace Of Base sold over seven million albums in the United States, while the German production team using the name Enigma sold four million albums in the United States. A sign of changes in the habits of record-buyers within Europe itself was the list of the top hundred chart singles and albums of 1994 compiled by the business publication *Music & Media* from the various national hit parades including that of Britain. The listing shows that 45 of the best-selling singles originated in continental Europe, compared with 35 in 1993. A further 28 came from the UK and only 29 from North America. Amongst albums, the figures were Europe 29, UK 26 and North America 45. In terms of language, 17 of the 100 albums were non-Anglophone. The languages included French, Spanish, German, Italian and Wolof. Only six of the singles had non-English titles, although many of the 94 other tracks were sung in what I have elsewhere called 'disco Esperanto', that is a dialect of English whose small vocabulary derives in large part from dance-floor slogans and soul music rhetoric (Laing, 1992).

There have been three principal genres of continental European music in the early 1990s. The first is the Anglophone pop/rock typified by Ace of Base and by Roxette from Sweden. There is also the rock-inflected ballad style associated in the United States with Michael Bolton and in Britain with Elton John. During recent years such European singers as Laura Pausini and Eros Ramazzotti from Italy and Patricia Kaas from France have achieved pan-European popularity while singing in their own languages. The third genre includes the various forms of new dance and rap music. In addition to these there are distinctive European-based elements of 'easy listening' (James Last from Germany), hard rock/metal (the Scorpions, also based in Germany), so-called 'world music' (the Gypsy Kings from France, More Kante and other West African musicians based in Paris or Brussels), jazz and avant-garde musics.

Dance networks

In the remainder of this essay I want to point out some features of just one of the genres of European music: the complex of dance forms. I shall restrict my comments to three aspects: texts (recordings), forms and sites of production, and the distinctive networks through which the music operates.

Texts

According to country music historian Bill C. Malone, 'Cotton-Eyed Joe' was a fiddle tune which originated in the late nineteenth century either among black musicians or the 'black-face minstrelsy' of white vaudeville troupes. By the 1930s the piece had become a staple element in the repertoire of western swing bands which combined elements from a range of musics under a zany cowboy image. Among those with whom it was particularly associated was Adolph Hofner, a Texan bandleader whose grandparents had been born in what is now the Czech Republic. Hofner's own first language was 'Bohemian' and his repertoire included Czech waltzes and polkas as well as 'Cotton-Eyed Joe' (Malone, 1985). At the beginning of 1995 the fastest-selling single throughout Europe was 'Cotton Eye Joe' by Rednex. Apparently recorded in an American studio, this version of the tune was created by Dutch producers who allied the melody to contemporary dance beats and a somewhat imprecise variant of square-dancing which was featured on the video created to accompany the record.

At one point in 'Is anybody listening?', Lawrence Grossberg criticises simple models of centre and periphery in the field of popular music by posing the 'real question' which is 'what kind of sounds travel? From where to where? What are the enabling and constraining conditions of such mobilities and stabilities?' In any discussion of such a phenomenon as 'Cotton Eye Joe', these seem to me to be the right sort of issues on which to focus. What does this playful Dutch production do to the fiddle tune passed from minstrelsy to Tex-Czech music? Is it an ironic re-working, a parody, a cartoon-like tribute to the Western movies which form part of the staple programming of Europe's growing number of satellite and cable film channels? And the name Rednex, with its rap-derived re-spelling of a nomenclature most Europeans would see as a negative description of poor whites in the Southern States. How does that name signify?

The whole of the European dance movement itself is also at one level the product of the complex mobilities of musical forms in the present era. The techno recordings which first inspired the new dance producers and DJs of Europe were created by black sonic experimenters in Detroit. In turn these producers had drawn on the work in electronic music of German artists of the 1970s such as Kraftwerk and Can. Finally, some members of a new generation of German techno producers have short-circuited the transatlantic crossing of two decades by proclaiming themselves the direct heirs of Kraftwerk and the guardians of a purely German genre of modern pop music. The Russian formalists used to talk of literary history advancing by the 'junior branch' or by the 'knight's move'. By this they meant that new forms of the novel or poetry often derived from despised or unvalued elements in the writing of a previous era. Tracks like 'Cotton Eye Joe' and its predecessors among European dance tracks have in general been ignored by both critics and the mainstream music business. As the modern equivalent of 'AM bubble-gum' and as prime examples of a situation where 'you like the music you dance to', the genre was for a long while derided as without the seriousness or staying-power needed by rock's next step forward. Within the past couple of years, however, this new 'junior branch' of popular music has become the site of some of the most innovative work in sound-production and recording. This has occurred primarily through an unforeseen rendezvous between the new generation of producers and the genre of ambient music founded in the 1970s by Brian Eno and others. In Britain, groups such as the Orb and Future Sound Of London have developed an 'ambient house' which encompasses lengthy pieces incorporating found-sounds, samples and sometime contemplative social criticism.

Production

The ambiguities and complexities of the new European music take a different form when the mode of its production is considered. In many ways the division of labour has regressed to that of American systems of the 1960s and earlier. One model seems to be that established by Phil Spector, where the producer controlled all aspects of a recording and its presentation through live performances or appearances. Like Spector with the Ronettes, the Italian producers of Black Box (whose 'Ride On Time' remains a founding classic of the pop-dance genre) act as puppet-masters for a production performed by a photogenic and well-drilled vocalist. Sometimes, as with the now notorious Milli Vanilli, the 'artists' are revealed as lip-synching rather than singing in their own voices. Other 'groups' like Snap or Technotronic have constantly shifting personnel with new rappers or vocalists for almost every single. This antique division of labour also tends to be gender and race specific. A considerable number of the dance acts as presented to television audiences include black (often US-born) rappers and female vocalists. But there is a contrast here between the traditional format of production houses in Frankfurt or Milan and the active participation of female and black rappers and club DJs.

Networks

In contrast to the more monumental concept of 'formation', it seems more apt to speak of 'networks' in describing such musical phenomena as the European dance movement, particularly in discussing the flow of affinities across national and continental borders. The system associated with the platinum triangle is more hierarchical and vertically integrated with its centre at the point where the multinational record company and the equally transnational supergroup or superstar form their symbiotic link. Though uneven, the distribution of power within the horizontal networks associated with European dance and many other musical forms such as jazz or 'world music' is far more diffuse. Such networks might possibly be seen as contemporary examples of the *rhizomes* described by Deleuze and Guattari (1983).

The flow of affinities across these networks is in part geographical. The key centres of production shift from country to country (Belgium to Italy to Germany to the Netherlands) as well as from genre to genre. This is another contrast with the monolithic platinum triangle where there is a geographical hierarchy mirroring that of institutions. The one-way lines of flow go to New York, Nashville, Los Angeles, London.

There is also at one level a multiplicity of these dance networks, defined by the ever-increasing genre distinctions. Within dance the bifurcation began when house emerged alongside techno and the splitting has continued with the identification of both new and hybrid genres. But all the networks intersect in such key institutions as clubs and DJs, studios, large live events (raves), radio stations, record stores, record labels, fashion and clothes stores, drinks and drugs. Nor are these networks or rhizomes isolated from other social dimensions or formations. For example, the major record companies attempt to insert themselves at the level of distribution of recordings and to exercise control over the direction of the musical flow. And the dance music networks are capable of political intervention if they need to fight for the right to party, as in the campaign against Britain's Criminal Justice Act.

Conclusions

What is the significance of the rise of these geographical blocs for the plantinum triangle and particularly Britain and the United States? Much of the British role in the global musical economy over that past thirty years has been as an exporter. In particular, the major record companies have used Britain as an extra talent source for first the US rock music market and then the global one. As a result, the popular music of Britain has been distorted to emphasise transnational guitar rock music in the mode of the Rolling Stones, Pink Floyd, Dire Straits, U2. Music, like the punk styles of the late 1970s, which is not palatable to large American audiences is regarded as having failed in its duty to contribute to Britain's balance of musical payments.

While Britain's place in the platinum triangle has been mainly as this repertoire source and a test-bed for the US music market, there is another 'Britain' in the networks of new dance music, where the lines of force reach to Europe as well as to a now marginalised North American club scene. That dance club scene is marginalised in part because of its openness to music which has the 'mobilities' mentioned by Grossberg. Elsewhere, American music culture in the mid-1990s seems defined by 'stabilities', by growing audiences for two highly introverted American genres. The two musical forms which have increased in popularity (as measured by record sales) the most are country music and rap. And while these have shown unexpected 'mobilities' in colonising new audiences amongst guitar rock's traditional constituencies, unlike guitar rock or soul music, both country music and rap have little or no direct resonance abroad (while rap has inspired young musicians elsewhere, American rap artists in general have not found comparable foreign audiences to those for Bon Jovi or Whitney Houston).

References

Bradby, Barbara (1993) 'Sampling sexuality; gender, technology and the body in dance music', *Popular Music* 12, 2: 155–76.

Bradby, Barbara and Torode, Brian (1984) 'Pity Peggy Sue', *Popular Music* 4: 183–205.

Clarke, John (1975) 'Style' in Resistance Through Rituals, *Cultural Studies* 7–8: 175–92.

Cubitt, Sean (1984) 'Maybellene: meaning and the listening subject', *Popular Music*, 4: 206–21.

Deleuze, Gilles and Guattari, Felix (1983) *On the Line*, New York: Semiotext(e).

Gillett, Charlie (1970) *The Sound of the City*, New York, Outerbridge & Dientsfrey.

Grossberg, Lawrence (1994) 'Is anybody listening? Does anybody care? On talking about "the state of rock"', in Andrew Ross and Tricia Rose (eds) *Microphone Fiends: Youth Music and Youth Culture*, New York and London, Routledge.

Laing, Dave (1985) *One Chord Wonders: Power and Meaning in Punk Rock*, Milton Keynes, Open University Press.

Laing, Dave (1992) '"Sadness", Scorpions and single markets: national and transnational trends in European popular music', *Popular Music* 11, 2: 127–40.

Levin, Mike (1995) 'Chinese pop music lovers show a taste for rock', *Billboard*, 21 January, p. 45.

Malone, Bill C. (1985) *Country Music USA*, Austin, University of Texas Press.

Marsh, Dave and Jon Swenson (eds) (1979) *The Rolling Stone Record Guide*, San Franciso, Straight Arrow Press.

Negus, Keith (1992) *Producing Pop: Culture and Conflict in the Popular Music Industry*, London, Edward Arnold.

Sartre, Jean Paul (1976) *Critique of Dialectical Reason*, London, NLB.

7 Vron Ware

Purity and danger: race, gender and tales of sex tourism

It is precisely that longing for . . . pleasure that has led the white west to sustain a romantic fantasy of the 'primitive' and the concrete search for a real primitive paradise, whether that location be a country or a body, a dark continent or dark flesh, perceived as the perfect embodiment of that possibility.

bell hooks[1]

Black guy wanted, West Indian, 30 to 36, attractive, honest, GSOH, reliable, for one to one relationship. I am a white, young 48, female, petite, very caring and romantic.

Caring white female, 24, average looks, likes cosy nights in, seeking white male, 23–30, for loving long-term relationship. Must be honest, homely and reliable.

Loot[2]

The funny thing about this story of hypocrisy and brutality is not just that you can't stop people fancying each other across any kind of racial barrier. The real irony is that the myths could almost have been designed to spark off some of the most intense sexual experiences ever.

No fruit has ever been quite so forbidden. What person of spirit could fail to crave such a taste? And how sweet is this poem of contrasts between gleaming black skin and creamy pink flesh. How tender the refuge from the terror and rage of the world. How piercing the intrusions of apprehension and guilt.

Mike Phillips[3]

This piece was originally inspired by various British newspaper reports in national and locally based tabloids; it is the result of puzzling over familiar constructions of white femininity and black masculinity that appear in popular culture but which are rarely commented on or critically analysed by feminists. The crude racism often signified by these images is effective, I believe, in continuing to shape widely held perceptions of racialised and gendered identities. My argument here is that these perceptions appeal to memories of the long histories of racial slavery and colonialism, which partly accounts for their 'familiar' and 'common-sensical' force. In my discussion of two sets of media reports I want to emphasise the importance of bringing a historical perspective to an analysis of these rather routine and often apparently trivial representations of black and white masculinities and femininities. Trying to make connections between the social construction of racialised and gendered difference in the UK and North America, I am aware that understanding the source and power of these images is only a small step towards dismantling them. In the final part of this piece I want to address the question of feminism and political agency against racism.

In Spike Lee's film *Jungle Fever*, which demonstrates the inadvisability, if not the impossibility, of a loving sexual relationship between a black man and a white woman in contemporary urban America, there is a particularly tense scene in which the black father figure delivers a passionate speech denouncing the role of the white woman in slavery. In the voice of a preacher inspired by an anger that clearly embarrasses his wife, his son and his son's new, white, girlfriend, he raises the spectre of the white woman placed on a pedestal by the white man in order to control and humiliate the black man and to have free access to the black woman. His speech might well have been inspired by a passage from Malcolm X's autobiography – the subject of a later Lee movie:

> I had told how the antebellum white slavemaster even devilishly manipulated his own woman. He convinced her that she was 'too pure' for his own base 'animal instincts'. With this 'noble' ruse, he conned his own wife to look away from his obvious preference for the 'animal' black woman. So the 'delicate mistress' sat and watched the plantation's little mongrel-complexioned children, sired obviously by her father, her husband, her brothers, her sons.[4]

The father's diatribe in *Jungle Fever* has the effect of adding to the battery of 'racial common-sense' which ultimately prevails, destroying the affection that the young couple seemed to have had for each other. However, the speech is also instrumental in bringing the historical memory of racial slavery to the attention of not just a younger generation within the narrative but the cinema-going public as well, summoning up for both audiences vivid images of the terror of white supremacy. It hardly needs restating that these images work through gender as well as race, and that they operate in systemic relation to each other. Black and white masculinities and femininities are constructed not as simple binary pairings – such as the white woman being 'pure' while the black woman is 'animal' – but in a more complex and asymmetrical pattern of interconnected and self-similar attributes. It is important to stress that the asymmetry refers to the values and privileges encoded by 'whiteness' as well as by constructions of masculinity, although not necessarily by both simultaneously. In her recent book *Transformations*, Drucilla Cornell makes a similar point:

> an understanding of this asymmetrical relationship would also deny that color can be reduced to a set of positive characteristics separate from the chain of signifiers in which it is given meaning. In other words there are not just 'white' and 'black' women who are just there and can be reduced to their 'whiteness' and 'blackness' as if color could signify separately from the matrix of desire in which it is given meaning. What it means to be 'white,' in other words, can only be grasped in relationship to the privilege of being 'white' within the differential articulation of 'white' and 'black' womanhood.[5]

Cornell goes on to assert that it is important to 'grasp the oppressiveness of the so-called meaning given to whiteness which identifies "it" with a fantasized feminine desirability characterized by inaccessibility and so-called virtue'. Her discussion is partly based on the constructions of racialised masculinity and femininity that legitimated the practice of lynching as a form of racial terror in the 1930s, constructions that derived their power from the social and political relations of Southern slavery. In *Beyond the Pale* I tried to show that it was the very oppressiveness of this particular construction of white womanhood that alerted some women, forty years earlier, to the fact that racism could also involve the subordination of 'white' women.[6] It is worth repeating here that this analysis of the intersection of race and gender was first suggested by an African-American woman, Ida B. Wells, who lambasted the concept of Southern chivalry as a means by which the white man legitimated his authority over white women as well as the black population of the South.[7] Her subsequent journey to Britain in the 1890s to campaign against lynching provides a fascinating example of the transatlantic dialogue between women on the politics of women's emancipation and anti-racism.

Although it is my intention here to explore contemporary images of white femininity that refer back to earlier historical periods, I think it is a crucial part of the argument to show how these historical construc- tions – produced by the intersection of racial domination and female subordination – are articulated (and contested) differently according to time and place. So far I have discussed these constructs in the context of racial slavery, which is entirely appropriate when talking about North American history and memory, particularly the United States. While Britain shares this history of slavery, the historical memory of this system of racial domination has been transformed by nearly two hundred years of colonialism. Making sense of contemporary patterns of racism found within Britain requires an understanding of the more recent histories of imperial domination and the various forms of resis- tance that finally overthrew them. By this I am not saying that the institution of slavery was not fundamental to the project of building the empire, or that there was some kind of disjuncture between the two forms of white supremacy. Certainly for those British citizens of Caribbean origin it would be hard to separate the two in any case. The process of interpreting the imagery of racialised and gendered subjects that recurs in British culture ought to refer as much to the memory of empire as that of racial slavery.

This point may be illustrated by the critical situation existing in some parts of Britain today. In September 1993 a member of a fascist group was elected as a representative in local government for the first time in over fifteen years. The British National Party (BNP), which had not even come near winning an election since it was founded in the early 1980s, was successful in gaining a seat in an area of east London known as the Isle of Dogs. Their propaganda, including a newsletter called *Island Patriot*, is mainly directed against the community of Bengalis settled within the same borough. According to a police report the number of reported racial incidents rose nearly 300 per cent in just four months after the election in the Isle of Dogs, and the perpetrators appeared to be mainly white men in their twenties and thirties. Racist violence is cer- tainly not a new phenomenon in urban Britain, but the combination of organised physical intimidation and brutality being carried out by a group democratically elected to represent a local constituency had not been seen since the late 1970s. Fortunately, the fascist councillor lost his seat in new elections in May the following year, but the BNP continue to campaign in the area. Meanwhile, south of the river in the boroughs of Greenwich and Bexley, where the BNP headquarters was located, four young black men have been murdered in the last few years, each one as a result of unprovoked attack by gangs of white males.

One particularly atrocious incident that took place in Essex made the headlines briefly when the case came to court in 1994. Three white men were jailed for three to five years after being found guilty of attacking a black man and his white female partner. They first abused the woman, Lynn Woodard, calling her a 'nigger lover' and a slut, and then stabbed Ken Harris, who came to her defence, and ran him over repeatedly with his own car as he lay wounded on the ground. The judge at the trial said, 'The only reasons for this attack was that he happened to be black and she white'. These brief details are intended to provide a context for talking about racism in a manner that links theory very closely with questions of political agency. Of course contemporary racism is mani-fested in other forms than physical violence, but what role does femi-nism have to play in the politics of abolishing racism when the principal actors asserting white supremacy appear to be men – as they do here? How does an understanding of the past help to create political strate-gies to suit today's infinitely complex and dangerous situations? Clearly the Bengali community under attack in the East End of London has a historical relationship to Britain through colonialism rather than through being enslaved. The racist meanings attributed to Asian modes of masculinity and femininity express ideas not just derived from constructions of their 'race' and sexuality but their religions as well. The discourses of Orientalism have supplied images of exoticism, passivity and irrationality, for example, which often represent the degree to which the cultures of 'the East' (wherever that is) are unfathomable and therefore threatening to the Western mind. Gender as well as class play crucial roles in mediating notions of difference between northern European and Asian ways of life: ideas about what constitutes Asian femininity and masculinity, for example, are formed in relation to ideas about white femininity and masculinity. Where Asian women are represented as submissive to their husbands, oppressed by the demands of a patriarchal family network, the implica-tion is that white women are, in contrast, liberated, independent and free to move around wherever they choose. However, the point is not to identify fixed meanings in the imagery of either racially coded feminin-ities or masculinities, but to be aware of the interconnectedness between these different constructions and the way that they can articulate pow-erful messages about cultural difference and white supremacy. Jane Flax expresses the complexity of this process in her essay 'Minerva's Owl':

My current understanding of race/gender is a dynamic, disorderly, yet systemic one. Everyone is marked within and by race/gender systems (although differently). Gender and race categories, practices, and concrete historical beings are in multiple, unstable, contingent, and deeply determining relations with one another.[8]

The constructions of Bengali – and by extension Indian and Pakistani – masculinity and femininity which emerge in discourses of racism in Britain today have been refined throughout the processes of colonisation, decolonisation, migration and settlement. Yet despite the differences between this history and the history of African Americans through slavery, emancipation, the Civil Rights Movement and contemporary racism in the United States, it is still possible to identify similarities or connections between these 'dynamic and disorderly, yet systemic' constructions of black and white masculinity and femininity. This convergence is particularly visible in the construction of the vulnerable white woman threatened by the predatory black man, a couplet that can be traced throughout the history of white supremacy. The ideology of the black male as a kind of beast lusting after innocent white women erupts at significant moments in different geographical locations. It helped to legitimate the practice of lynching in the United States after the abolition of slavery; it surfaced under the heading of the 'Black Peril' in South Africa between 1890 and 1920, causing the Association of Women's Organisations to demand 'the social segregation of the races'.[9] Another example – which I have discussed in more depth in *Beyond the Pale* – was the first Indian Uprising, also known as the Indian Mutiny in 1857.[10] As a result of the rumoured slaughter of hundreds of defenceless Englishwomen at the hands of the Indian sepoys, Indians were thereafter commonly referred to, both in Britain and in the Raj, as 'niggers'.[11] Despite the multiplicity and instability of meanings attached to 'race' and gender, the white supremacist imagination is still capable of a very limited repertoire.

In this next section I want to consider ways that contemporary popular culture contributes to the construction of white femininity – or how 'white' women are represented as racialised and gendered subjects. In this instance I have chosen to discuss images that appear primarily in written form, that is, in the print media rather than on film or television. The examples are taken from two different accounts of sex tourism involving 'white' British women in West Africa: the first in the *Sun*, Britain's most popular tabloid newspaper, read by an estimated five million people daily, and the second in *Marie Claire*, a glossy magazine with a commitment to a version of middle-class lifestyle feminism, with the words 'For women of the world' tucked inside the front cover and a circulation currently of 340,000 in the UK.[12] The similarities and contrasts between the representations of white femininity and black masculinity in each case are particularly useful in showing the adaptability of these constructions, depending on the 'race', class, age and gender of the audience for whom they are intended.

The exercise was initially provoked by a three-part series in the *Sun*. The first episode appeared on the front page one Monday morning with the huge heading: 'Mud-Hut Rat Stole My Wife'. The text described how a 39-year-old Sandra Anderson 'set up home in a mud hut with a tribal prince after husband Frank took her on a Gambian holiday'. Inside, the text continued to describe her adventures – and her husband's reaction – under the caption 'It's like a mix of Shirley Valentine and Out of Africa . . . with more romance'.

Later that week the second part of the feature appeared, dramatised by a large, half-page colour picture of eight black men, with dreadlocks, guitar and cheerful smiles, supporting the weight of a horizontal young white woman, all bare legs and arms and smiling happily. The picture is captioned in large letters: 'All because the ladies love black magic men' – an immediately recognisable but inverted reference to a series of adverts about Cadbury's chocolate in which a heroic white man is seen battling against all kinds of odds to bring a woman friend a box of 'Milk Tray' chocolates. The text accompanying this picture, introduced by a smaller shot of the same woman with 'Jimmy' the man who 'charmed' her, is headed: 'Beach Boys in Gambia say holiday Brits can't get enough sex in the sand'. It begins: 'They're tall, dark and handsome – and British women just can't resist the magic of Gambian beach boys. The hunky charmers spend their days chatting up the holidaymakers and their nights making love to them in the sand.'

The article is actually written by the woman who appears in the two pictures; as well as providing the pictorial evidence of the scene she describes, she also positions herself as the innocent holidaymaker in order to research the background to the 'mud-hut love affair'. Her account is framed by the sentence 'As I soaked up the sun on the beach, the smoothtalkers showed why they are so successful' and ends with 'But I'm one woman who didn't fall under the black magic spell . . . the photographer and I had a job to do'. The feature runs across two pages and consists of interviews with the Gambian men whom she met on the beach explaining why white women were so easily swept off their feet by black men. Their reasons included the women's inability to resist being flattered, stroked and praised for their 'ivory' skin, their excitement at the prospect of having outdoor sex, and the novelty of 'having had a coloured man'. Before the first cross-heading the author felt bound to state that 'No British man I've ever met could have matched either their charm or their cheek'. Throughout the article the Gambian interviewees compare themselves to British men, either directly or indirectly with remarks such as 'Most British women have never been with a black man before but once they have, they just can't help themselves coming back for more' or 'From what I can see, British men don't do this very much [tell women how beautiful they are], which is probably why their women can't get enough from us' – and of course the obligatory favourable comments on the size of black men's penises. The man known as 'Jimmy', having described his techniques of seduction in minute detail, goes on to assert confidently that 'It doesn't matter whether a woman is with her husband or not, they usually still want to flirt, and love all the attention from local men'.

The following day a third, page-length feature appeared with the heading: 'Gambian Rat Stole My Wife Too!' with the subheading 'I even gave him money to buy rice'. Pictures of 'The Wife', 'The Husband' (who is shown reading the original story on the front page of the *Sun* earlier in the week) and 'The Lover' (a blurred figure of a man in uniform with dark glasses) introduce the characters in this second example of a British woman doing a 'Shirley-Valentine runner into the arms of Gambian lover'. What is interesting in this episode, apart from the bizarre account of how this woman made the decision to stay with her new lover in Africa, is the way in which she is described. 'Prim teacher Barbara Ferrier, 42, fell for a black PC 19 years her junior . . . Grey-haired Barbara is living in a primitive concrete compound in shanty town Serrakunda . . . she cooks on a charcoal fire . . . and the loo is a hole in the back yard.' In a short interview further down the page, headed 'Love at First Sight', she denied that it was 'just the sex' that made her decide to leave her husband, saying that it was 'fate' that had taken over her life.

Most astonishing of all, alongside the third episode of the series, the *Sun* published details of a competition to 'Test your Marriage in Africa'. By answering the question 'What is Gambia's capital?' entrants are 'dared' to put their marriages 'to the ultimate test' by winning seven nights in a top hotel in the country. The entrants must be over eighteen,

Figure 1   From the *Sun*, 12 February 1994

married and free to travel before a certain date, and by implication white too.

This type of tabloid journalism is classic in the way it sensationalises a story with elements of 'racial' promiscuity and titillating details of unorthodox sexual encounters. The writers rely on all the familiar images of black male sexual athletes, inhibited white Englishmen and 'prim' but seducible white Englishwomen. Yet even if the two examples of the 'runaway' wives had been entirely fabricated, the feature still refers to a phenomenon that is recognisable enough, captured in cultural forms such as 'Smile Orange' (a comic play and film written from the point of view of Jamaican waiters working in a hotel for wealthy white and often single female tourists in the Caribbean) and of course in the oft-cited Shirley Valentine, although her lover was not black. The exchange relationship whereby the men earn money, or are 'kept' in return for providing single women with sex and company, was made quite explicit in the *Sun* articles. It was certainly clear to the men, both black and white, that the women were expected to 'bankroll' their African lovers in return for their attentions. At no point was it suggested that the Gambian men found white women particularly beautiful or alluring apart from their wallets. This no doubt contributed to their 'cheek' as well as their self-confidence.

At first sight the *Sun* reports might seem harmless enough, given that no one was hurt (apart from the two husbands) and no crime was committed. This form of sex tourism, involving opportunities for mutual exploitation between consenting adults, is qualitatively different from the exploitation and physical abuse of women and children in Thailand and Sri Lanka by white Western men. However, there are two sets of interconnected problems that arise from this type of writing. The first concerns the way that the images of each set of players – black men, white men, white women and black women – have been made to fit crude racialised figures that match certain kinds of behaviour with essentialised notions of masculinity and femininity, black and white. The African men are constructed as sexually powerful, their superiority over white men existing in the shape and appearance of their bodies; they are also denounced as 'rats' which suggests associations with dirt, disease, squalor. They are sexually interested in white women, not because of their appearance but because of what they symbolise in terms of wealth, and they see it as a challenge to 'steal' them away from their husbands. The white men in this scenario are represented through the eyes of the African men as sexually unsophisticated, and relatively powerless once they are on holiday and therefore removed from the world of work, home, and other normal social structures. White women are constructed as belonging to their husbands; they have no power to resist the sexual advances of the professionals (apart from the sleuth who was not in holiday mode) and their own sexuality is evidently repressed through lack of experience and opportunity. Although it is evident from the newspaper reports that the women made conscious decisions to leave their husbands and live with other men, they are not represented as 'bad' women or as being 'oversexed' themselves. Instead there is a curious impression that they are the innocent victims of the 'black magic' worked on and in their bodies. In some ways black women are the most significant presence in this narrative because of their total absence. They do not 'fit' in this sequence of events, which has several implications: first, that if black women are on holiday they may not be so easily fooled as white women and in any case do not receive the same kind of attention; second, that in their roles as wives, sisters and mothers they do not have access to the same kind of tourist economy as their menfolk; third, that they behave in such a way at home that their men actually prefer to mix with white women who give them less trouble and allow them to dominate. However, it could also be argued that the absence of black women reflects the marginality of all women in this particular story; the real drama is perhaps between the different modes of black and white masculinity which articulate contesting forms of male power and express them through the bodies of women as they circulate across the line of colour.

These constructions of racialised masculinity and femininity that I have suggested here clearly represent a problem in that they perpetuate deeply held racist ideas about how men and women behave. In doing so they give shape to notions of bestiality and other forms of deviant sexuality associated with 'racial' difference that have troubled the white imagination since the development of modern racism. The second set of problems that flow on from this becomes evident when this discourse of race, sex and seduction is placed alongside that of race and violence against women. In the same edition as one of the episodes described above, a short piece appeared about a man who was convicted and jailed for raping two women, a nun and a social worker. The rapist who was described as 'a drug-crazed sex fiend', 'evil', and a 'crack addict' was nowhere referred to as 'black'. A small picture of his face inserted into the text was sufficient evidence to link his crime with his 'racial' type. The two different stories together contribute to a more complex but

mutually reinforcing representation of racialised and gendered categories. However, the significance of these constructions is also changed
by the context in which they are read. Obviously crime reports appear
soon after the details become known to the press, but why did the
Gambian feature appear in that particular week in February 1994?
Perhaps a better question would be to ask, how is it likely that people
will read it in today's political climate? Who do readers identify with?
What does it say about the state of British racism that a story like that
appears over three days in the most popular tabloid newspaper at this
time? And is there any connection between the racism expressed in the
pages of the *Sun* and the attack on Ken Harris and Lynn Woodard?

If the *Sun* version of the Gambia story works by appealing to a traditional populist view of the social relations of 'race' and gender, the
report of the same phenomenon in *Marie Claire* seems to bend over
backwards to offer a more critical and detached account while using
some of the same ingredients: white women old enough to be
grandmothers purchasing sex and romance from young black men of
vastly different economic and cultural backgrounds in an exotic location.[13] This version of the story works in this context by appearing to
offer a sensationalist narrative of an assertive but vulnerable female
sexuality with which its readers will be entirely familiar. However, the
story begins and ends from the men's point of view, offering a semi-soci-
ological view of the economic relations that force them to sell their services in such a desperate manner. Although the women's motives are
described in their own words, the effect of the whole piece is that their
assertiveness is a sham and that many remain victims of male duplicity,
both at home and in their new-found paradise. Despite the very obvious
differences between the coding of the two stories, the net result appears
to be the same: black men are cast as predators, white women remain
passive victims and the conclusion is that such dangerous and desperate liaisons simply cannot work. Furthermore, the inability of the
Marie Claire piece to offer any insights into the social relations of
'race', as well as class and gender, suggests, as I shall argue shortly, that
readers are expected to apply their own prejudices and fantasies to
make sense of what is going on.

In spite of sharing these same spicy ingredients of interracial sex, at
first sight the feature in *Marie Claire* gives a very different impression
to the one in the *Sun* and is entirely congruent with a sophisticated, pro-
feminist fashion magazine. Its headline for a start is 'Seeking Sex in the
Gambia', laid in bold black type over a double page photo of three

'We make love on the beach. Ebu's not that experienced, so I have been teaching him'
Doris with Ebu

Figure 2   From *Marie Claire*, May 1994

white women each entwined with a black man. The introduction on the same spread suggests the significance of age in this scenario: the women are described as 'a 58-year-old art dealer', 'a grandmother' and '62', while their husbands and boyfriends are 25 and 26. A caption in the corner announces 'You don't ask for sex but the men seem to know you want it. They say things like, "Would you like to see the real Africa?" It's all very discreet.' The next two pages feature large colour shots of couples kissing with eyes closed, one with the caption: 'We make love on the beach. Ebu's not that experienced, so I have been teaching him.' Picked out of the text in large type is the observation: 'In the discos lacquered grey heads happily bob along bouncing dreadlocks'. In the pages of *Marie Claire*, the 'prim' and 'grey-haired' Barbara Ferrier might have come across as a different kind of woman altogether.

Further on through the feature, however, these images of assertive, joyful, older, 'white' female sexuality, that make such arresting viewing to anyone scanning the pages of the magazine, are disrupted by a note of doubt as the images and captions start to suggest the reality of some of the exchanges taking place between the young men and their various partners. The prospect of easy friendship and casual interracial sex depicted on the first page of the article is complicated by highlights from the text such as 'Most of the men want to find a woman who will send them money and take them to Europe' or 'Ellen has seen a lot of women fall for Gambian men. "I suppose it's better than Valium," she says.' Turning to the text itself which is tightly wrapped round the extraordinary images and quotes, it becomes clearer why the joy of finding sex in the sun comes with a heavy price attached.

Interestingly the article comes under the heading of 'reportage' which suggests rather a racy style of journalism. It is written by a female journalist who approached her task in a more detached and seemingly impartial manner than her counterpart at the *Sun* in that she has not included any mention of her own experiences. However, her opening paragraph is totally explicit about who are the active partners in this game, despite the brazen headline. Readers are invited to watch the arrival of a planeload of British tourists through the eyes of two young Gambian brothers and then to imagine them 'cruising' the beach 'eyeing the burning white flesh draped over the sunbeds', assessing which are the newcomers by their degree of whiteness and by the eager look in their eyes when they are approached. At the same time it is explained that the young men are 'bumsters' who earn their living by selling sex to middle-aged and elderly female tourists. Though the article mentions the fact that many European women come to the Gambia for sex, the focus is on the ones who are 'caught unawares by the charms of the Gambian men'. In other words, those who fall under the spell of the black magic and who are 'easily seduced by the attentiveness of the young suitors'.

What is strange about this scenario is the discreet absence of any mention of 'race'. Where the populist tabloid wades right in and speculates on the relative charms of black and white men, *Marie Claire* would prefer to deflect the whole topic of 'race' and racism by focusing obsessively on the age difference between the men and women, which is also apparent by looking at their bodies. Indeed, throughout the text the only other references to 'race', apart from the observations on white flesh at the beginning, is the comment that British women are kinder than Swedish women who 'just want to get a black man' and that having a white woman, old or young, gives Gambian men status. The emphasis on the attractiveness of the men also works as a code for their exotic appeal: 'During the day . . . it's common to see women in their fifties and sixties strolling hand in hand with beautiful young men, and on Gambia's long palm-fringed beaches the women go topless and flirt with handsome teenagers'. Or, as one woman is quoted as saying, 'It was very empowering as a woman to be able to have my pick of a bunch of beautiful men'. Is the reader expected to believe that youth confers some special degree of physical beauty on Gambian males, or is it something about their dark skin that makes them appear so attractive to European women? Surely here the reader is being asked to apply her own 'romantic fantasy' about the pleasures and dangers of 'the primitive paradise'[14] in the name of some kind of post-feminist liberation.

This deafening silence on the 'race' angle – except that which is communicated by the pictures – is intensified by the lack of any information about the history of the Gambia. The writer explains that it is 'one of the world's poorest countries' where life expectancy is, on average, forty-four and infant mortality is 135 per 1,000. There is no suggestion that these shocking statistics – which immediately place the obsession with the women's age in a different kind of perspective – might have something to do with the fact that the Gambia was one of Britain's former colonial possessions. The nexus of post-colonialism that connects the two countries today is obscured by framing the young men's desire to go to Europe as a rather devious opportunism, since they are earning their plane tickets by selling their bodies to tourists. The fact that the women can fly between Britain and the Gambia as often as they please is entirely taken for granted. Clearly the editors of *Marie Claire* were too squeamish to speculate on the appeal of cultural difference that entices European women to the shores of West Africa, but I think the framing of the Gambia as a backward country that appears to have no history betrays a more unforgivable ignorance about how to handle the politics of race, class and gender.

There is only one voice in the whole feature that ventures a critical comment on the exchange taking place. A tour organiser who witnesses many relationships between British women and Gambian men observed that:

> it rarely works when the boys go to Europe. The British Embassy here has loads of letters from women in the UK complaining that the boys have stayed in bed all the time, or disappeared – mostly with someone younger. There are horror stories, too, of boys being held prisoner by women who only use them for sex. Some of the boys are only sixteen; they must be ter-rified. It's a statement about our society. We corrupt them, they don't corrupt us.

This comment does not seem to fit with the accounts provided by the men interviewed in the article. Most have a completely mercenary approach, and are forced by economic hardship to find gullible women who will send them money and take them to Europe. Their easiest prey seem to be older women 'facing up to the loss of their youth' or whose husbands have either lost interest in sex or betrayed them for younger women. The vulnerability of these women radiates from the pages, and although most of them claim to enjoy the excitement of rediscovering sex, it is more the attention and companionship that they say they are addicted to. Their readiness to be taken in by promises of love and fidel-ity is made plausible by the loneliness and frustration they experience at home. The final paragraph of the article underscores their despera-tion by quoting a woman who intends to return to marry and help her husband set up a business: '"What have I got to lose?"' she asks, echoing her contemporaries. The piece ends by suggesting that her future husband might well ask himself the same question, thus cementing the image of the woman as having fallen hook, line and sinker for the bait prepared for her.

I find it significant that the *Marie Claire* feature leaves the reader with the same kind of message about white femininity and black masculin-ity as the *Sun*, despite the very different approaches and the different audiences, the former being middle-class, waged and female, and the latter predominantly working-class, both male and female, waged and unwaged. The convergence between the two genres suggests that these racialised and gendered constructions have a powerful appeal that can work across class, and that they are able to create and reassemble communities of desire, antipathy and identification between groups of people who appear to have little in common.

In my discussion of these representations of sex tourism I have focused on racist constructions of white femininity and black masculinity that are haunted by images and themes produced in earlier historical periods. I have argued here and elsewhere that a historical perspective is needed to take these constructions apart and examine how they are expressed in contemporary cultural conflict. In the final part of this piece I want to address the question of how and why feminism should respond to these images and the forms of domination to which they contribute. In her discussion of the race/gender system to which I referred earlier, Jane Flax proposes that: 'How these representations result or enter into social relations and institutions that profoundly *affect* concrete men and women (differently) can be crucial feminist concerns'.[15] Feminists ought to be equiped with special insights into this process since struggles over representation of femininity have been at the heart of the movement for women's emancipation. But without an understanding of the intersection of gender with race these struggles have not challenged the ways that representations of femininity can also articulate racism. Consistent with my focus on constructions of white femininity I want to consider how these might be most effectively challenged by the 'concrete' women who are most affected by them. In other words I am thinking about strategies that might be appropriate for feminists who are identified as 'white', and who decide to interrogate and disavow their whiteness as part of a broader attempt to bring about the abolition of white supremacy. I recognise that this careful wording emphasising choice concerning one's 'racial' identity may appear to side-step the rather obvious material consequences that flow from the lack of choice that most people have in this matter in their everyday lives, but I am anxious to avoid talking about 'white' feminism and 'black' feminism, which makes it sound as if feminist politics are inevitably determined by one's skin colour. Other terms are needed for a politics that seeks to build solidarity among women of different cultural, ethnic and class identities.

There is another problem in the way that racism is often represented as exclusively affecting the people constructed as racially subordinate rather than those who are racially dominant. Expressions such as 'people of colour' can create a misapprehension among people without 'colour' that they exist somehow outside the structures of race and racism. To draw attention to the social construction of whiteness is to struggle against its normativity. Of course this is not to say that whiteness is seen as normal or invisible to those who have not been identified as having the 'open sesame of a pork-colored skin'.[16] Analysing whiteness as a discourse can provide a basis for developing political strategies against white supremacy, although as I have argued it is more useful to analyse it as a gendered category rather than an abstract genderless one.

In order to interrogate the seeming passivity of women in cultural conflict between men and to demonstrate how racism positions social groups in systemic and hierarchical relation to each other – black, white, masculine, feminine – feminists need to show how critical it is for a politics of emancipating women to include active participation in the politics of abolishing racism as well. Since the figure of the white woman has been used historically to legitimate certain forms of racial oppression, it is important to study the relationship between those constructions of white femininity produced in the past and those which appear in the present. Thinking about how 'concrete' women (and men) are affected by representations of white femininity which refer back to the histories of slavery and colonialism opens up a space to start challenging those images.

Notes

Thanks to Paul Gilroy for showing me his copy of the *Sun* and for offering useful insights; and to the MA Cultural Studies students at Thames Valley University for helpful comments on the Gambia phenomenon when I first tried this out as a talk.

1 bell hooks, 'Eating the other', in *Black Looks* (South End Press, Boston 1992) p. 27.

2 Both quotes are from the 'Contacts UK' section of *Loot* (the 'Free Ads paper') 2 September 1993.

3 Mike Phillips 'Ebony–Ivory' in *Elle* (UK) October 1991, pp. 91–2.

4 *The Autobiography of Malcolm X* (Penguin 1964), p. 394.

5 Drucilla Cornell, *Transformations* (Routledge 1993) p. 192.

6 Vron Ware, *Beyond the Pale: White Women, Racism and History* (Verso, London/NY 1992), Chapter 4 'To Make the Facts Known'.

7 Alfreda M. Duster, ed., *Crusade for Justice: The Autobiography of Ida B. Wells* (University of Chicago Press 1970) esp. pp. 70–1.

8 Jane Flax, *Disputed Subjects: Essays on Psychoanalysis, Politics, and History* (Routledge, NY/London 1993) p. 28.

9 Cecillie Swaisland, *Servants and Gentlewomen to the Golden Land* (Berg, Oxford/Providence 1993) pp. 94–5.

10 *Beyond the Pale*, pp. 38–42, 138–9.

11 V. G. Kiernan, *The Lords of Human Kind* (Weidenfeld & Nicolson, London 1969) pp. 47–8.

12 This figure was obtained from the press office at IPC magazines. *Marie Claire* is published in several other languages, such as French and Spanish, and each is edited as a separate magazine.

13 *Marie Claire*, May 1994, pp. 12–18.

14 hooks, 'Eating the other'.

15 Flax, *Disputed Subjects*, p. 28.

16 George Schuyler, *Black No More* (Northeastern University Press, Boston 1989) p. 35.

8 Maria Pini

Women and the early British rave scene

> To me, the scene has totally changed my life. I felt like it was almost a cult – a following sort of thing. The scene was like a whole society – a different society. You were yourself – you had your own identity – but you were also part of the whole group. (Miriam)

> I'm really sorry I found it so late. It's a scene where I just really feel quite at home. This is the first time that I really felt this is what I wanted from clubs. (Helen)

> I would feel totally comfortable going to a rave solo. Unlike discos and many pubs – people may look at you as being there to pick someone up. I would feel very self-conscious going alone to clubs. But, I wouldn't hesitate to go raving on my own. It's fine for a woman to go to a rave, pop anything they want to, skin-up a huge joint and no one bats an eyelid. (Ann)

For well over a decade now, feminists involved in researching youth culture have sought to contest the familiar association of 'youth' with masculinity. This has involved highlighting the extent to which the category of youth is structured (within academia as much as within pop journalism) around a particular (and often romantic) concern with questions of 'deviance' and 'resistance', and a prioritisation of musical production and stylistic 'innovation' (McRobbie, 1991). Despite this feminist attempt to shift focus away from the 'street' and the 'gang', and to move beyond an exclusive concern with questions of cultural *production*, there is still a considerable absence of work on girls' and young women's lived locations within, and experiences of, youth cultural practices. The almost complete lack of academic interest in social dance, for instance, clearly illustrates the extent to which women's activities and experiences are largely 'written out' of youth-cultural histories (McRobbie, 1984; Ward, 1993).

Academic accounts of the early British rave scene tend to be limited either to historical analyses of rave's evolution as the latest youth culture – with little sustained attention given over to the actual location of women within this – or to semiotic readings of the scene in terms of its cultivation of a particular 'style' (Redhead, 1994). With the notable exception of Angela McRobbie's *Shut up and Dance* (1994), none of the existing academic works on this scene, or on clubbing more generally, seriously address the position of girls and women within rave. Whilst some of these accounts point to the differential positions of men and women within rave, they do not attempt to examine where and how women *are* located within it (Redhead, 1994; Thornton, 1994). No work that I know of on rave looks at the type of 'self' encouraged within this, or at the role of 'clubbing' within a wider life-context. Neither do they fully address questions of sexuality and pleasure, or direct adequate attention towards what goes on on the dance-floor – the place where most women are located. In short, they do not address the issues which I suggest are most important to an understanding of women's involvement within this scene. Although this chapter cannot address all of these themes in adequate detail, it represents an attempt to open them up.

As with previous youth cultures, women within rave tend not to be located at the levels of musical production, event organisation, drug distribution and hence profit-making. These are predominantely male sites of experience. Neither do they fit the 'folk devil' image generated by early panic-press reports. And yet, thousands of women *are* involved in the practices of 'rave', and, as the opening statements from interviewees suggest, many women *do* feel centrally invested in the identities this scene seems to afford. But these factors seem to remain largely insignificant within accounts of the scene. In this sense, women's invisibility can be seen as twofold; their marginality doubled by a perspective which attends solely to the more visible – and traditionally more 'meaningful' – levels of involvement and so reconstructs male experience as the 'significant' object of its story. It is of little surprise, given this received framework of concerns, that feminist commentators on rave have tended to lament its apparently retrogressive tendency. Angela McRobbie states,

> Indeed rave seems to overturn many of the expectations and assumptions we might now have about youth subcultures, and for this reason, reminds

us of the dangers of looking for linear development and progression, in let us say, the sexual politics of youth. Girls appear for example to be less involved in the cultural production of rave, from the flyers to the events, to the DJing than their male counterparts. We can in no way be certain therefore that the broader changing climate of sexual politics is reflected in rave. (1994: 168)

Although McRobbie is clearly justified in pointing out the male domination of production within rave, girls' virtual exclusion at this level should not stop us considering their involvement at other levels – an involvement which is often experienced as being 'liberating', and one which, I will argue, can be seen as positive in feminist terms.

Whilst Sarah Thornton (1994) presents an excellent analysis of the relations between the 'underground' ideologies of youth cultures and media constructions of these cultures, her analysis does not consider the actual position of the many women involved in rave, or the complex of meanings this scene can have for them. Thornton quite rightly suggests the extent to which notions of subcultural 'authenticity' are tied to masculinity and, although (as I argue later) women also often make sense of their involvement in rave in terms of a 'mainstream' / subculture divide, this distinction is important inasmuch as it relates to perceptions of sexual relations and not just to male constructions of 'cool'.

In what follows, I will draw upon material collected in a series of in-depth interviews with (mainly) women involved in the early London rave scene. (It is important to point out that this analysis is dealing with the *early* rave scene, and represents just part of ongoing research on femininity and club culture in general.) I am suggesting that women's lack of involvement at the levels of rave production should not blind researchers to the fact that for many women, rave represents an undoing of the traditional cultural asssociations between dancing, drugged, 'dressed-up' woman and sexual invitation, and as such opens up a new space for the exploration of new forms of identity and pleasure. In short, if, as Rumsey and Little (1989) argue, women have traditionally been denied the kinds of 'unsupervised adventures' celebrated within previous youth-cultural scenes, then I am suggesting that rave allows for such adventure. Further, within rave, producing the 'self' out of a relentless drive for the maximisation of pleasure is central. Being 'ecstatic' has in many ways replaced previous youth-cultural 'styles of being': being 'political', being 'angry', being 'hard' and even (certainly at the very beginning of rave in London) being 'fashionable'. Physical and mental enjoyment becomes a central point of involvement. In many ways, open displays of 'happiness', auto-erotic pleasure, 'friendliness' and enjoyment of dance are traditionally more closely associated with femininity, and gay male culture (Dyer, 1990). In this sense, rave can be read as a challenge to heterosexual masculinity's traditional centrality, and for this reason alone is worthy of attention.

Researching rave: identity and textuality

To explore these issues I have embarked upon a kind of 'identity ethnography' (McRobbie, 1992) which involves an exploration of the personal meanings an involvement with the practices of rave has for the women interviewed, and the particular 'subjectivities' encouraged within this scene. In drawing upon personal accounts, I am not claiming to have gained privileged access to the essential 'truth' about rave. Rather I am giving a reading of accounts which are themselves partial, provisional and located readings and reports. My focus is upon how particular understandings and experiences are produced, generated and reinforced within this scene. The notion of 'textuality' is used to suggest that far from being basic to the activities involved, certain emotions and experiences are actually 'bound up' with cultural narratives and organisational practices, which make up the background of, and give meaning to these practices (Curt, 1994). In this sense, 'experience' is lived, negotiated and understood through a variety of 'storying practices' and it is through such processes that identities are produced.

My particular reading, then, aims to elucidate the stories or 'texts' through which women experience rave, and hence through which the rave experience is constituted. To speak of rave as 'textualised', however, need not imply a prioritisation of 'interpretation' or personal accounts (or language broadly) over other more material aspects such as the organisation of machinery, music, visuals, and the role of drugs, money, etc. Rather, rave can be conceived of as a material and discursive assemblage, involving the organisation of time (such as the fact that events go on all night), space (including the lay-out and decoration of venues), and bodies (including dance, drug-taking and so forth). The discursive personal accounts which I deal with in this piece are inseparable from this material ensemble.

This emphasis on 'texts' within rave is partly influenced by the work of Maria Milagres Lopes (1991), who in a study in Puerto Rico uses the concept of a 'text of fear' to illustrate the interrelationship between the discourses of authorities and the press, and the personal fear experiences of the public. Centrally Lopes is concerned with how even the subjective understandings of actually being assaulted are not inherent to the act but prescribed and re-told in context-specific ways. 'Each story', she argues, 'is part of a larger one which reproduces itself in each individual storytelling.' In the same way, personal experiences and accounts of rave can be thought of as 'textualised'.

Hence, in this piece I am using the notion of a 'text of excitement' to get at the production and generation of a sense of 'excitement' by the scene and the reproduction of this excitement within personal accounts of involvement. These accounts, therefore, should not be thought of as simply 'about' an experience which is otherwise separate and discrete, but as partly constitutive of the rave experience itself; as part of the complex web which makes up what it means to 'rave'. Secondly, and having outlined this 'text of excitement', I want to suggest certain central themes (or interconnected threads) which I believe go some way towards accounting for the fact that women seem to enjoy equal location within this 'text of excitement' as their male counterparts. Among these are what I am calling, first, rave's 'text of sameness', and second, rave's intertextuality with 'New Age' discourses and the active production of an ecstatic mind/body/spirit/technology assemblage. Finally, I want to bring this all back to the central question of this work: why is it that women speak of rave as being so sexually progressive, and as providing the space for new forms of subjectivity?

Rave's 'text of excitement'

For those directly involved, and even for many looking on from the sidelines, the early rave scene was surrounded by an air of thrill, illegality and mystery. Aside from the panic generated by the early press around the use of drugs, the occupation of unsafe, abandoned warehouses and the motorway convoys, there were the excited accounts of participants who adopted new 'raver' identities and talked repeatedly about how nothing could ever be as good as dancing on 'E'. Indeed as Miriam (quoted above) suggests, there was a general feeling that what had developed was a kind of 'cult' of devotees prepared to go to great lengths and expense to rave. As Sonia remarks; 'I can't believe how far we would travel. And *then*, you didn't even know for sure whether it would even be on when you got there.' The notion of having somehow gained 'cult' membership was reinforced by a general feeling that ravers could identify fellow-ravers, outside of actual events. Sue says that,

> I was standing at the tube station and looked down the platform at this guy
> wearing head-phones and I just knew he'd been raving – we made eye-to-
> eye and he smiled . . . that was the really good thing about it – feeling part
> of something.

Driving for miles, into the night, only to find that an event had been can-
celled by police did not seem to put people off. On the contrary, this was
all part of the 'buzz'. Elaine says:

> It was like an underground movement and the excitement of finding the
> rave, and the uncertainty was a real buzz . . . meeting other car-loads of
> people all looking for the same rave was really good – it was like an 'us and
> them' situation between the ravers and the police. Getting to the ware-
> house and seeing all the people waiting and popping 'E's, hearing the
> music, was all a real high.

Mary says, 'I drove for miles – but I didn't mind. It was exciting 'cause
you kept imagining what it would be like'. The senses of mystery and
excitement were heightened by the variety of pirate radio stations which
called out to 'children of London' announcing phone numbers, code
names and meeting points from which various 'magical mystery tours'
would begin on their 'Orbital convoys'.

The generation of this panicked excitement was also reinforced by
the actual set-up of events. Dark, badly ventilated and often over-
crowded rooms, dripping with condensation were usual venues. As
interviewees suggest, success of an actual event was often understood
in terms of numbers, where the more the better, and the more crowded
the venue the more intense the experience. Added to this general 'intensity' and taking the crowd even 'higher' were DJs screaming for everyone to 'Go fucking Mental'. Hillegonda Reitveld accurately describes
early 'Acid House' music as having 'a rather schizophrenic feel to it; the
texture of the baseline continually changes and voices and other fragments of stolen sound make a "disembodied" appearance' (1994: 23).
The use of strobes and 'dry ice' can also be seen as serving to create a
general scene of 'disembodiedness', slowing down, and fragmenting the
movements of dancers, giving the whole crowd the appearance of a
complicated mechanical circuit.

Obviously central to the production of 'excitement' was the heavy
use of 'Ecstasy', and the bodily 'rushes' associated with it. All of the
women interviewed here had used the drug at the start of their involvement in rave, but many had stopped using it after about a year. Almost

all of them, however, claimed that taking 'E' at least once was necessary in order to fully experience the pleasures involved in raving. Also, many stated that having experienced 'E' once, they could re-capture the sensations and feelings of this without actually being on the drug – that is, they could feel similarly 'Ecstatic' through simply being in the rave environment or through listening to a particular music track.

This 'text of excitement' is comparable to Lopes's 'text of fear' in that it is not only generated by the authorities and the media, but also actively produced and reinforced by the set-up of events themselves. Further, this larger story can be seen to reproduce itself in individual accounts of the scene. Experiences of 'E' and rave events were churned through what Foucault calls an 'endless mill of discourse', where much of the excitement was actively generated outside of actual events, in the almost obsessive accounts of how good the last event was, or the enthusiastic anticipation of the next one, and the long and unpredictable process of actually getting to this.

This 'text of excitement' can be supplemented with that of a mutually dependent 'text of fear', because in many ways the set-up of events appeared to actively play on and heighten senses of panic and anxiety. This was obvious in a range of practices, from the ways in which 'bouncer outfits' seemed to exaggerate the potential for danger, to the ways in which DJ chants often played on the possibilities of someone having a 'bad trip'. As Mark points out:

> Yeah, it's interesting that the bouncers are always outside the rave; you get a very strong sense of being policed before you go in – which is again strange. It's a counter-cultural tenet – it's gotta be outside the law – but there's obviously a very definite law being set-up.

Elaine indicates the way in which particular fears are actively played on by DJs:

> That was the time when the DJ kept screaming on about going mad and he kept saying 'do you know what you've taken?' . . . I was getting really freaked out and it was nearly impossible to get away from it all. And he just kept shouting down the mike that you were going mad and that.

All of this took place within the context of the dark, crowded space where often people had bought 'pills' from strangers and spent at least some time anticipating the effects. 'Coping' with the obvious anxieties and keeping these at bay became a theme. A statement by Jim illustrates this:

I suppose it's whether you can control it . . . some people can't take it. Some can't . . . um . . . some people's personality can't cope – they can't control the rush. I've been close to it but I've stopped it – it's the paranoia at the back of your head. It always gets to you. Sometimes you do a pill and think 'fucking hell, I wonder if I'll be alright on this one'. You can be scared but at the end of the day, you just got to put it aside and say 'bollocks' to it.

Anxiety and fear, rather than really appearing as obstacles to be overcome, seem central to the particular pleasures involved, providing the opportunity of seeing yourself as 'able to handle it'. Indeed, as the women quoted below indicate, feeling nervous or anxious were all part of the 'thrill':

> Well, when you got in there, there were a lot of blokes going 'E, Acid, coke' and it made you a bit uneasy. It was all very hot, very dark – lights everywhere and loud, pumping, pumping music – lights everywhere and smoke everywhere. (Miriam)

> I always got really bad nerves – excitement nerves – every time before a rave. I nearly made myself sick. (Ann)

> I got such bad butterflies in my stomach every time – just thinking about it – all day before a night out. (Joanne)

Similarly, uses and understandings of technology within the scene also worked towards a heightening of excitement and fear. The body abandoned to machinery was central and clearly suggested by the computerised and mechanical music, which was seen as taking over the body. The early 'Trance Dance' illustrates this ideal of an absolute absorption in music. Fliers also sold events on the power of their machinery. Themes of space exploration and technological progress feature strongly in these. Many outdoor events often included funfairs, and here machinery could take over the heightening of bodily pleasures and intensify these further.

In the sense outlined above, rave can partly be seen in terms of a celebration of excitement and pleasure. I have elucidated these themes in terms of a 'text of excitement' to show how rave can be seen as threaded through with a particular set of narratives which operate as much on the organisation level as they do at the level of personal experience. This is certainly not to suggest that this is the *only* way of experiencing this scene, or that *everybody* would experience a sense of excitement in this same way. On the contrary, pointing to the 'textuality' of rave enables us to see how a particular manner of textual engagement is required for a full 'appreciation' of the scene.

Rave's emphasis on excitement and thrill is common to many youth cultures. My argument, however, is that unlike many previous scenes, women within rave draw upon a 'text of excitement' as much as the boys and young men involved. It is difficult to overstate the extent to which interviewees insist upon rave's 'progressive' sexual politics, and the degree to which they view rave as providing a new space in terms of sexual relations. To offer simply a few examples of responses to the question of how rave was different to other club scenes interviewees had been involved in:

> It was *totally* different to other scenes . . . because . . . well, the only thing that I thought was similar was the fact that there was music. I saw clubs very much pick-up joints where you got men just staring at you, or coming up to chat you up. (Miriam)

> It was strikingly different to other club scenes. There was no alcohol around, so little aggression and little emphasis on chatting people up and the 'cattle-market' element of, say, disco, didn't seem to be around. (Ann)

> Well, they were hugely different . . . It's a completely different scene. They seem very unaggressive – they're friendly in a completely different way from people being friendly when they're completely pissed-up. Um . . . the men – even in kind of 'hard-core' clubs aren't sort of . . . predatory and they're not there to pull. (Helen)

The absence of heterosexual 'pick-up' ('coping off', being 'chatted-up' and so on) is central to many women's accounts of rave's appeal to them. Most mention a general lack of aggression, and many contrast 'E'-type clubs with scenes which involve heavy alcohol use. In many ways, the appeal of rave is bound up with the perceived absence of particular kinds of masculinity, and the dance-floor relations associated with traditional dance clubs.

The erosion of difference and the constitution of particular mind/body/spirit relations

In order to briefly explore the discursive construction of these seemingly different gender relations, and to suggest what seem to be new forms of gendered subjectivity, I want to elucidate the two interwoven themes mentioned above.

Firstly, rave can be seen to be partly organised around a 'text of sameness': a phrase which I am using to get at the assemblage of themes which stress rave's non-oppositionality, its accessibility to everyone and its potential to break down social boundaries. The following interviewee statements clearly illustrate this text:

> Rave attracts all sorts of people: black and white, women and men – from all classes. (Ann)

> Rave tended to bring everyone together. (Helen)

> Everyone was in it together and there was an instant sort of bond. (Miriam)

To reiterate this theme in the words of Primal Scream:

> We are unified because together we have power,
> Gospel, Rhythm and Blues and Jazz – all of those are just labels.
> ('Come Together')

'Unisex' clothes and the whole 'dress-to-sweat' emphasis of the scene are important factors in the perceived erosion of sexual differences. Nearly all of the interviewees mentioned this aspect as central to their understandings of rave as progressive in terms of sexual politics. Although this perceived erosion of social differences is related to the empathetic effects of 'E', many enjoy 'raving' without this. For this reason it becomes implausible to attribute the emergence of this theme solely to the drug – the drug is just one part of the ensemble.

The breaking down of boundaries applies not only to social differences, but is also related to ideas of breaking down individual boundaries, so that the raver can describe losing her sense of 'self' and becoming part of something 'bigger', as Miriam's statement at the start of this piece illustrates. Catherine describes this as an 'ideal state' to be worked towards: 'It's a very strange sensation really – an ideal state is where you're not centred on yourself. You're part of the whole crowd of people – like your identity is a much broader one.' And Jane says:

> You're part of something, and that feeling of being inside something that's bigger than yourself is really lovely . . . and the whole thing was just an organic whole together, and you could fit into that, and be part of this organic whole. So, although you are aware of yourself, you're in something bigger than yourself. And so you can just spread out and – especially when you're on 'E' – your boundaries are just so stretched out, it isn't you any more – it's a whole thing.

Ann articulates this theme in terms of being involved in a 'team': 'I felt like part of a big team and when I felt a little tired after dancing for about five hours, I couldn't stop as I'd feel I was letting the side down'.

Although many of the interviewees accepted that rave has become more fragmented since the late 1980s, all insist that, in the 'early days', race, gender, age, sexuality and other differences played no central role in dividing the scene. One interesting aspect of this 'text of sameness' is the extent to which it can be seen as operating in direct opposition to any 'politics of difference'. Indeed, individual 'identity', as suggested, is seen as being largely eroded within an event. However, when we look to the fact that early rave, unlike say contemporary 'Jungle', was a predominantly white, working-class culture, and at the obvious 'differences' which get glossed-over by the ideal of 'sameness', then it becomes clear that what I have been referring to as this 'text of sameness' *is* as much an 'ideal' or a 'representation' of relations as it is a 'reality'. The rave experience, then, can be viewed as being bound up with a range of self techniques (such as working towards a blissful absorption of the self into the dancing crowd) which encourage a certain manner of textual engagement. Location within this text is not something which comes 'naturally'. Rather, reaching the desired state is, as many song lyrics and DJ chants will tell you, something you have to 'work for'.

A key aspect of this 'governing' or 'managing' of experience is brought out, I would argue, in a theme of 'positivity', which is simultaneously a 'policing' of 'negativity'. This 'ethics of pleasure' is highlighted in a number of interviewee accounts which stress the importance of the right attitude, which includes avoiding the power of 'negative vibes' to 'bring you down' (and which seems, at times, to mean refusing to acknowledge 'difference' or tensions). In many ways Jazzie B's lyric, 'Enrich your positivity – no time for negativity', sums up this aspect of the early scene. As the statements below suggest, this 'positivity' wears thin when confronted with tensions, or resistance:

> No one wanted to hear I was having a bad time. They'd all been really nice up until then. I felt really bad and no one would listen – they all just kept dancing and avoiding me. (Elaine)

Similarly, Peter gives the following account of being sold a 'dud E':

> So I went back down to that person and said 'that drug didn't work'. Suddenly lots of people in the room started looking uncomfortable and shifty. He turned around to look at someone, who looked at someone else,

trying to imply that I didn't fit, or I didn't seem to be part of the scene. And I knew well that the 'E' wasn't working for the others either, but they just didn't want to 'bring down' the atmosphere and so just carried on as if it *had* worked and told me 'it's only money'. They all slipped away, and danced and acted as though it really didn't matter. Not just that – they actually seemed to go out of their way to make me feel bad about caring.

This 'positivity' aspect, along with ideas which stress the power of rave to break down social and individual boundaries, relates to the second theme I mentioned above: rave's intertextuality with certain 'New Age' discourses (I am using the term 'New Age' broadly to refer to what Andrew Ross describes as a set of ideas claiming an 'alternative world-view, distinct from orthodox rationalism', 1992). Specifically, certain understandings of the self within rave resonate with particularly 'New Age' discourses on mind/body relations. I argued that the 'text of same-ness' involves ideas about the erosion of differences, and a construction of the individual body as part of 'something bigger'. These ideas cor-relate with 'New Age' stress on the interrelation of mind/body/spirit. The body in rave is commonly conceived of in terms of a holistic mind/body, and participants stressed the absence of any clear separa-tion and the connectedness between themselves and others. Just as the 'text of sameness' strives to challenge external and interpersonal boundaries between selves, in this configuration, internal and intra-personal boundaries are challenged. Any prioritisation of mind over body, or 'rational thought' over pleasure, is seen as an 'imbalance'. As Catherine states, 'You don't need to *think*. You just *feel*. You have to just get into *feeling* the energy and all the things going on around you.' The stress on 'feeling' rather than 'thinking' is a theme clearly illustrated in an advertisement for the 'Vibrasound Machine' – one of the many attractions at the 1990 'Mind, Body, Spirit' conference held in London. This promises 'relaxation and altered consciousness through the fusion of science with the senses':

> State-of-the-art electronics and frequency transducers transform music in to a total sensory stimulating experience that we call 'sensory resonance'. Sensory resonance helps turn-off the brain's *analytic* component . . . and allows the user to experience consciousness rather than conceptualising it.

This 'holistic' mind/body of rave is also not separate from 'spirit':

> Rave dancing is like putting you in contact with the spiritual world too – it's like meditation. It's not just the physicality of it, or the mental bliss. It's

more than that. When you dance, you feel more whole. Yes, you're far more whole when you're dancing. I'm talking specifically about 'E' dancing in raves. (Miriam)

Rave then, can be seen as a 'body' culture, but this 'body' is no longer separate from mind and spirit. Rather, emphasis is on being 'in touch' with all of these at once. Hence the rave event is seen as breaking down standard mind/body dualisms. 'Thought' and 'rationality' within such configurations are seen as potentially obstructive to the achievement of full pleasure, and indeed any prioritisation of these is seen as signalling a conspicuous imbalance of mind/body relations. In speaking of the pleasures of dance, Miriam contrasts this to reading and writing: 'When you read or write, you don't use your body – you don't move it'. Hence, the body/mind in rave becomes sensitive or 'open' to 'vibes', 'spirituality', non-verbal communication and so on. The outer boundaries of the mind/body are thus extended – or 'stretched' as Jane put it earlier – and made permeable. This body thus becomes a rather more 'cyborgian' one, not separate from its environment, but an integrated part of this circuit (Haraway, 1991). As Miriam puts it: 'You're not separate from the music – the music *is* you. You are part of the music and . . . there's no relationship even 'cause you're one.' As with the Vibrasound machine, technology – in the form of music and 'visuals' – is seen as 'working through' the body. Similarly, non-verbal communication gets characterised almost as a form of 'telepathy' (in fact, the name of an early London club). The following statement by Miriam is typical:

> You didn't have to communicate with anyone verbally – it was very much a non-verbal communication . . . You'd just be dancing and you'd look round and look at someone in the eyes and you knew that that person was experiencing exactly the same as you were experiencing and there was a direct sort of bond with that person.

Talking becomes, in this context, an unnecessary excess and this is illustrated by the standard one-liners which characterise rave conversation (i.e. 'You up?' 'What are you on?' etc.). 'Touch' and particular modes of looking seem to largely replace verbal-conversation. Taking this particular mind/body 'higher', onto a different plane of consciousness, becomes central.

To draw towards a close, I want to mention a final (clearly related) theme: that of the constitution within rave of a particular 'ecstatic' mind/body/spirit/technology assemblage. Foucault points out that:

Technologies of the self . . . permit individuals to effect by their own means or with the help of others a number of operations on their bodies and their souls, thought, conduct and a way of being, so as to transform themselves in order to attain a certain state of happiness, purity, wisdom, perfection or immortality. (1988: 14)

Rather than directing attention towards an individual performer or performance, rave works to direct it towards the individual dancing body. The holistic self of rave becomes the primary target to be 'worked', 'pleasured', 'drugged', 'taken higher' and, in Foucauldian terms, otherwise 'produced'. Having stamina, the 'right attitude', and being 'positive' are simultaneously sought-after states and the techniques through which a particular mind/body/spirit/technology assemblage is produced.

Hillegonda Reitveld (1994) speaks of the 'undoing' within rave of the constructed 'self'. I would suggest that once undone, the 'self' within rave is then reconstructed in terms of a particular mind/body/spirit/ technology assemblage. The 'self' is no longer a neatly 'bounded', individual self. Rather, involvement and pleasure are experienced in terms of connections between self and others, and between mind, body and machine. Individuality or 'self-consciousness' are seen as actually getting in the way of full enjoyment, and as suggested above, a certain 'positivity' seems to operate to maintain the notions of 'sameness' and unity which prop up this understanding of self.

A significant feature of rave, then, is its provision of resources which can be used to produce a seemingly different state of 'selfhood'. One important implication of the stress on producing and maintaining the collective self described above is the extent to which this signals a shift away from sexual pick-up. Indeed, rave pleasures seem to be largely about 'incorporation' and the erosion of individual differences, so that the raver speaks of herself as part of something 'bigger'. Arguably, what has also been eroded in the processes of 'melting into' the whole, is the space, or position, for the objectification of the 'other'. Related to this is the apparent development of a new 'gaze': modes of looking which seem not to be based on objectification and separation, but rather on incorporation and unity. In this sense, the rave dance-floor breaks down the divide between audience and performer and provides the possibility of being both simultaneously. These particular 'scopophilic' pleasures and the pleasures of being watched were stressed by interviewees.

You could look at everyone, and everyone – especially my friends – looked gorgeous. Women and men – they just looked so engrossed in their bodies and so into the music and almost unaware of anyone else – until they looked up and caught your eye, and it was amazing – like a peak. (Catherine)

Yeah, and it's a 'showy-offy' thing as well and probably um . . . sort of . . . I don't know. I say 'showy-off' because 'E'-type clubs are so much more *about* dancing. You watch other people dance and they watch you. (Helen)

The pleasures of looking seem to largely cut across gender differences. Indeed, it seems to be precisely because these forms of looking are not seen as being tied to sexual objectification, and hence pick-up, that they are so enjoyed.

Women and rave: some conclusions

In this piece, I have tried moving away from the more traditional foci of youth-cultural studies and attempted to direct attention towards issues of subjectivity and experience. Taking women's own personal accounts as my starting points, my aim was to illustrate the kind of 'selves' encouraged within rave, and to outline the practices and 'texts' which can be seen to make for an understanding of rave as sexually pro-gressive. In general, I would argue that rave's appeal to women is tied with its opening up of new modes of 'looking', its set-up of particular interpersonal relations and its encouragement of new understandings of 'self'. Women within this context feel freed from traditional associa-tions of dancing with sexual invite, and in this sense rave seems to repre-sent an 'alternative' space.

To return to Sarah Thornton's work, many of the women interviewed did indeed make sense of their involvement in rave in terms of an opposition between rave and more 'traditional' or 'mainstream' club-scenes. But there is more to this than simply the construction of self as 'cool' and of the scene as 'underground'. Rather, many of these women articulate their involvement within rave, and the pleasures it is seen to afford, in terms of an implicitly feminist dissatisfaction with traditional sexual relations and particular forms of masculinity. For instance, Jane speaks of other social-dance scenes as 'pick-up cities', and describes the kind of feelings she associates with these;

There was always a feeling that you could fail – if you didn't get picked-up, and also, if you didn't get picked-up by the right person – then what was the point? There was always the idea, when you got approached of 'oh God, are they going to demand something from me that I'm not going to give – meaning a snog, or a fuck, or a date, or a phone-number or whatever.

The rave dance-floor, I would argue, is one of the few spaces which afford – and indeed, encourage – open displays of physical pleasure and affection. Explicit displays of 'ecstatic' happiness, and the relentless drive to achieve this, have never been so central to a youth culture's meaning. Arguably rave represents the emergence of a particular form of 'jouissance', one which is more centred on the achievement of physical and mental transformation and one which is possibly best understood as a non-phallic form of pleasure. Many of the interviewees *did* speak of rave pleasures as being 'sexual', but many had difficulty in clearly 'languaging' what this 'sexual' was. I would suggest that this is because these pleasures do not clearly 'fit' standard, patriarchal definitions of sexuality, and eroticism. To illustrate this difficulty:

I kind of see it as a place where I can feel sexually about other people, but it doesn't actually go anywhere . . . It doesn't *have* to go anywhere 'cause that's it really. (Catherine)

It's not sexual, but orgasmic . . . I wouldn't say it was sexual. It's different from being sexual. It's orgasmic in the sense of being very intense and reaching a peak. (Miriam)

Well it's sexual kind of . . . no, it's *not* sexual – it's different. (Helen)

When I go raving . . . it's very . . . um . . . well, one word that really comes to mind is auto-erotic . . . because you're getting off on yourself. And you can dance quite sexily and you can enjoy it . . . and you can get really into being a sexual being. It can be sexual, but it's a kind of self-contained sexual, so that auto-erotic spreads out – out of the erotic – and into a whole personality thing. (Jane)

Also Jane points out that although she might normally feel 'guilt' around certain forms of self-pleasure (and here, she mentions masturbation), auto-eroticism within rave is normalised:

But, somehow it's sanctioned more in a club – 'cause if you look round you think other people are doing it too so, it's OK. It's normalised because like, *everyone* is doing it and you can always see somebody out there with less clothes on than you and dancing *way* more sexy than you – and all you think is 'wow, they look like they're having a good time' – and it actually helps you to as well.

Hence, what seems to emerge within rave is a space for new modes of femininity and physical pleasures. In terms of how this space fits within a wider life-context, many interviewees described the rave scene as providing a space for the expression of 'other sides' of themselves. As Jane puts it;

> It's about letting go of being conformist, and being professional and proper and . . . 'together'. It's 'other' to presenting that face of you. It's not necessarily the dark side of you – but it's the messy side of you . . . It's about something you do which isn't about working. It's about the time you spend doing things which are about freedom.

To close then, despite women's relative absence at the levels of rave production and organisation, at other levels rave can be seen as indicating an important shift in sexual relations, and indeed might suggest (with its emphasis on dance, physicality, affection and unity) a general 'feminisation' of 'youth'.

References

Curt, B. (1994) *Textuality and Tectonics*, Open University Press, Buckinghamshire.

Dyer, R. (1990) 'In defence of disco', in S. Frith and A. Goodwin (eds) *On Record*, Pantheon, London.

Foucault, M. (1988) 'Technologies of the self' in L. H. Martin, H. Gutman and P. H. Hutton (eds) *Technologies of the Self*, Tavistock Publications, London.

Haraway, D. (1991) *Simians, Cyborgs and Women*, Free Association Books, London.

Lopes, M. M. (1991) 'Text of fear in Puerto Rico', Discourse Analysis Conference, Manchester University.

McRobbie, A. (1984) 'Dance and social fantasy', in A. McRobbie and M. Nava (eds) *Gender and Generation*, Macmillan, London.

McRobbie, A. (1991) 'Girls and subcultures', in A. McRobbie, *Feminism and Youth Culture*, Macmillan, Basingstoke and London.

McRobbie, A. (1992) 'Post-Marxism and cultural studies', in L. Grossberg, C. Nelson and P. Treichler (eds) *Cultural Studies*, Routledge, London.

McRobbie, A. (1994) 'Shut up and dance', in A. McRobbie, *Postmodernism and Popular Culture*, Routledge, London.

Redhead, S. (ed.) (1994) *Rave Off*, Manchester University Press.

Reitveld, H. (1994) 'Living the dream', in S. Redhead, *Rave Off*, Manchester University Press.

Ross, A. (1992) 'New Age technoculture', in L. Grossberg, C. Nelson and P. Treichler (eds) *Cultural Studies*, Routledge, London.

Rumsey, G. and Little, H. (1989) 'Women and pop: a series of lost encounters', in A. McRobbie (ed.) *Zoot Suits and Second Hand Dresses*, Macmillan, Basingstoke and London.

Thornton, S. (1994) 'Moral panic: the media and British rave culture', in T. Rose and A. Ross (eds) *Microphone Fiends*, Routledge, New York.

Ward, A. (1993) 'Dancing in the dark', in H. Thomas (ed.) *Dance, Gender and Culture*, Macmillan, Basingstoke and London.

Designs on masculinity: menswear retailing and the role of retail design

Menswear represented one of the more dynamic retailing markets in the mid to late 1980s. A central part of this dynamism stemmed from the innovations in garment design which transformed the 'look' of menswear across the three key blocks of the market in this period (the designer, middle and mass markets). There were some consistent themes in these innovations. From the circuits of the designer shows, two dominant versions of menswear emerged. On the one hand, menswear was constructed around body-conscious styles which drew on the stylistic ensembles of 'street style' and its appropriation of elements of sportswear and workwear. These designs, exemplified in the collections of the French designer Jean Paul Gaultier, valorised 'tough' outerwear (like the MA-1 flight jacket) and figure-hugging lines, and emphasised a new muscular masculine frame. On the other hand, there was a reinvention of classic menswear, especially in suit design. These harked back to the broad-shouldered jackets and looser trousers of 1940s and 1950s suit design. Giorgio Armani's designs were influential in this regard, offering wide but not aggressive profiles in a characteristically 'loose' cut. Both versions of menswear at this end of the market – as both Gaultier and Armani testify – gave a prominence to the name-label, often worn (in the case of Gaultier's sportswear-inspired tops) as a visible design feature of the garment.

These developments in high fashion or designer menswear were paralleled in the middle and mass markets. Next, the middle-market multiple, in both its choice of cuts and fabrics, consolidated a version of classic menswear, particularly around the suit and in its outerwear and casualwear. The Burton Group and Marks and Spencer, the most important mass-market retailers of menswear, offered ranges which drew on similar design innovations for a mass market. The sportswear influence on menswear – from hooded tops, track-suit bottoms, the strength of name-label sportswear and footwear – was particularly influential on the garment ranges sold by the Burton Group's Top Man, while Marks and Spencer produced new ranges of suits in a less waisted, more contemporary cut using new fabrics and colours.

The innovations in garment design, certainly at the high fashion end of the market, owed much to a renewed interest in menswear from designers. What figured strongly in this was an excitement about the possibilities of menswear; the fact that there were, in the words of the designer John Richmond, more barriers to be broken down.[1] Allied to this new enthusiasm was a perception, much cited by both menswear designers and retailers across the menswear market, that significant shifts were taking place in the culture of young men. What this was producing as far as trade insiders were concerned was new groups of style-conscious men prepared to commit time and money to clothing without the fear of being labelled outlandish, effeminate or gay.[2]

The intersection of both these factors within the industry set the terms for the production of some new masculine identities through the design codes of menswear. Thus, within the designer market, for example, Armani carved out an understated, self-confidently masculine image through his garment designs: a masculinity that was, in the words of Dejan Sudjic, 'discreetly modern, discreetly affluent'.[3] Within the same market, Paul Smith, on the other hand, represented a highly contemporary version of English masculinity, reworking classic English menswear through quirky details and references to the immaculate neatness of mod style. In the middle market Next represented a new white-collar masculinity at work and leisure, explicitly coding a range of identities for its get-ahead man as he moved from the world of work to the domains of leisure: 'Tycoon', 'Portrait of a Gentleman' and 'Long Island Weekend' were some of the 'looks' produced in 1989, for example.[4]

How we might want to read the cultural significance of these versions of masculinity thrown up by the new designs in menswear is an important issue. It is not, however, my focus here.[5] Rather, I want to reflect upon a set of practices of design and presentation which helped to forge these masculinities in the first place. Underlying this emphasis is the assertion that the meaning of particular menswear garment designs – including, centrally, the codes of masculinity associated with them – were dependent on a wider set of practices of representation associated with their circulation. Thus, from catwalk shows and catalogues to the marketing of the name-label, press and television advertising, fashion photography and the retail outlet, the circulation of menswear tied the meanings of particular garment designs into a wider set of meanings. In this chapter I want to centre-stage one of these sites of circulation: shops or retail outlets. My central concern in what follows is to detail the ways in which the coding of shop space brought to bear specific cultural values and meanings on the garment designs. Underpinning this coding of shop space were the practices of retail design and the expertise of retail designers. Focusing on the work of these practitioners offers us a way into how shops functioned as sites of representation, resignifying the meaning of garment designs and organising the coding of masculinities at the point of sale. Who, then, were retail designers and what was retail design?

Retail design and retailing strategy

Retail designers were one of the ascendent professional identities of the 1980s. As specialist design businesses like Fitch-RS (formerly Fitch and Co.), Michael Peters Group, David Davies Associates, Allied International Design, Peter Saville Associates, Pentagram and Din Associates grew through the decade, retail design contributed strongly to the public profile and success of many of these companies.[6] Retail design itself was a recognised specialism within the industry and involved the production of detailed drawings of the way shops would be fitted out and the space of the built environment organised. The rise in professional status of specialist retail designers stemmed from a number of developments. Gardner and Sheppard identify the progressive centralisation and more systematic organisation of shop display and shop design by High Street multiples (such as Marks and Spencer) from the late 1950s and into the 1960s as a key development (Gardner and Sheppard, 1989: 79). They suggest that this set the terms on which multiple retailers began to buy in retail design services and in turn provided a market for specialist retail designers through the 1970s and into the 1980s. More importantly, as we will see shortly, the ascendency of retail designers was rooted in the decision of retailing strategists to privilege retail design as the single most important selling technique within retailing. It was this decision which gave retail designers a new higher public profile in the 1980s.

The development of a distinctive set of retail design practices in the 1950s and 1960s was an important legacy shaping retail design in the

1980s. Gardner and Sheppard, correctly I think, pick out Terence Conran's design for Habitat as a significant turning point in the development of a deliberately *design-led* approach to selling in which retail design figured strongly. It is worth briefly identifying the elements of Habitat's approach which have informed more recent practice. Conran started up Habitat with a shop in the Fulham Road, London in 1964. Two prime motivations shaped its launch. On a very practical level Conran – essentially a furniture designer – had been frustrated by the way retailers were selling his designs.[7] Habitat, in this sense, was an attempt by Conran to present his designs more effectively at the point of sale. In addition, Habitat was driven by Conran's mission to bring 'good design' to a discerning public and to educate consumers in the appreciation of 'good design'.[8] Both these elements fused in Habitat's approach to design-led selling. Conran brought together a set of domestic objects – furniture, furnishings and homewares – in a strongly coordinated range of materials and colours; lots of natural finishes, timber, earthenware, rush matting, basketware, wool and cotton, as Gardner and Sheppard note (1989: 78). Importantly these domestic objects were displayed in a warehouse-like shop and arranged either as piled up 'stock' or set out in room displays. The room displays were particularly innovative as an approach to selling. Gardner and Sheppard quote a long-standing associate of Conran's, Oliver Gregory, who signalled the break marked by this mode of display. Gregory suggested, 'twenty years ago furniture wasn't displayed, there were no surprises – all you saw was a sea of cubes three feet high' (1989: 78).

The setting out of room displays made very visible the coordinated nature of Habitat's range. Here were the clean, simple lines of 'modernist' design combined with the reclaimed rusticity of Conran's beloved Provence. Conran was, in addition, very clear that this product range was aimed at a specific set of consumers; as he put it: '(I) don't try to satisfy every taste' (1989: 77). Gardner and Sheppard suggest that Habitat was principally aimed at 'consumers in the 20–30 years old age group, who were relatively affluent, probably professional or white collar, and living away from their parents or recently married' (1989: 79).

For my account these are the seminal elements of Habitat's innovation: the coordination of products through the design and display techniques used at the point of sale and addressed to a specific group of consumers. Conran's skill, in fact, was to more rigorously put into practice concepts (if not the design vocabularies) which had been emerging in fashion retailing from the mid-1950s and into the 1960s, most prominently through the development of boutiques. Mary Quant had opened Bazaar in 1955, while in Carnaby Street John Stephen established His Clothes in 1959. Stephen's boutique concept for His Clothes reworked the 'look' of the shop in order to speak to particular consumers, conceived very loosely within the rubric of *fashionableness*. Nik Cohn, reflecting on his sojourns through Carnaby Street in the 1960s, caught the new exuberance of fashion retailing (and specifically menswear retailing) that His Clothes embodied: '(He) made his shops like amusement arcades. He had records blaring as loud as they could go, kaleidoscope window displays, garments hung around the open doorways and spilling out across the pavements . . . Inside there was more infinite brightness and newness and glamour' (Cohn, 1971: 66).

Granny Takes a Trip in the Portebello road and Barbara Hulanicki's Biba similarly emphasised the profusion and excitement of clothes and accessories through retail design and display techniques. These boutiques drew upon more than one set of cultural references and targeted quite different consumers. The relatively cheap range of products and the dark colours and intoxicating exotic atmosphere of the shop space for which Biba was celebrated, for example, was very different from the interior 'look' of Granny Takes a Trip and the product range which it offered. All of the boutiques – from Bazaar through His Clothes to Biba – looked different from the clean lines and spaciousness of Habitat's interiors. Nonetheless, all of them created retail spaces for loosely defined consumer constituencies in which the interior 'look' of the shop was central.

By the mid-1970s the experimentations of small, metropolitan fashion boutiques and Conran's more systematised approach through Habitat were registering in wider design discourse. James Pilditch, writing in *Retail and Distribution Management* in January 1974, attempted to synthesise the lessons of these experiments in retail design into an approach applicable to a wider range of retailers. For Pilditch retail design was the central solution to the 'problem' of retailing. That is, it was a way to 'improve sales and profitability' (1974: 26). Two linked themes – echoing some of Conran's ambitions – concerned Pilditch. Firstly, he suggested retail design could play the role of 'helping define and create a personality for a retail outlet'. In a nice phrase Pilditch saw this as involving the need to 'find a corner of the (public's) imagination', (1974: 27). Retailers, then, and especially multiple retailers, could differentiate themselves from competitors not only through 'price cum quality', but through establishing an 'emotional' response from the consumer through the shop design in the form of graphics, display techniques and lighting. Secondly, Pilditch argued that 'the more fundamental work design can do for retailing is to help it to be first into the changing consumer-dominated world. We can forecast that shopping will become more specialised – not by product but by type of consumer' (1974: 28). Retail design, then, functioned to represent the shop's 'identity' and to address that 'identity' to a specific market of consumers. Pilditch's comments were specifically addressed to mass-market retailers. In his polemical assertion of the pivotal role retail design should play in solving the 'problem' of retailing, Pilditch identified Burtons as a mainstream retailer which was receptive to this design-led approach to selling.

The Burton Group's long-term designers, Fitch-RS, were assertive advocates of retail design as a powerful marketing tool. Rodney Fitch, founder, chairman and joint managing director, started his career, like a number of other high profile designers of the 1980s, with Conran Design, before establishing Fitch and Co. in 1974. The company grew rapidly over a ten-year period, servicing a range of clients: The Midland Bank, Heathrow Airport, Asda, Esprit du Vin, for example. Fitch, together with Fitch-RS's director of information, James Woudhuysen, were articulate in putting forward in a range of forums an elaborated rendering of design strategy in retailing. They argued that design was fundamentally a 'strategic business resource' which could be used by retailers in four principal ways. Firstly, to differentiate; secondly, to focus or segment operations; thirdly, to reposition stores; and fourthly, to represent stores as brands, fixing their image (Fitch and Woudhuysen, 1988: 19). They cited the work Fitch and Co. undertook for Midland Bank as an example of differentiation. Here the bank used a major overhaul of its interior design to set itself apart from other banks and building societies following changes in the regulation of financial services. The redesign emphasised the bank as a more customer-friendly retail outlet against the austere traditions of bank design. Fitch's work for Debenhams, on the other hand, aimed to reposition the store through the redesign of the shop interior. Starting with the flagship store in Oxford Street, London, the redesign aimed to shift '[Debenham's] dull and worthy image' (Gardner, 1987), and counter falling sales and an ageing customer profile. The design represented a 1980s rehash of the department store in its heyday; shopping defined as overblown spectacle, playing off all the right cues about luxury, glamour and status.

What is of most interest to this account, however, are Fitch and Woudhuysen's comments on the practice of focusing or segmenting through design. They were very direct about design's role. As they put it, 'Design is a key weapon with which to implement the basic strategy of market segmentation' (1987: 19). To produce the desired segmentation, Fitch and Woudhuysen emphasised the dialogical ambitions of retail design:

> Design is about capturing the consumer's imagination . . . Designing is about needs and desires, about social circumstances; it is about touching people in their hearts as well as their pockets . . . We should be concerned with what people want rather than with what we can sell them. A good designer, therefore, will conduct a continuous . . . enquiry into the consumer's visual, tactile and spatial consciousness. (1987: 15)

It is this concern with the cultural values at work within the realms of the 'visual, tactile and spatial', which Fitch and Woudhuysen signal in this quote, that gives retail designers a set of coordinates through which to segment consumers. Choice of colours, materials and techniques of display and lighting, then, are the vehicles for the coding of specific cultural values and the forging of a mode of address to particular groups of consumers. In this sense, Fitch and Woudhuysen explicitly understand retail design as working through the organisation and incitement of identity. This design practice amounts to the construction of shops as sites of representation in a very deliberate way.

Fitch and Woudhuysen were not alone in this advocacy of the role retail design could play in retail segmentation in the 1980s. One design company was particularly successful in using these formulations of design strategy and retail segmentation in its work with retailing clients. This was the design company DDA. DDA was formed in 1982 by David Davies, a highly ambitious graduate of Kingston Polytechnic's 3-D design course. Davies moved rapidly between jobs in the late 1970s and early 1980s (including a spell at Conran Design) before deciding, at the age of twenty-six and with no premises or clients to his name, to form DDA. Davies's decision was indicative of the business culture of the UK design industry in the early 1980s. In setting up on his own and initially working from home, then renting a small studio, hiring one or two designers to work for him when work came in, and quickly finding a partner to consolidate the company, Davies was representative of a mode of operating and commercial organisation typical amongst the small businesses which dominated – and continue to dominate – the UK design industry. The ambitious Davies, however, timed his move into self-employment well. By 1986, DDA had grown rapidly, expanding to fifty staff. This rose to 130 staff in 1988, making DDA one of the largest design companies in London at the time.[9] The meteoric growth of DDA was underpinned not only by the quality of its design work, but also by the marked increase in the demand for design services during this period – in particular the increasingly rapid turnover in the life-cycle of shop interiors. It was the business generated by one client in particular which was central to DDA's growth. The client was Next. The relationship between the two companies was integral to each of their fortunes and, although it was Conran Design which produced the first retail interior format for Next, it was DDA which was responsible for producing the trademark Next retail design and for developing the programme of shop design and development between 1983–86. I want to reflect on the retail design produced by DDA for Next as a way into considering the specific cultural values mobilised by retail designers in the selling of menswear.

Design vocabularies and menswear

Next was formed as a line of womenswear shops in 1982 following the acquisition of Kendalls by the men's tailors Hepworths in May 1981. Central to the expansion of Next into menswear – which came with the launch of Next for Men in August 1984 – was the application of the concept of 'affordable collectables' first deployed in the development of the original womenswear concept (Davies, 1989: 64). This approach to menswear put a premium on a relatively restricted range of clothes, while organising these into loose collections. The marketing ethos here was about presenting a fairly tightly integrated 'lifestyle' package. These 'collections' were quite explicitly pitched between established menswear chains and upmarket menswear. George Davies, Next chairman and chief executive until the end of 1988, and architect of the Next strategy, put this approach as follows:

> I'd looked at a variety of menswear chains – Dunns, Fentons, Colliers, as well as Hepworths – and I'd seen that everyone was turning out the same drab and uninspiring merchandise. The clothes were very traditional and without any of the stylishness the Italians, say, were producing. In London there were one or two expensive shops like Paul Smith and Woodhouse where stylish garments were being sold. But elsewhere, there was nothing

other than Top Man, which catered only for the young, and besides wasn't
an upmarket operation. (Davies, 1989: 74)

For Davies, then, these were upmarket clothes at affordable prices. In his
account of the Next story, he emphasises – and it is theme reiterated
throughout his account – that considerable effort was made to provide
a 'look' that was 'fashionable and stylish, and the prices accessible'
(1989: 59).

Absolutely pivotal to both the intial formulation and the expansion
of the business was the construction and careful regulation of Next's
'image'. Davies outlined the basis of this concern as follows:

> One of the things that has struck me was the lack of image among the
> retailers I'd visited. I would visit ten stores in an afternoon, and when I'd
> finished I'd have real trouble distinguishing one from another in my
> memory – all of them were quite lacking in any identity . . . Image was
> uppermost in my mind at the outset, and I knew that image must start with
> the shop fitments. (1989: 49–50)

In setting in motion the process of producing what was to become a
highly influential shop design, Davies drew inspiration from the early
Benetton stores in London. He was impressed by the way Benetton
broke with established conventions of display: 'Unlike everyone else,
they weren't using window dummies to display the merchandise – they
simply draped it over black plastic fittings' (1989: 48). Next followed
this innovation as part of its approach to the retail interior: an approach
that aimed to be, in Davies's favourite phrase, 'upmarket from the shop
fittings to the sales girls, who were dressed in Next merchandise and
looked wonderful' (1989: 64). The designs produced by DDA were very
distinctive. Central to the design of the Next menswear interiors
(including the point of sale materials and packaging) was the use of
space and materials. The frontage of the stores gave the first indication
of this: a large window set in a dark matt grey frame beneath the trademark signage, Next, in lowercase lettering. The window displays,
framed by this frontage, were similarly uncluttered. A combination of
garments were displayed on abstract mannequins, backed, often, by
large display or show cards that gave written accounts of the merchandise range. The display cards, featuring details of the clothes being
worn as well as the accompanying copy, played off the themes of space,
colour and line in the shop through their layout and lettering. Inside,
the lighting, colouring and organisation of space were distinctive. Here

Figure 3 Next for Men window display and frontage, Princes Street, Edinburgh, 1989 (Photo: Sean Nixon)

were the features that formed a coherent design vocabulary: bleached wooden pigeon holes and dresser units; downlighting spotlights; gently spiralled staircases with matt black bannisters. The 'edited' collection of clothes was displayed in a range of ways. Around the sides of the shop slatted wooden units displayed a few folded jumpers next to hangers with three jackets: socks were folded in pigeon holes or individual shoes perched on bleached wood units. A dresser unit commanded the central space of the shop, standing upon a classic woven carpet. Such features acted as centripetal counterpoints to the displays of clothes that were set against the walls and encouraged customers to circulate around the shop. The design of the shop interiors, then, combined a number of distinctive stylistic borrowings to produce a shop space in which the assertively modern idioms of cruise-line aesthetics sat alongside the warmer English colourings of dark wood and brass detailing.

The connotations of 'upmarketness' and exclusivity that DDA's formats established were rooted, in part, in the quality of the materials used. The polished woods and solid metal chosen were materials conventionally ruled out of court in middle and mass-market retailing following the developments in synthetic materials (such as moulded plastics) in the 1960s and 1970s. The choice of these fine quality materials for the shop fittings drew upon an influential vocabulary which had emerged within design practice in the late 1970s; Mark Landini, then of Fitch-RS, and Rasheid Din of Din Associates, whom I spoke to in 1989, both identified the consolidation of minimalism in architecture and product design as formative to this design practice. Landini spoke of the importance of the German electrical goods manufacturer Braun, and their early 1970s designs in matt black and chrome, in establishing certain precepts in the 'look' of design materials for a generation of young designers finding their professional feet in the 1980s. More significantly both men – talking about the importance to their work of materials like granite, polished wood, distressed metals and very subdued colours – identified the design emerging from Japan in the early 1980s as seminal.

Rei Kawabuko and the Comme des Garçons design loomed large here. The interior design of the Comme des Garçons shops was dramatic in its austerity and 'stillness'. Typically, the shops were harshly lit with a minimum of clothes displayed on units stripped of detailing or sculpting. Kawabuko saw this as part of a 'new understanding that the shop as much as the clothes should carry the designers' message'

(Sudjic, 1990: 111). Rasheid Din underlined the importance of these elements:

> It was the Japanese influence . . . that was the main visual image of the early 80s and that was obviously to do with the minimalism, with the lack of references to any particular period or style or colour and that had very much to do with the strength of designers like Comme des Garçons . . . and about a kind of translation of interiors from Japan to this country. That's where everyone was looking for inspiration. It was incredibly shocking when that came out. (Din, 1989)

Din deployed elements of this design vocabulary in his own work for Next, as the store evolved the 'look' of its outlets in the late 1980s. Din had initially been approached by David Davies to contribute to the design of a small Next hairdressing salon in March 1986. When Next ended the relationship with DDA later in 1986, George Davies contacted Din and asked him to become more centrally involved in developing a range of new projects. The most important of these was the design of Department X, a flagship store in Oxford Street, London, aimed at a slightly younger group of consumer than the core of Next's business. It was in the design of Department X that Din put into practice a harder-edged design in the fitting out of the Next retail interiors. The central concept of Department X was to construct it along the lines of a mechanised warehouse in which the storage and retrieval systems for goods were made into a central design feature of the shop. The materials chosen underscored the mechanised structure of the store. Industrial-looking sheets of pressed metal, chain-link fencing and a bare concrete-coloured finish to the walls, together with the use of glass-topped, pale wood counters, produced a striking shop interior.

The Japanese influence was not the only one informing the turn to minimalism in the vocabularies of retail design. A less austere, but equally influential, minimalism was developed by the Czech-born architect Eva Jiricna. Her work also shaped the parameters of retail design vocabulary in 'high fashion' outlets in the early 1980s. Jiricna's design came to prominence through her close collaboration with Joseph Ettegunie for his Joseph shops. The shops featured an identifiable set of carefully controlled colours and materials: pale plaster walls, light marble or stone floors, lots of glass cabinets, matt metal fittings and spotlight brackets, and large windowed frontage.

The minimalism of Kawabuko and Jiricna was supplemented by a further design vocabulary which informed the design of menswear retail interiors in the mid to late 1980s. This vocabulary was drawn from the fittings and fixtures used in traditional gentlemen's outfitters. One retailer was particularly important in 'rediscovering' this design vocabulary at the beginning of the 1980s and in establishing its importance: this was Paul Smith. Smith celebrated a nostalgic image of the shopkeeper in his whole retailing ethos and in the design of his retail outlets. As he put it, 'I prefer the individuality and oddness of corner shops or food shops, or shops where old and modern utilitarian items are sold together . . . I enjoy seeing how people sell things, whether it's pots or pans in Greece or fruit and vegetables in Marrakesh' (Blackwell and Burney, 1990: 99). This enthusiasm for the detail of selling was applied to the collection of objects which embellished the Paul Smith shops: 'old cameras, glass soda siphons; plastic radios, old stamp albums . . . train sets', and toy robots (*Arena*, No. 33, 1992: 154). These curios added to the mahogany fittings salvaged initially from old chemists and perfumiers, which formed the shell of the shops, together with the polished wood and glass cabinets, and the woven rugs which covered the shop floor. All these elements evoked the feel of an English gentlemen's outfitters in the interwar years, mixed with references to more recent (1950s) childhoods.

World Service Limited, the designer menswear shop established in Covent Garden, London in 1986, was another menswear store which made much of the same 'retro' menswear outfitters elements in its retail design. In its small oddly shaped interior, wooden pigeon holes and glass fronted cabinets figured prominently together with props such as leather bound suitcases and classic cigarette cases. These design elements were mobilised to capture what its owners and designers O'Reilly and Prendergast saw as 'the spirit of the well-travelled man' (*Arena*, No. 8, 1988: 133).

The influence of minimalism and of references to gentlemen's outfitters was not restricted, however, to the retail design of the designer and middle-market menswear retailers. It also crossed over into the mass market, most clearly in the retail design of the Burton Group's Top Man. The Burton Group's interest in retail design grew from their attempts through the 1970s to refocus their business through the segmentation of their retail operations. The launch of Top Shop, the womenswear stores aimed at 16–25 year olds, in 1970 marked the beginning of this process. By 1980 this segmentation of their portfolio was quite well established. The 1980 Annual Report, however, was undemonstrative on the subject: 'The Burton Group consists of a number of retailing chains and each with a distinctive face to the public'. (*Burton Group Annual Report*, 1980: 1).

By 1985, the language of segmentation was altogether more confident. Gone was the reference to 'the public' and its implied sense of a limited differentiation within a mass market. Speaking of its menswear concerns, the report suggested:

> the market is fragmenting strongly. Within mainstream purchasers of menswear . . . three principal classes of customer have been identified. This type of market stratification, not by socio-economic class alone, but by consumer preferences and lifestyles, is fundamental to the Group's approach to the marketplace. (*Burton Annual Report*, 1985: 7)

The 1987 Annual Report went further still in justifying the process of segmentation:

> The British shopper, wishing to express individuality and a sense of style, continues to demand a wider and increasingly specialised range of products and services. The Burton Group has built its success on meeting the specialised needs of the largest and most profitable sectors by developing a widespread but integrated portfolio of national and small space retail chains . . . Everyone knows the standard age, sex and socio-economic categories (can) be used to segment markets. But things aren't that easy. Rather than squeeze people into boxes that don't fit, we have thrown away the boxes and now use more creative and flexible ways of grouping customers. We look at their attitudes to living, how they want to live and express themselves. What their aspirations are . . . What sort of shopping experience are they seeking . . . For each group we develop a shopping experience that meets their requirements. (*Burton Group Annual Report*, 1987: 1 and 10)

In segmenting their portfolio – which consisted of Burton Retail, Alias, Top Man, Radius, Champion Sport, Principles for Men, Principles for Women, Dorothy Perkins, Secrets, Top Shop, Evans, Harvey Nichols and Debenhams by 1987 – and in developing the appropriate 'shopping experiences', the Burton Group emphasised the value of retail design: 'We constantly consider and innovate new ideas for shop formats . . . related to customer needs' (*Burton Group Annual Report*, 1987: 10).

The Burton Group's concern to innovate in shop formats impacted very clearly on the fitting out of Top Man. It moved away from its boutique-inspired interiors towards a more restrained mode of presentation by the late 1980s. Fitch-RS's redesign in 1989 broke with the earlier, dominant 'look' of Top Man. Introduced with the launch of the chain in 1977/78, and developed through the 1980s, this format emphasised the quantity and diversity of the merchandise on offer: lots of clothes bulging from hangers on floor-standing displays, lit under high voltage lighting. The shop frontage and graphics, as well as the fittings, evoked what Landini aptly described as the feel of the disco or *Top of the Pops*. These elements drew from the visual style of 1960s boutiques. In particular the Top Man signage and logo proclaimed a brusque exuberance through its bright, plastic chunkiness. The Fitch-RS redesign attempted to rework this retail design so that it spoke to a slightly older consumer. In came, not surprisingly, bleached wooden floors, slatted wooden units and a less 'busy' organisation of space. Significantly the typography of the Top Man logo moved towards a more restrained format.

The Top Man redesign – and its selected appropriation of the design vocabulary developed in 'high fashion' menswear retailing – is testimony to the ironies of the drive to segment through retail design. Although it represented very much the mass-market end of menswear retailing and its shop interiors would not have fooled the cognescenti familiar with the interiors of Comme des Garçons or Paul Smith, the Top Man redesign did consolidate a certain continuity in the coding of retail interiors across the different menswear markets by the end of the decade. These designs consolidated two dominant repertoires of cultural values: a sense of 'modernity' and a sense of 'tradition' in the presentation of menswear. From the stark, austere minimalism of Comme des Garçons to the softer dark wood interiors of Paul Smith, menswear outlets mixed, to varying degrees, the aesthetics of non-reference and placelessness of an aggressive modernity with the nostalgia of a particular re-imagined Edwardian past. It was precisely these codings, however, as I suggested at the outset, which helped to fix the meaning of the garment designs to some specific representations of masculinity at the point of sale. Each of the menswear retailers which I have mentioned, then, had designs not only on signifying cultural values like 'exclusivity', 'conservatism' or 'modernity' in the marketing of its products to groups of male consumers, but also on representing particular versions of masculinity to them.

Conclusion

There are a number of points that I want to draw out in conclusion from this reading of retail design practices and the coding of shop space

Figure 4 The Burton Group's Top Man store entrance and signage, 1989 (photo: courtesy of Bill Webb, Fitch-RS)

Figure 5 Interior displays, Top Man, 1989 (photo: courtesy of Bill Webb, Fitch-RS)

which they produced. Firstly, although I have privileged the work of representation which takes place at the point of sale (the shops), it is important to reiterate the significance of other sites of representation in the circulation of menswear. Fashion photography (most importantly in the form of magazine editorials), television and press advertising, shop and mail-order catalogues as well as catwalk displays, all constitute key moments which bring to bear their own representational practices on the resignification of the garment designs. In the marketing of designer name-labels, for example, press advertising was especially important in fixing the meaning of garment designs and the codes of masculinity associated with them. Fashion photography within popular magazines, especially the style magazines and general interest men's magazines, also exerted a strong influence over the resignification of the garment designs. The elaborated nature of these images – involving location as well as studio settings and the selection of a range of film stocks and types of lighting, for example – established important new levels of signification in the representation of menswear. The casting of certain types of men to model the clothes was also crucial to the overall signification of masculinity produced in relation to the garment designs. In the mid to late 1980s, the casting decisions taken within magazine fashion photography, in fact, exerted a strong influence over the wider field of codings of masculinity associated with the circulation of menswear. This included, significantly, the photographic representations which were mobilised on display boards in retail outlets. My key point, then, is that the representations produced at the point of sale need to be grasped as part of a wider regime of representation in which the new menswear designs signified.

Secondly, although I have centre-staged retail design in my account of the coding of shop interiors, it is important to insist on the way retail design interlinked with other retailing practices to produce these codings. Merchandising is worth mentioning in this respect. The selection of a range of garments for the point of sale by merchandising teams, clearly impacts upon the representations of masculinity which can be produced within the shops. We glimpsed something of this process in relation to my comments on Next. The selection and coordination of the garments was at the heart of its retailing strategy. These merchandising decisions were shaped by calculations about Next for Men's target customers and in turn set some of the terms for the kind of codes of masculinity projected by Next for Men. Merchandising practices are also worth mentioning in a further sense, however. They direct us towards the relationship between retailers and wholesalers and manufacturers; that is, the wider economic structures of the clothing sector. This is important because – certainly in the case of middle and mass-market menswear – the targeting of specific consumer segments was associated with retailers placing new demands on manufacturers. Looming large in this were demands for shorter runs and for shorter lead times, as well as for more collaborative input from the manufacturer concerning the garment designs. These demands amounted to the formation of a culture of flexible specialisation within retailing, one which, given the relative power of multiple retailers over manufacturers, drove the implementation of new flexible production techniques amongst manufacturers. Focusing on the way retail design was deployed by retailers to target more segmented markets, then, throws light on a deeper restructuring of consumer markets in which it was precisely these new strategies at the point of sale which drove the economic restructuring. In this sense it is clear that the masculinities signified at the point of sale in shops like Next for Men and Top Man were an integral part of this culture of flexible specialisation within retailing.

Thirdly, throughout this chapter I have emphasised the ways the coding of shop space added cultural values and meanings to the garment designs. However, I would also want to insist that the coding of shop space structured particular techniques of use for customers. A central part of this was the regulation of the movement of customers within the shops. The positioning of cash desks, display stands and lighting stem from well established conventions within retail design concerned with guiding the movements or flow of shoppers into and around shops. More than that, the retail designs I have discussed put a premium on the organisation of forms of consumer spectatorship. The elements of shop interiors which I detailed – the polished wood, the solid-metal fittings, large plate-glass windows, showcards, props and spotlighting – addressed shoppers primarily in visual terms. That is, they formally organised ways of visually apprehending the clothes and shop space. Grasping the organisation of these processes – the forms of movement and looking – is important to understanding the shopping experience offered by the retail outlets I have discussed.

Fourthly, putting the practices of retail design at the heart of my account has meant working against the more familiar entry-points into the analysis of fields of culture associated with contemporary cultural analysis. In particular, it has meant challenging the mode of mapping fields of culture which fail within the terms of a more purely textualised form of analysis. Although I have laid stress on the meaning of shop space, and read it for the significations at work, it has been the institutional practices and forms of expertise which have been as important to my account as the meanings they produced. Bringing into the account these practices points us towards the commercial institutions (in this case the design companies and retailers) which shape and regulate specific fields of culture and which form a central set of determinations on the production and circulation of any kind of 'text' within these fields. To centre-stage these institutional practices, however, is not to advocate the return to more conventional accounts of cultural institutions and organisations found within political economy or the mainstream sociological work on cultural industries. Rather, as I have hinted at in this chapter, it is to push for a more dynamic sense of the relationship between 'texts' and institutions in which the discursive practices which govern and regulate the production of particular representations are given a more central place in the analysis. Paying attention to these practices has other consequences. It directs us towards the practitioners who wield these forms of expertise. In the example I have focused on here, that has meant retail designers. It is cultural intermediaries like these, expert dealers in the symbolic and technical aspects of culture, whom more attention should be focused on in cultural analysis. Cultural critics need to know more about these intermediaries given, as we have seen in relation to menswear in this chapter, the increasingly important role they play in the circulation of goods and services.

Notes

1 John Richmond, quoted in 'Men's Where?', *The Face*, Vol. 1, No. 55, 1984, p. 86.
2 See, for example, the quotes from Paul Smith and Patrick Safarti in 'Men's Where?'.
3 Dejan Sudjic, *Arena*, No. 6, 1987, p. 31.
4 These titles are taken from the 1989 *Next Directory*.
5 I have argued elsewhere (Nixon, 1994) that the new designs in menswear formed part of a wider regime of 'new man' imagery. Although there was more than one version of the 'new man', I suggest that the significance of these shifts at the level of representation stemmed from the way they marked out a highly stylised version of masculinity characterised by the combination of an assertive masculinity and the sanctioning of sensuality. Importantly, these versions of masculinity offered men more intensive forms

of narcissism around the body and appearance, and extended the possibilities of masculine spectatorship in relation to forms of individual consumption. At their most ruptural the new masculinities coded in relation to the new designs in menswear opened up a space for an ambivalent masculine sexual identity, blurring the fixed distinctions between gay and straight men.

6 The UK design industry – especially those companies with large investments in retail design – suffered rapid losses with the downturn in consumer spending and the increase in interest rates from 1989. For a discussion on the impact of these developments, see, 'Going public, going bust', *Design*, January 1991: 13–20.

7 Carl Gardner makes this point in *New Statesmen and Society*, 9 March 1990, p. 9.

8 On Conran's mission to extend popular interest in design, see Jane Lott's review of, B. Philips, *Conran and the Habitat Story*, in *Design*, May 1984, p. 6.

9 On DDA see, *inter alia*: 'Next step for Davies', *Creative Review*, July 1986, pp. 24–6; 'On the spot', *Direction*, November 1988, pp. 32–4; 'Beyond Next; new English traditions', *Design*, April 1988, pp. 38–9. DDA went into receivership on 15 November 1991. *Design Week* noted that the accountants KPMG Peat Marwick were 'brought in as a receiver because of DDA's legacy of bad debts and over-expansion in the 1980's'. *Design Week*, 22 November 1991, p. 3.

References

Blackwell, P. and Burney, D. (1990) *Retail Future*, London.

Cohn, N. (1971) *Today There Are No Gentlemen*, London.

Davies, G. (1989) *What Next?*, London.

Din, R. (1989) Unpublished interview, London.

Fitch, R. and Woudhuysen, J. (1988) 'The strategic significance of design', in E. McFayden, *The Changing Face of British Retailing*, London.

Gardner, C. (1987) 'The new retail theatre', *Design*, No. 460 (April).

Gardner, C. and Sheppard, J. (1989) *Consuming Passion, The Rise of Retail Culture*, London.

Nixon, S. (1996) 'Hard looks: masculinities, the visual and practices of consumption in the 1980s', University of Lonfon Press, London.

Pilditch, J. (1974) 'The changing face of design', *Retail and Distribution Management*, January/February, pp. 26–9.

Sudjic, D. (1990) *Rei Kawabuko and Comme des Garcons*, London.

Zeitlin, J. (1988) 'The clothing industry in transition', *Textile History*, Vol. 19, No. 2, pp. 211–38.

More! New sexualities in girls' and women's magazines

Feminist scholarship on women's magazines

For over twenty years feminists have singled out girls' and women's magazines as commercial sites of intensified femininity and hence rich fields of analysis and critique. So established is this interest that it can be read in its own right, as part of the history of the development of feminism in the academy. This was as true in the 1970s as it is now in the 1990s when feminism has fragmented and splintered and given way to various feminisms. The purpose of this chapter is to offer an account of these changes in feminist analysis in conjunction with the equally visible, indeed quite dramatic changes which have taken place across the landscape of the magazines over the same period.

In the mid-1970s feminist attention to girls' and women's magazines saw the magazines as exemplifying oppression. The glossy advertisements did nothing but convince readers of their own inadequacies while hooking them into the consumer culture on the promise that they could buy their way out of bodily dissatisfactions and low self-esteem. The magazines promoted romance as the means by which women should interpret and practice their sexuality. Inevitably this required submissive and compliant behaviour in relation to men and as I argued in my early work on *Jackie* magazines (McRobbie, 1991) it produced a neurotic femininity since men could never be trusted to remain faithful and other women, even best-friends, would as a result always represent competition. The problem pages repeated and confirmed this narrow field of feminine interests. Even the enjoyment of fashion and pop music seemed to be defined in terms of the presence or absence of a 'boyfriend'. It was a completely claustrophobic world which appeared to be quite resistant to change. There was no interest in improvements in women's position in society, only within the already established parameters of conventional femininity. Thus the *Cosmopolitan* brand of liberation throughout the 1970s and into the 1980s only meant better or more sex for women. And from the mid-1980s onwards the whole field of magazines shifted towards seeking improvements for the individual. Self-improvement became the underlying principle, with some gestures being made to better careers and financial independence.

By failing to depart from the proven old formulae of commercial femininity the magazines could be accused of deep conservatism. On the other hand, if we read them closely, there are substantial degrees of change within the admittedly narrow parameters, that also seem worthy of comment. For example there is an energy and vitality in magazines like *Just Seventeen*, a self-confidence and openness to the world rather than a retreat from it. At any rate this is what I (and some other feminists) have been arguing over the last few years in relation to magazines like *Elle, Marie Claire, Just Seventeen, Mizz* and many of the other new titles (see Winship, 1987; Stuart, 1990; McRobbie, 1991, 1994; Driscoll, 1995). There are as many other feminists, however, for whom commercial magazines remain quite unacceptably and irrevocably sexist. Condemned for, among other things, the assumption of heterosexuality as normative, the magazines are more or less dismissed by writers like Jackson (1996). Women and girls, she implies, would be much better off without them.

Stuart (1990) and Brunsdon (1991) have both characterised the early critical relation between academic feminism and commercial 'women's genres' as an opposition between feminism and femininity. The argument in this chapter is that there remains an important relation between feminism and the world of girls' and women's magazines, even though the more stark opposition between feminism and femininity, as Brunsdon and Stuart both show, has given way in recent years to something more fluid and something which is also more challenging. To feminists like Jackson commercial magazines function like a red rag to a bull. To others they remain interesting, a kind of barometer of how womanhood and girlhood are currently represented in the popular media. Responses to these cultural forms also have the ability to regenerate polarities and oppositions within feminism (as this chapter itself reflects), while at the same time the magazines themselves demonstrate an ongoing engagement with many feminist themes and issues.

In the pages that follow these dynamics will be explored more fully. The magazines in a sense provoke 'us' feminists into asking urgent questions not just about the changes we can see around us, but also about the changes we want to see; the magazines we would ideally like girls and women to read, or at least the kinds of publications that would be somehow better than what is on offer at present. The popularity of magazines like *More!* also prompts us to consider our own effectivity as feminists. Have we managed to have any impact in re-defining what women and girls nowadays want? How do we now stand in relation to the outside world of 'ordinary women' and commercial culture?

In media and cultural studies, scholarship on magazines has occupied a less central and prestigious place than scholarship on other media, partly because magazines remain a narrow sector of the global communications industry. In addition, because the focus has until recently been on women's magazines (rather than men's magazines, though this is now changing, see Nixon, 1993) the debate has been conducted more rigidly along the lines of gender than other areas of study. In other words it has remained a debate among women. We can characterise the feminist critique of magazines as taking place in four stages. These are, first, the 'angry repudiation' stage; second, the theory of ideology approach; third, the question of female pleasure; and fourth, the 'return of the reader'. It is my intention in this chapter to add to this a further three levels of analysis. These are: the question of the meaning of the new sexualities in the 1990s, now so visible in these cultural forms; the relation to feminism; and the re-conceptualisation of the production–consumption relation.

Let me first say a few words on the early four stages of analysis. The 'angry repudiation' is self-evidently that formative moment in feminism when it was necessary to condemn the false and objectified images of women in the mass media. Not only were these images designed to make women attractive for male consumption, they also did this by hooking women into consumer culture, since to achieve this ideal it was necessary to buy an endless stream of gadgets, devices and 'artificial aids'. The overall message to women by feminists at this point was to stop buying magazines and therefore free themselves from this kind of pressure. This is exactly what liberation meant: to be free of the paraphernalia of oppression.

The second, more academic stage of analysis drew on Althusser's theory of ideology (1971). This acknowledged that the power of ideology was not just confined to female culture but was both pervasive and normative across the whole of society. In fact it was the key means by which dominant social groups retained their power and influence. Ideology worked by naturalising and universalising meanings and values which were in fact socially constructed. Ideology also ensured the smooth reproduction of the existing relations of institutional power in society. By pointing to the huge field of influence of ideology, feminists moved beyond the earlier and elitist assumption that 'ordinary women' were simply duped by capitalist society into a kind of false consciousness, unlike their feminist counterparts who had somehow managed to break free and find true consciousness. Instead we were all implicated in the spider's web of ideology. Ideology 'interpellated' us, it gave us a name and a place in culture, and through these means our inner selves, our sense of self, and our 'subjectivities' were also constructed.

Magazines played an important role in this process because in these forms were found the meanings appropriate to being a woman. Study of magazines and of other associated material, such as advertisements, thus represented an exploration into the heartland of 'sexual difference'. The impact of the post-structuralist writing which followed Althusser in terms of its availability in the United Kingdom took this argument further and suggested that we now move beyond ideology since the concept itself suggested some underlying or hidden true state of being which could somehow be arrived at, and which would then represent some kind of ideal or essential state of feminist womanhood. Instead of seeking to uncover the truth behind ideology, the question now was to consider the power of meaning. This meant looking at the battle in these magazines to define what it is to be a girl or a woman in contemporary society. As Driscoll has recently put it, the teenage magazine 'as a source of advice and a site of information exchange, sells its own necessity by emphasising the unavoidable, all-important difficulty of unguided feminine adolescence and the untrained adolescent feminine body' (Driscoll, 1995: 189). Magazines are therefore forms of discourse. They are commercial sites which have a tremendous investment in the representation of women. But so also is feminism according to this mode of thinking a discursive formation and, as a political force, it too is given over to representing women. Post-structuralist feminism has argued that there is and can be no truth of womanhood just as there can be no single or true feminism. Power resides in the currents of meaning which condense at key cultural sites in society including magazines. Hence one important task for feminism is to show how magazines compete to construct the subjectivities of millions of female readers by producing these great bundles of meaning on a weekly basis. So familiar are these that they enter our unconsciousnesses producing desires and pleasures even when consciously we might not want them to.

Feminist psychoanalysis can be seen then as ushering in the third stage in this field of study (although, as is already clear, these stages do not follow a strictly chronological order). The question of female pleasure coincides with a glimmering of an admission on the part of a few feminist writers that, like many other women, they have in fact something of a love–hate relationship with these comics and magazines. The fantasy of the perfect body, the wonderful romance, the glamorous lifestyle continue to have a presence in our lives even when we try to deny it. This admission begins to break down the lines of opposition between 'feminism' and 'femininity'. The fact that reason and political analysis tells us that femininity is bad for us while the unconscious continues to produce guilty pleasures evokes at least a complexity when it comes to thinking about how we consume commercial culture.

Feminist psychoanalysis also demonstrated the difficulty of psychic change and the complicity of feminists with their own desires even when these are understood as harmful. Rose's work showed how femininity as a normative structure of gender identity was never as assured as patriarchy required it to be (Rose, 1987). This then accounts for the repetitive anxiety in commercial culture to keep on trying to tie it down, to secure this otherwise meandering sexual identity to its correct place in the symbolic order. There is also an urgency in the invoking of femininity in the pages of the magazines. Hence the same old stories, the same problems, the same kinds of responses. This insecurity at the heart of culture about how women ought to be, also allowed feminists to prise open contradictory dynamics within a field which had hitherto been seen as a seamless web of oppression and objectification. This then allows feminists like Driscoll to say of teenage magazines that 'It does not do justice to the complexity of adolescent women, or these magazines, to discuss their production only in terms of her commodification' (Driscoll, 1995: 194).

The pleasure question had a resounding impact in the feminist academy. First, it put feminists on a more equal footing with 'ordinary women' once it was recognised that most of us seem to share many of the same pleasures. This also allowed feminists to feel more connected to the outside world of women. During the austere stages of feminism this had seemed impossible and so it was with a sigh of relief that it was now once again possible to be part of a women's culture rather than just a feminist culture. This engagement also allowed feminist researchers to re-investigate in more depth the field of female pleasure. This had two productive effects. First, it allowed feminists to rescue popular cultural forms from their low status as trivial and insignificant, not even worthy of study in media or cultural studies, and second, it also pointed to the political opportunities that seemed to arise in gaining pleasure from, for example, autonomous, even clandestine, readings of romantic novels. Radway's study (1984) showed how this private reading gave her female respondents not just an escape from housework but also a kind of alternative to their perceived dissatisfactions in their 'real-life' sexual relations. In short, it produced an openness to thinking about or imagining change from within the isolated conditions of being a housewife.

In magazine scholarship female readers are also granted more power. Frazer (1987) demonstrated (as did Beezer et al. 1986) that my own earlier work on *Jackie* magazine wrongly assumed that ideology actually worked in a mechanical, even automatic kind of way. By carrying out interviews with groups of *Jackie* readers, Frazer showed that instead of accepting the meanings, the girls actually negotiated them, arguing with the magazines and taking issue with what they were saying. And finally Walkerdine (1990) rounds up this argument by bringing herself in as reader and arguing forcibly and convincingly that the power of the text over the working-class girl/reader remains overwhelming. For Walkerdine, a young girl's comics do nothing but encourage submissiveness and feminine passivity. All sorts of miseries and injustices are to be tolerated for the prize of being a 'good girl'. In contrast, my own argument (1991, 1994) is that magazines for slightly older girls have, by the late 1980s and early 1990s, shifted decisively away from this kind of docile sensibility, replacing it instead with a much more assertive and 'fun-seeking' female subjectivity. This is signalled in the disappearance of romance. The magazines even seemed to have absorbed a sprinkling of feminist ideas, especially on the problem pages. At this point then there is a loosening up of the opposition between feminism and femininity. The question is what do we make of this process of detachment, how do we critically navigate the new less familiar spaces within which female subjectivity now finds itself being constructed?

Shagging, snogging and having a good time

I want now to provide an account of the three additional levels of analysis needed to develop a fuller understanding of the changes in girls' and women's magazines and what these mean for contemporary feminism. What I have called 'new sexualities' is possibly the most visible evidence of the changing world of magazines. These are images and texts which break decisively with the conventions of feminine behaviour by representing girls as crudely lustful, desiring young women. For this new kind of (typically heterosexual) girl, frank information, advice and knowledge about sex is a prerequisite for her adventures as a 'serial dater' (*Just Seventeen*). And so the first task to consider here is what is going on when oral sex and the quality of orgasm are the cover stories in magazines read by girls as young as thirteen years old ('Blissed Out: Treat Yourself to the O to Mmm of Orgasm', *19*).

In a few scattered articles and chapters published in the last year or so there has been a recognition that young women in the United Kingdom have somehow changed in their attitudes and behaviour, especially in leisure. Sheila Henderson, for example, writing in *Druglink*, describes how young women have participated fully in the Ecstasy culture of recent years, dealing it, taking it and, as we know from the tragic death of Leah Betts, also dying from it (Henderson, 1993). Girls seem to have thrown off the old notions of ladylike behaviour and talk frankly about wanting to 'get out of it', or to 'get off their heads' on drink or drugs. Susan Speer's ethnography of a girls' night out in Newcastle also describes their enthusiasm for getting so drunk that all their sexual inhibitions disappear. As one girl says to her:

> Seven times out of ten I would be thinking about the possibility of getting a snog. There's other aims too other than getting a snog . . . One night you might be looking for a man, another night you might be going out with the girls . . . (Speer, 1994: 28).

Likewise Beatrix Campbell reports recently in the *Guardian* (Campbell, 1996) how girlfriends arrange their evenings of drinking or drug consumption to allow one person in the group to remain sober and in control and therefore able to deal with unwanted male attention or drink or drug-related accidents. These kinds of reports have led some feminist journalists to suggest that girls have simply become 'loutish and laddish'. If this is so, the question is why? Where does the encouragement come from to act in this way, and what kind of confidence and enjoyment does it give to girls to have won the freedom to act like boys?

If we look back to the magazines, especially *More!* and *19* (both read by girls much younger than the officially targeted age), we find an exact replica of this kind of talk. The new girls' magazines are all about 'shagging, snogging and having a good time'. The magazines are not alone in this respect. Late night TV shows for young people, in particular

Channel Four's *The Girlie Show*, relish what happens when girls turn the tables on men. Usually this involves subjecting male 'victims' to the same kind of scrutiny and lascivious comment as has been the norm for women. School toilet humour provides the entertainment for live audiences who join the leering, mocking female presenters in the ritual humiliation of young males.

However, it is the magazines which have attracted the critical attention of politicians and moral guardians. In February 1996 Tory MP Peter Luff, a 'concerned father of a teenage girl', presented a private member's bill to Parliament (which subsequently failed) requiring that girls' magazines carry age-specification warning stickers on their front covers.[1] This was because he had inadvertently come across what he described as obscene material in *Sugar*, the magazine read by his thirteen-year-old daughter. Information about oral sex (i.e. how to do it), which was what he complained about, was also carried in a number of publications at about the same time, including the popular 'family magazine' *TV Hits*. Luff was worried about the fact that this aggressively promoted material was being read by much younger girls than the publishers were willing to admit. In fact teenage magazines are always read by an age range below the target readership the editors officially aim at, for the simple reason that they perform the role of guides to girls as to what is in store for them at the next stage of growing up. So magazines like *More!* are indeed consumed most avidly by fourteen-year-olds. What the moral guardians of recent months found inside the pages of these publications were features like the now notorious 'Position of the Fortnight' showing a line drawing of a couple experimenting with different ways of having sex. The accompanying text gives more precise directions. In addition, magazines like these carry explicit information on masturbation (male and female), sex games, sex toys, and an endless supply of sexual advice. In fact it is the sort of 'explicit' material found in adult sex videos or manuals. More significantly, many of these features carry the logo of condom manufacturers in the bottom corner of the page and editorially they are presented in the context of a safe sex message.

Information is therefore combined in magazines like these with a kind of traditionally 'naughty' humour. Most of them borrow their editorial style from the downmarket tabloids, especially those which, like the *News of the World*, specialise in gossip and sex scandals. Typical *More!* headlines include, for example, 'Revealed Claudia's Sexy Secrets' or 'I Read His Diary and Discovered His Dirty Secret' or 'Nanny, With

Knobs On'. *Marie Claire*, despite being targeted at an older audience, also uses this tabloid style of journalism. Some of its lead stories include 'I Know He Has A Mistress', 'My Brother is My Lover and We Have a Child' and 'The Married Man with Sixty Eight Other Women'. This kind of shock-horror headline now has become the staple of the girls' and women's magazine market. Like so many other forms of the youth-oriented media this 'quoting' of the sleazy tabloids, this borrowing from the downmarket true confession kind of publication is presented in a vaguely ironic way. There is an assumption that we the readers are not so naive as to imagine that these captions are not a jokey parody of a kind of debased or downmarket literature, the sort of material that sophisticated readers and young people would nowadays laugh at. And so the house-style of the magazines is that they parody the silly tabloids and the sleazy porn magazines. This is clearly signalled through the use of exaggerated and 'over the top' headlines that would otherwise be inappropriate to the women's magazine genre. The assumption is that readers know and recognise the quality of pastiche. The editorial trick is, of course, that the readers get the joke. Everything in magazines like *More!, Sugar, 19*, and *Just Seventeen* has a stagey feel about it. Irony is pervasive and every individual who appears in the magazine, from the well-known star or celebrity to the unknown reader having a make-over, is, in a more self-conscious way than would have been the case in the past, performing a role, with the act of performance permitting some degree of distance from what it is she or he is doing. The dominant editorial style is ironic and this licenses a kind of all-round exaggerated silliness with by-lines for features presenting male pin-ups including 'Yabba Dabba Drool: Men to Make Your Bed Rock' (*Looks*). Underlying this is the idea that 'we' can all participate in the fun of the 'Snogger of the Week' competition because 'we' all know that none of us takes it seriously.

This process of creating ironic distance from the 'sexy' contents of the magazines and thereby securing a new kind of closeness between the editors and the readers, is also a new way of saying 'we are in touch with our readers and this is what they want'. This is 'our' way of having fun. It is also the means by which the magazines now try to achieve the intimate, almost conspiratorial feel which has long been their most important feature. The magazines and the readers can bond together and line up together against the outside (adult) world! But does this new way of speaking really reflect a different kind of relationship? I would argue it does. This new form of 'girls' camp' allows readers to identify with the stars, to enjoy being a fan, to enjoy having fun, without finding themselves trapped into traditional gender roles. Irony gives them some room to move. It says 'let's enjoy drooling over Noel or Liam Gallagher, or Boyzone. This is after all what girls' magazines are all about.' 'We' girls can participate in the fun of being a fan, especially now that it is acknowledged that in 'real life' these lads are probably boring, sexist, possibly even gay. Even the act of 'being a fan' is now conducted self-consciously; there is a clear element of self-parody which also allows the girls to be fans without being simply 'stupid girls'. The magazines too even manage to create a distance from the genre they inhabit by also engaging in self-parody. They are continually quoting their own tradition, in a mocking, humorous way.

However, while it may be possible to account for the popularity of the magazines in these stylistically grabbing terms, this does not account for the bold, brazen and provocative new sexualities. Why this abandonment of romance in favour of foreplay, condoms and sexual pleasure? Let me acknowledge the usual (often cynical) explanation which is that sexy covers and copy sell more copies and that in the competitive world of magazine publishing circulations, profits and advertising revenue are what keep editors in their jobs. This provides the crude explanatory factor in the competition to sell magazines but it does not explain the distinctiveness of the sexual meanings now found in these publications. The fact that sex sells tells us nothing about the social relations of sexuality which underpin this field of representation.

I would argue that to understand these we need to take into account two factors: first, the tragedy of AIDS and its consequences; and second, the impact of feminism. AIDS and HIV have produced a new more explicit sexual culture which is itself the product of government-approved awareness and prevention programmes. Whether magazine publishers and editors act responsibly in this respect by speaking to readers in their own language, even though as the Luff case demonstrates this might be too uncomfortable to many parents, or whether they merely exploit the freedom to publish what some might see as semi-pornographic material for young female readers and thereby reap the profits, is open to question. (This point is pursued in the concluding section of this chapter). However, what we do know is that it is now widely accepted by professionals in adolescent health education that magazines of this sort provide a highly effective environment, much more so than sex education lessons, for getting the message across about safe sex.

The second factor which needs to be more fully explored is the impact of feminism itself on these publications. The approval by women (most of whom would define themselves as feminists) working in health education indicates that the contents are recognised as having some value by professional feminists. In addition, in the days running up to and following the Luff Bill, various women (including mothers, teachers, family planning counsellors, doctors and other health workers) who, although they did not speak as feminists, nonetheless spoke in the language of feminism, strongly defended the magazines in public. This again suggests an interesting and hitherto unexplored social relation where an older generation of women enter the public sphere to defend the pleasure-seeking sexual identities of a younger generation of girls. At the same time the place of feminism inside the magazines is debatable. My own argument is that it has a mediated and important presence mostly in the advice columns and in the overall message to girls to be assertive, confident and supportive of each other. It is also present in how it encourages girls to insist on being treated as an equal by men and boyfriends, and on being able to say no when they want to. For writers like Stevi Jackson the magazines only provide girls with the same old staples of heterosexual sex, body anxieties and 'the old idea that girls' sexuality is being attractive and alluring' (Jackson, 1996: 57). So there are no great advances here, she is saying. What I would say in contrast is that feminism exists as a productive tension in these pages. As Brunsdon has argued in relation to a number of Hollywood films including *Working Girl* (dir. Mike Nicholls, 1988) and *Pretty Woman* (dir. Garry Marshall, 1990), there is both a dependence on feminism and a disavowal of it (Brunsdon, forthcoming 1997). In the new 'girlie' culture this is taken further and there is also a desire to be provocative to feminism, which now stands as a reference point in culture, a source of interest, common sense but also regulation and adult authority. 'They' appear to have something of a love–hate relationship to 'us', as indeed we do to them.

Feminism and *More!*

The most straightforward way to respond to these magazines, as a feminist, is to condemn them. They try to convince their readers that nothing is more important than sex and having a boyfriend and that alongside this only the world of shopping and consumption offers opportunities for leisure and enjoyment. In addition, even when they carry features on gay and lesbian sexuality this is always done in an obviously sympathetic or liberal way which only confirms the status of heterosexuality as the norm. Jackson's short commentary, in the light of the Luff Bill, follows this fairly conventional feminist pathway. I want to suggest here, however, that this kind of response avoids the challenge posed by the magazines by treating them as more or less the same and almost equally as bad as their predecessors, and also by understanding them as coherent texts, without contradictions, or disruptions or uncertainties. Nor can this critique engage with the enormous popularity of the magazines (*More!* is currently read by almost ½ million readers) at any level other than the readers being pressured to buy them in the same way as they are pressured by the magazines to buy feminine products.[2] Can we really account for the enjoyment of so many young people in such dismissive terms? The main problem with the conventional feminist attack is that it avoids reflecting on the relation feminism might have with the girls who read these publications and indeed with the female journalists and editors who produce the magazines. This in turn generates an enormous polarisation between 'the feminists' and the magazines and their readers, a relationship which is neither politically useful, nor actually substantiated if we look more closely at the magazines. It is a politically flawed approach because it does not explore its own agenda, it does not ask what feminism actually wants young women to be like these days, nor does it hint at what women's magazines would look like if they correspond more to a feminist agenda. It offers almost no opportunities for intervention or even dialogue with either the female producers of magazines or the consumers. But in the ideal feminist world of 'feminist' magazines, what would go and what might be allowed to stay? Who would make these decisions? This kind of feminism seems to have no interest in interrogating its own foundations, its assumptions and its categories of both 'women' and 'girl'. And yet it is obviously driven by such assumptions and such categories. Nor does it have any sense of feminism itself representing a field of power or regulation. It shows no interest in the consequences for feminism when feminists occupy positions of relative power and influence, in education, in the academy and elsewhere. It certainly never imagines that the editors of magazines like these might also think of themselves as feminists. Perish the thought! But 'we' feminists are many and diverse, and who is to say who the real feminist is? Many of us are now probably seen by younger women as figures of authority. And is it any wonder then that younger generations of women and their magazines join forces in rebelling against us too, as well as the moral guardians who condemn their reading material?

My instinct is to see this as healthy and interesting. It forces us feminists to at least think about what it is we expect of young women. Do we really want them to be like us, do we want to reproduce ourselves? Surely this would be a narrow, dangerous and historically unviable ambition? In fact Jackson finds it hard to present her negative case against the magazines unequivocally. She admits that the 'advice given on heterosexual sex in the problem pages is often sensible' (Jackson, 1996: 58). She also concedes that there are 'more serious articles about both sexuality and other aspects of life . . . The readers of these magazines certainly know far more about coercive sex, sexual exploitation, rape and incest than previous generations.' Is this not exactly what feminism has argued for? In which case it would seem that the magazines are doing a good job. Indeed one could go further and suggest that even within the narrow, almost exclusive focus on sexuality there are strong signs of the influence of feminism. The idea that sexual pleasure is learnt, not automatically discovered with the right partner; the importance of being able to identify and articulate what you want sexually and what you do not want; the importance of learning about the body and being able to make the right decisions about abortion, contraception etc., the different ways of getting pleasure and so on, each one of these figured high in the early feminist agenda, the sort of material found in books like *Our Bodies, Our Selves* (Boston Women's Health Collective, 1993), the volume which started off as a feminist handbook and went on to sell millions of copies across the world.

The real issue upon which Jackson's case rests is the place of lesbianism in the sexual content of the magazines. I have argued elsewhere (McRobbie, 1996) that lesbian issues are now addressed much more directly by the magazines. Indeed *Just Seventeen* recently ran a three-page feature on 'Girls Who Fancy Girls', the first time as far as I can see that the idea of lesbian desire has actually been acknowledged in the younger girls' magazines. However, Jackson is right to point out that heterosexuality is still the norm. The whole cultural field of the magazines takes heterosexual desire as constituting a framework of normality. There is no explicit information about the fine details of lesbian sex, no position of the fortnight for lesbian lovers. This point then marks the limits of permissible sexualities within the field of the magazines. Lesbianism remains, for younger readers, a social issue rather than a sexual desire. But does this mean we turn away from the magazines, dismissing them entirely on these grounds? Surely this too is an issue that has to be thought through more seriously. What would it take for a commercial magazine to promote lesbian desire alongside and equal to heterosexual desire? And what then might be the relation between feminist critics and the version of lesbianism now presented as normative? That is to say, what kind of lesbianism does Jackson have in mind when she points to its marginalisation? What if it found a place for itself as normative on the pages of the magazines through the currency of gay and lesbian consumption, i.e. the 'pink pound'? Is so-called lesbian chic compatible or incompatible with feminism?

There is no underestimating the harm done and the injury caused by the endless invocation of femininities which violently exclude the desires and the identities of young lesbian women. But this very act of exclusion also poses important political questions. Does it produce and reproduce lines of division within feminism; that is, between heterosexual feminists and lesbian feminists? Or is it even more complicated than this? How, for example, do lesbian feminist mothers feel about their daughters avidly reading these magazines? How would a feminist like Stevi Jackson deal with female students, gay and straight, defending the magazines against her criticism? These seem important questions to me and the only way they will be answered is by opening up the magazines to a wider debate. One way of initiating such a debate is to play a role as an interested party, to explore how the magazines are produced and by whom, and also to consider how different groups of young women consume them.

Re-conceptualising the relations of magazine production and consumption

Where has feminism, over the period I have described here, found a field of intervention, if not in education? Possibly the only direct channel for the wider dissemination of feminist debates on women's and girls' magazines is actually through the process of teaching. Whether it is women's studies, cultural studies or media studies, introducing women students to a critical analysis of material they have only read in their leisure time and in the privacy of their homes, also means interacting with groups of consumers of the magazines, since it is rare to find students who have never bought or read at least some of these publications. How they respond to this encounter between feminism and their own cultural forms now appearing in the more formal environment of the university curriculum, is something of a litmus test for feminism, in much the same way as Brunsdon has argued female students responding to the feminist analysis of popular Hollywood films (including women's genres) often represent a force of challenge to feminist scholarship (Brunsdon, 1991).

However, the question of how we 'teach the media' goes beyond simply arguing the feminist case in relation to particular cultural forms or genres. Not only do effective pedagogics depend on listening to and responding to students, they also mean recognising the many differ- ences between them and us. I will put this more concretely. Over a period of thirteen years in two London institutions I taught students for whom working on a magazine was a not unrealistic ambition. These were hard-working and motivated art students, graphic design students, fashion students and media studies students. I could not have done my job effectively and certainly not established a good rapport with them had my approach to the magazines been that of condemnation. I could certainly be critical, but I had to work with the principle that the mag- azines would not transform themselves suddenly one day into feminist magazines bereft of advertising, beauty products, pictures of pin-ups and problem pages: i.e. they would remain bound by the genre. I also had to start with the principle that a job on a magazine is a perfectly reasonable goal for young women being trained in media studies today, and that indeed by working inside the institutions opportunities might well arise for 'changing them from within' (as it used to be put). Over this period dozens of graduates from these courses have found work in the big publishing companies. I cannot think of a single women's or girls' magazine whose (full-time or freelance) staff does not include some of my ex-students.

My own political realism (or accommodationism as some no doubt would see it) was to recognise that getting a good job is important for women leaving college and that at least some of the courses they are taught should provide them with material, ideas or information as well as critical and theoretical perspectives that will be useful to them when they start looking for a job. Several students who over the years had done research projects in their final year on magazines duly reported to me how useful this had been in interviews since they were able to impress the panel with their knowledge and research skills in the field. The realism in my support for their job searching was based on my feeling that it is better to participate in the field of commercial cultural production as an art or media graduate than to be left outside it armed with criticism but on the dole. I also understood the attraction of work in what they viewed as an exciting and glamorous environment. Given the battles women have had to fight to get their foot inside the door of the big media corporations I was hardly going to pour cold water on their enthusiasm. At the same time I could see that the students themselves were often cynical about working on a magazine. They were openly sceptical about how much they thought they could change them, but they still wanted the opportunity to try.

If we follow through this interventionist and alliance-building approach and take into account similar approaches by other feminists teaching in these areas then it is quite conceivable that many young women working on the magazines today are the products of these courses. They have been exposed to feminist ideas in the seminar room and have had the opportunity of arguing with and against them on many occasions. If we add to this the way in which feminist issues have also had an impact on the everyday practices of a number of other important social institutions, including health and welfare, social services, the family and the law, then it is not unreasonable to suggest that feminism exists as a strong point of reference for the whole way in which women's and girls' lives are now presented in the popular mass media and in magazines in particular.

Building bridges with women working in the magazine field also gives us insight into how feminist and more broadly 'women's' issues are negotiated outside the academy. It allows us to see the obstacles editors and journalists come up against when they try to introduce material which the management consider inappropriate or unsuitable. This is not to suggest that the new women's and girls' magazines now serve as an alternative to the old feminist magazines like *Spare Rib* or *Everywoman*, or that all women journalists and editors are self-proclaimed feminists. But many are, and many well-known feminists write regularly for the magazines and even those women who conform more to the 'career feminist' image generally have more interesting views about the experience of women working in the commercial field than most of us 'public-sector' feminists imagine. (So perhaps it is also time we disaggregate and reconsider what we mean by the label 'career feminist'). However, where feminism is viewed as moralistic and condemning of young women having fun and enjoying heterosexuality, it is true that the magazines adopt a more provocative tone. One underlying tension then is that between the magazines and a certain image or representation of 'feminism'.

Overall this kind of approach also calls for more research on women journalists and editors as cultural producers. There is still almost no information or analysis available on magazine journalism as a career for women, although there are many accounts of the textual meaning of images found on the pages of the magazines. Nobody, it seems, has thought to study the people who put these pages together, who argue about lay-out, captions and emphasis, who make decisions about how to 'do' a story on young lesbians, who challenge the senior editors and management (usually male) by giving frank information to readers about oral sex, and who at the same time emphasise the 'fun' element in magazines. To explore more fully the representation of the 'new sexuality' and to really engage with the style of the magazines which allows a sense of ironic distance from the material they are presenting, it would also be necessary to ask the writers and designers what it is they think they are doing. What is their relationship to feminism? How aware are they of its influence? My own recent research on the British fashion industry has only touched on these themes. But the research does show the editors to be responsible, feminist-inclined and committed to covering all issues relevant to their readers' lives despite opposition from chief executives and advertisers. Indeed it was this kind of adventurous brief which forced one of the early editors of the newly launched *Just Seventeen* to make a direct appeal to the readers to enable her to produce a magazine which, as she put it, 'no longer spoke down to its readers':

> We commissioned a large market research survey and we got thousands of girls to fill in a questionnaire and we were then able to deliver this material into the hands of the cynics and show them that girls didn't want romances and love stories any more. We could create a more up-to-the-moment magazine by getting rid of all the slushy stuff. (Morag Purdie, 1990)

However, I do not wish to imply that popular feminism is now the norm and that there are no battles to be had with the world of girls' and women's magazines. This is far from the case, as many of those working on them would also testify. To add a further twist to this discussion, when *Vogue* magazine recently ran a fashion feature showing models whose bodies indicated symptoms of anorexia, it was the advertisers who objected on the grounds that this encouraged young girls to develop eating disorders and they threatened to withdraw their accounts. The editor predictably appealed to the awareness on the part of readers that there is indeed a large gap between fashion fantasies and

real bodies. This shows that we should recognise 'readers' as social categories who play a key role in the politics of magazine production.
Editors appeal to the readers as part of their professional practice, especially when they are under fire from critics. They appeal to the group
with whom they have attempted to nurture a close and intimate 'big
sister' relationship, and the test is whether this group will remain loyal.
This is also an economic relationship since editorial jobs rely on
increasing sales. There should be no glossing over the hard-headed
calculations most editors have to make and the strategic deployment of
appeals to readers. In many ways the magazines exploit all the
characteristics attributed to conventional femininity while also nowadays paying lip-service to feminism. But the difference is that this latter
is now a viable choice and a viable combination. Indeed even the least
sympathetic, toughest Fleet Street-style journalists like Mandy
Norwood, the recently appointed editor at *Cosmopolitan*, cannot
really afford to ignore feminist issues. And Glenda Bailey, former editor
of British *Marie Claire* and currently about to launch its American
equivalent, gained her reputation by combining tabloid-style sensation-
alism with common sense feminism. She describes this formula as
follows:

> Women want to know the facts but they also want to be able to enjoy the
> fun. We are not just about sex . . . we also aim to inform our readers and
> they want to know about things that matter to them, even when it hurts.
> Everybody is interested in sex, we present it in a modern kind of way, we
> don't force it down our readers' throats. We manage to find the right
> balance between fascinating things that we might never think of doing but
> like to read about, and people's real life sexual experiences. We are not the
> tabloid press, we don't go out looking for sordid stories and we never pay
> for people to sell their stories. Anybody who does one of our first person
> features wants to share what has happened to them and does it voluntar-
> ily. We are influenced by issues like women's equality in every aspect of
> their lives, at home, at work and also in bed, because we want the best for
> women. (Interview November 1994).

If the traditional feminist critique of this field of mass media sets itself
up in stark opposition to the magazines, there is no straightforward way
in which feminists like myself now simply endorse the magazines
because they or their editors might claim to have taken feminism on
board. For a start this kind of feminism is a narrow and restricted political entity. It is the sort of feminism that benefits white First World

women without having very much to say to women who live in poverty and who produce many of the luxury goods, including fashion, for the consumption of women in the affluent West. As Vron Ware shows in her article in this volume (see Chapter 7), this is also a feminism which allows white women to find sexual freedom and self-expression through 'picking up' and having sex with impoverished Third World men. It almost cheers them on.

In conclusion it appears that the whole field of girls' and women's magazines comprises a socially constructed dialogic community inviting and involving a number of different female participants in a number of different roles. In this dialogue feminists and feminism find themselves embodying the role of mother or literally the 'agony aunt'. The feminist voice is almost maternal, it guides its wayward daughters, tolerating their rebelliousness and, by necessity, facilitating the pain and the consequences of separation. Perhaps it is only by being willing to let go, and relinquish its grasp over the truth, that feminism earns an important place for itself in the magazines. Otherwise it remains locked in a role of disapproval and condemnation, thereby minimising the opportunity for debate.

Notes

This is a revised and updated version of a piece of the same title which appeared in J. Curran, D. Morley and V. Walkerdine, eds, *Cultural Studies and Communications*, Edward Arnold, 1996.

1   The fate of the bill resulted, however, in a behind-the-scenes attempt to encourage self-regulation in the girls' magazine industry. At the time of writing a panel of experts is considering how guidelines might be drawn up to ensure responsible coverage of sexual matters.
2   March 1995 circulation figures are as follows: *Marie Claire* (monthly) 430,000; *Cosmopolitan* (monthly) 460,582: *Elle* (monthly) 230,000; *19* (monthly) 203,000; *More!* (fortnightly) 415,000; *Just Seventeen* (weekly) 162,000.

References

Althusser, L. (1971) 'Ideology and ideological state apparatuses' in *Lenin and Philosophy and Other Essays*, New Left Books, London.
Beezer, A., Grimshaw, J. and Barker, M. (1986) 'Methods for cultural studies

students' in D. Punter, ed., *Introduction to Contemporary Cultural Studies*, Longman, London.

Boston Women's Health Collective (1973) *Our Bodies, Our Selves*, Simon and Schuster, New York.

Brunsdon, C. (1991) 'Pedagogies of the feminine: feminist teaching and women's genres', *Screen*, Vol. 32, pp. 364–82.

Brunsdon, C. (1997 forthcoming) *Screen Tastes*, Routledge, London.

Campbell, B. (1996) 'Girls on Safari', *Guardian*, 15 July.

Driscoll, C. (1995) 'Who needs a boyfriend? The homoerotic virgin in adolescent women's magazines' in P. van Toorn and D. English, eds, *Speaking Positions: Aboriginality, Gender and Ethnicity in Australian Cultural Studies*, Department of Humanities, Victoria University of Technology, Melbourne, Australia, pp. 188–98.

Frazer, E. (1987) 'Teenage girls reading *Jackie*', *Media, Culture and Society*, Vol. 9, No. 4, pp. 407–25.

Henderson, S. (1993) 'Time for a make-over' and 'Keep your bra and burn your brains?', *Druglink* Sept, Oct, Nov and Dec, pp. 14–16 and 10–12.

Jackson, S. (1996) 'Ignorance is bliss: when you are Just Seventeen', *Trouble and Strife*, No. 33 pp. 50–60.

McRobbie, A. (1991) *Feminism and Youth Culture: From Jackie to Just Seventeen*, Macmillan, Basingstoke.

McRobbie, A. (1994) *Postmodernism and Popular Culture*, Routledge, London.

McRobbie, A. (1996) '*More!* New sexualities in girls' and women's magazines' in J. Curran, D. Morley and V. Walkerdine, eds, *Cultural Studies and Communications*, Edward Arnold, London, pp. 172–95.

Nixon, S. (1993) 'Looking for the Holy Grail: publishing and advertising strategies and contemporary men's magazines', *Cultural Studies*, Vol. 7, No. 3, pp. 466–92.

Radway, J. (1984) *Reading and Romance: Women, Patriarchy and Popular Literature*, University of North Carolina Press.

Rose, J. (1987) 'Femininity and its discontents' in Feminist Review, ed., *Sexuality; A Reader*, Virago, London, pp. 177–201.

Speer, S. (1994) 'One for the girls: covert observation of strategic interaction in Newcastle's Bigg Market', unpublished dissertation, University of Durham.

Stuart, A. (1990) 'Feminism: dead or alive?' in J. Rutherford, ed., *Identity: Community, Culture, Difference*, Lawrence and Wishart, London, pp. 28–43.

Walkerdine, V. (1990) *Schoolgirl Fictions*, Verso, London.

Winship, J. (1987) *Inside Women's Magazines*, Pandora, London.

Index